NATURALISM AGAINST NATURE
KINSHIP AND DEGENERACY IN
FIN-DE-SIÈCLE PORTUGAL AND BRAZIL

# LEGENDA

LEGENDA is the Modern Humanities Research Association's book imprint for new research in the Humanities. Founded in 1995 by Malcolm Bowie and others within the University of Oxford, Legenda has always been a collaborative publishing enterprise, directly governed by scholars. The Modern Humanities Research Association (MHRA) joined this collaboration in 1998, became half-owner in 2004, in partnership with Maney Publishing and then Routledge, and has since 2016 been sole owner. Titles range from medieval texts to contemporary cinema and form a widely comparative view of the modern humanities, including works on Arabic, Catalan, English, French, German, Greek, Italian, Portuguese, Russian, Spanish, and Yiddish literature. Editorial boards and committees of more than 60 leading academic specialists work in collaboration with bodies such as the Society for French Studies, the British Comparative Literature Association and the Association of Hispanists of Great Britain & Ireland.

The MHRA encourages and promotes advanced study and research in the field of the modern humanities, especially modern European languages and literature, including English, and also cinema. It aims to break down the barriers between scholars working in different disciplines and to maintain the unity of humanistic scholarship. The Association fulfils this purpose through the publication of journals, bibliographies, monographs, critical editions, and the MHRA Style Guide, and by making grants in support of research. Membership is open to all who work in the Humanities, whether independent or in a University post, and the participation of younger colleagues entering the field is especially welcomed.

### ALSO PUBLISHED BY THE ASSOCIATION

*Critical Texts*
*Tudor and Stuart Translations* • *New Translations* • *European Translations*
*MHRA Library of Medieval Welsh Literature*

*MHRA Bibliographies*
*Publications of the Modern Humanities Research Association*

*The Annual Bibliography of English Language & Literature*
*Austrian Studies*
*Modern Language Review*
*Portuguese Studies*
*The Slavonic and East European Review*
*Working Papers in the Humanities*
*The Yearbook of English Studies*

www.mhra.org.uk
www.legendabooks.com

# STUDIES IN HISPANIC AND LUSOPHONE CULTURES

*Studies in Hispanic and Lusophone Cultures* are selected and edited by the Association of Hispanists of Great Britain & Ireland. The series seeks to publish the best new research in all areas of the literature, thought, history, culture, film, and languages of Spain, Spanish America, and the Portuguese-speaking world.

The Association of Hispanists of Great Britain & Ireland is a professional association which represents a very diverse discipline, in terms of both geographical coverage and objects of study. Its website showcases new work by members, and publicises jobs, conferences and grants in the field.

www.legendabooks.com/series/shlc

# STUDIES IN HISPANIC AND LUSOPHONE CULTURES

# Naturalism Against Nature

*Kinship and Degeneracy in
Fin-de-siècle Portugal and Brazil*

Davⅰd J. Baⅰley

## LEGENDA

Studies in Hispanic and Lusophone Cultures 48
Modern Humanities Research Association
2020

*Published by Legenda*
*an imprint of the Modern Humanities Research Association*
*Salisbury House, Station Road, Cambridge* CB1 2LA

*ISBN 978-1-78188-524-6 (HB)*
*ISBN 978-1-78188-528-4 (PB)*

*First published 2020*

*Copy-Editor: Richard Correll*

# CONTENTS

# ACKNOWLEDGEMENTS

I would first like to thank Maria Manuel Lisboa, without whose generous support throughout my time as a student in Cambridge none of this work would have been possible. Prof Lisboa rescued me from the clutches of linguistics in my final year of undergraduate study, introducing me to *O primo Basílio*, and her enlightening teaching, guidance and friendship since has been second to none. I feel very privileged to have worked with her.

I would also like to thank, of course, Brad Epps, who during my postgraduate years greatly informed and refined my thinking. I have fond memories of our supervisions and owe much of the theoretical approach in this book to his teaching; it was also Prof Epps who happily suggested I read *Bom Crioulo* and Naturalist literature from Brazil.

I am sincerely grateful to Trinity Hall, Cambridge, for its support during my eight years as a student there. The college extended its generosity on countless occasions. I would like to thank Martin Ruehl in particular for his kindness and attention.

I am also grateful to several other academics who have helped along the way: Vivien Kogut Lessa de Sá, for her guidance in Cambridge; Sérgio Nazar, who kindly helped to orientate me in Rio de Janeiro; Leonardo Mendes and Helena Buescu, who both leant their time and provided illuminative suggestions for research; and, more recently in Manchester, Lúcia Sá, who has been a valuable friend and colleague these last three years.

I would like to thank the Biblioteca Nacional de Portugal and Biblioteca Nacional do Rio de Janeiro for granting me access to their archives.

Of course, I owe much to my friends in the UK and Lisbon who have supported me in various ways, and particularly to those in Cambridge who have entertained my enthusiasm for Portuguese culture, even reading, to my manifest delight, the novels of Eça de Queirós. Most of all, I am indebted to my family for their unshakable love and support over the years.

Finally, I would like to thank the Wolfson Foundation, who generously funded much of this research, including several formative trips to Portugal and Brazil.

D.B., Manchester, January 2020

# INTRODUCTION

## Nature, Culture and Naturalism: An Age-old Problem

The modern era has often founded its knowledge on an assumed opposition between 'nature' and 'culture',[1] the former imagined consistently as a space untouched, or waiting to be touched, by human influence. At the dawn of the industrial age, for example — shortly before the writers that concern us in this book — the Romantic poets idealised the vanishing countryside, roaming the Alps and Lakeland fells in search of experiences unaltered by the encroaching cities. Even today, we often speak of 'reconnecting with nature' (from Latin *natura*, or 'birth'), as though it were a distant abstraction in which our everyday lives play no role. Such disavowal of our influence upon 'nature' is sustained by numerous and complex social mechanisms. Human waste lies hidden from general view, seemingly disappearing only to remain in the geological record for millions of years. As Slavoj Žižek puts it, 'to guarantee the symbolic consistency of our "sphere" of life [...], something — some excremental waste — has to disappear'.[2] Mankind has positioned itself, symbolically of course, as an observer, consumer, protector, even destroyer of nature, but rarely as an integral, reciprocating part of its system, with increasingly perilous and visible consequences. Indeed, the growing environmental crisis in particular has spawned varied attempts to rethink the idea, or rather construction, of 'nature' and its multiple meanings in relation to the human.

One such meaning, as etymology would suggest, relates to cycles of birth, life and regeneration. Contemporary discourses of conservation tend to imply a bountiful, pristine 'natural world' threatened by the supposedly degenerative activities of mankind. It is a mindset that seems to reenact the original Fall from paradise and yet, paradoxically perhaps, reinstates a role for us as nature's custodian. Albeit in a different context, Carolyn Merchant argues that the Western desire to conquer, settle, plant and cultivate the Earth, most obviously in the presumed *tabula rasa* of the 'New' World, plays out a desire to return to the mythical Garden of Eden by restoring a world of plenty to the altered landscape.[3] Humanity is imagined on the one hand to be destroying nature, and on the other to be replenishing what has been lost through plantation, rebirth and (re)production, invoking a procreative, generative, one might say *heteronormative* vision of the human to justify the colonial logic of modern Western history. Culture, itself derived from Latin *colere*, to tend or plant, exists in opposition to nature and yet ought to imitate its supposed principles. A well-known example from Lusophone studies would be the theorisation (and later justification) of the Portuguese empire as a so-called 'Lusotropical' racial family, disseminating through the world and improving the 'nature' of indigenous peoples through miscegenation and procreation.[4] Colonial power is thus recoded as a 'racial and cultural gift'.[5] This book is concerned with querying such 'natural', 'degenerate' and heteronormative representations of the human in the (post-) colonial world. Analysing a movement famed for its quest for representing 'nature' — the assertively named Naturalism and its formulations in Portugal and Brazil — it assesses the latter's role in reinforcing, and ultimately disrupting and rethinking, this characteristic operation of power as experienced at the end of the nineteenth century.

Naturalism, at first glance at least, is particularly noteworthy for its tendency to represent the human in terms of nature and degeneracy, reproducing, in the process, longstanding notions of the former as existing in conflict with the effects of culture. If Romanticism, to which the movement in many ways reacted, idealised the rural, the pastoral and the sentimental, the Naturalists focused chiefly on the modern city, idealising supposedly objective, detailed narration with the aim of performing a 'scientific' study of human nature, typically driven by sexual desire and irrepressible inner passions. Arising in France under Émile Zola, the movement spread with great popularity, controversy and scandal through the Western world in its quest for universal, 'scientific' truth; no one described its essence more succinctly than Zola himself in his famous preface to *Thérèse Raquin*, where he compares the process of literary composition to the work of a surgeon:

> If the novel is read with care it will be seen that each chapter is the study of a curious physiological case. [...] I simply carried out on two living bodies the same analytical examination that surgeons perform on corpses. [...] I found myself in the same position as those artists who copy the nude body without feeling the least stirring of desire. [...] I was lost to the world, completely engrossed in my exact and meticulous copying of real life and the analysis of the human mechanism.[6]

Behind these statements lies a common assumption that there is an objective, universal truth accessible through careful, painstaking study — and, by the same token, that contemplating this 'natural' reality necessitates the renunciation of subjective human experience. Seemingly in contrast to the Romantics, any appeal to the sentiments ought to be controlled and disavowed even as it surfaces as a possibility. In its self-proclaimed search for *the* detached observation of 'nature', Naturalism rehearsed the nature–culture problem at a particularly high pitch, so much so that cultural production was idealised as the negation of subjective, 'cultural' influence.[7]

Naturalism thus formed part of a wider arc of epistemological approaches in the nineteenth century that drew on Positivist principles of reason and logic as the only valid route to truth. Itself born of the Enlightenment, Positivism, which was first formulated as a distinctive method by Auguste Comte, sought to apply scientific tenets of empirical observation, experiment and evaluation to all aspects of knowledge, in particular to society, discounting subjective impressions in the process.[8] The Naturalists then applied this theory to art and literature, with narrators imagined to be objective 'scientists' studying calculable social and human forces.[9] Rejecting the sentimental turn of the Romantics, they took as precedents the Realists, who also strove to portray the world objectively; indeed, they perhaps differed from each other only by degree, with the Naturalists claiming greater allegiance to methods from the natural sciences, transforming a literary 'tendency' into a 'doctrine' and 'way of seeing, of reflecting, of studying, of making experiments'.[10] Zola's surgical analogy, suggestive of penetrative incision, evidently invokes this experimental thrust, promising to reveal the 'truth', and indeed the 'secrets', of human nature.

Since its inception, the movement has generated great controversy and been critiqued from a variety of angles. In the beginning, readers and critics were scandalised by writers' willingness to confront issues traditionally considered taboo in polite society, especially — and most spectacularly — the language and politics surrounding sex.[11] More generally, the movement elicited accusations of immorality, since much of what was considered inappropriate for representation had now become a valid, or at least self-validating, object of study; as the French critic Hippolyte Taine, himself an inspiration for the Naturalists, famously argued, 'vice and virtue are products like vitriol and sugar',[12] and were at least as lucrative as these when presented to an enthralled bourgeois readership in narrative form.[13] The comparison of virtue to sugar is an interesting one as it exemplifies the problem identified by much of the criticism of the movement in more recent times: the transformation of what today are often termed 'social constructions' into physical, or indeed physiological phenomena, 'culture' being reimagined as 'nature'. Thus social prescriptions of gender could be depicted as inevitabilities of sex, and the historic subjugation of black people could be powerfully recoded as supposedly inherent racial inferiority.[14] Again, humanity's role in constructing and shaping the surrounding world could be conveniently denied by assuming the position of mere observer of nature. Perhaps the most significant piece of criticism to emerge of the Realist-Naturalist inclination to disguise the subjectivity of representation is Roland Barthes's 1968 essay 'The Reality Effect', which identifies seemingly superfluous details in Flaubert's *Madame Bovary* that are significant precisely for their apparent *insignificance*. Such details '*denote* the real directly[;] all that they do — without saying so — is *signify* it'.[15] Barthes's formalist approach to the movement thus forms the basis for more recent criticism, often focused on the tendency to represent subjective impressions as 'natural' phenomena. That is not to say, however, that the movement partook uniformly of this naturalising process, even in the case of Zola himself.[16] One of the many contradictions of Naturalism is that whilst it tended to naturalise geopolitical inequalities,[17] it also dispersed with ease and great influence across nations and regions placed differently within the resulting hierarchies.[18] How the Naturalists dealt with this contradiction in the relatively marginalised countries of Portugal and Brazil will be a central concern of this book, and one I will return to shortly.

The apparent necessity, or at least convenience, of representing culture as nature in the latter part of the nineteenth century, particularly in relation to race, gender and sex, coupled with the great financial success of Naturalist works, belies the wider social context in which the movement was implicated. With the industrial revolution and the emergence of a global capitalist system exported through empire and colonialism, the nineteenth century bore witness to great upheavals in demographics and social structures throughout the Western world, giving rise to new discourses of control and resistance. In Europe, the mechanisation of the means of production led to the rapid growth of the working classes and the cities in which they lived, alongside the bourgeoisie whose wealth they worked to create. Women were now increasingly incorporated into the means of production, no longer solely as mothers, and slowly acquired the structures to support and educate themselves, so much so that by the 1870s there was talk of unmarried, 'surplus women' in Victorian England, alongside debate on how to deal with the 'problem', an implicit testimony to their increasing independence, if also continued stigmatisation.[19] The aristocracy, meanwhile, slowly lost influence in the economy, sometimes precipitously so in the various republican and liberal revolutions that rocked the continent from 1789. At the same time, vast global empires and 'underdeveloped', newly independent states provided the produce for use in European industry, often made by slaves, until the practice was finally outlawed in Brazil in 1888, the last country in the Western Hemisphere to do so. The incorporation of women and people of other nationalities and races into this newly globalised market brought great wealth to some, but with it a tendency, in many intellectual circles, to justify the *social* hierarchies on which they depended as *natural* phenomena.[20] These relations of dependency and exploitation are of considerable importance to this book, in that they inform the overarching claim that Naturalism was adapted and disrupted on the cultural margins of the world in such a way that critiqued the construction of those very margins.

Before I move on to Portugal and Brazil in more detail, however, further comment is warranted on the widespread preoccupation, at the time, with sex, gender, race and above all the body, onto which the patriarchal ideology of the age was inscribed.[21] As Elaine Showalter has demonstrated, the *fin de siècle* in particular, as the upheavals of the century gathered pace, was characterised by a generalised perception of cultural and national decline that manifested as 'sexual anarchy', with a series of sexual scandals, panic about the spread of syphilis, hysteria and national-racial 'degeneration', perhaps prefiguring concerns surrounding the degradation of a supposed virginal, fecund 'natural' world articulated a century later.[22] As I will explore further in the first chapter, the concept of degeneracy was extensively theorised and formalised in the *fin de siècle*, establishing hierarchies of race, gender, sexuality and nationality based on the application of Darwin's groundbreaking theory of evolution to society. Thus different social groups, at different stages of evolution, would supposedly compete, like animal species, for survival.[23] Ideas of 'natural' and 'unnatural' bodies flourished; this was the age of freak shows, of circuses and colonial exhibits, in which supposedly abnormal bodies could be presented for observation, spectacle and control.[24] One of the most significant pieces of scholarly work to emerge in this line of enquiry is of course Michel Foucault's *A History of Sexuality*, which traces the origins of the concept of sexuality and its historically 'deviant' protagonist par excellence, the homosexual. As Foucault demonstrates, the term 'homosexuality' was first coined in 1879, and the concept of homosexual as a particular social 'type' was gradually consolidated over the course of the nineteenth and early twentieth centuries,[25] often with recourse to physiology,[26] becoming a privileged site around which the bourgeoisie created systems of knowledge, power and control. A 'will to know' — reminiscent of Zola's surgical examination, perhaps — promised to reveal the 'secrets' of sexuality, a quest that invoked other markers of supposed deviance and degeneracy. By the *fin de siècle*, sexologists in France and Germany began to categorise different kinds of homosexual, ranging from the *petit-jésus*, an adolescent young man introduced to prostitution, to the *entreteneurs*, 'hardened' pederasts for whom the dangers of the pursuit were part of its appeal.[27] As Stephens argues, 'categories [of deviance] never managed to contain adequately the content they purported to describe',[28] resulting in an exponential number of deviant bodies that were paradoxically required to sustain the notion of a 'normal' and 'natural' human being. Unsurprisingly, it was the bourgeoisie, the class that benefitted most from the changes of the past century, that had the most to gain from the proliferation of discourses used to identify and isolate entities that did not conform to its ideology. Thus the delinquent, the mad, the hysterical, the darker-skinned, the promiscuous and the licentious were cast as naturally different and inferior, atavistic forms of *Homo sapiens*, in an attempt to justify the precarious social privilege of the dominant class — a fraught task, of course, given that the threat of contagion, through disease,[29] miscegenation or the conditioning effects of nurture,[30] loomed large. As we shall see in the first chapter with the case of *O Barão de Lavos*, Naturalist literature often participated in the *fin-de-siècle* frenzy surrounding the 'deviant' body, reflecting but also criticising, at times, the socioeconomic and geopolitical context that rendered the naturalisation of sexual, racial and national hierarchies particularly convenient.

Although I will return often to degeneration theory and Positivist approaches to race, sex and nationality, I would like to introduce an example here that demonstrates the peculiar relevance of *fin-de-siècle* pseudoscience to Portugal and Brazil, and indeed to southern nations distanced from centres of dominance more generally. This is the theory of the 'Sotadic Zone' developed in 1886 by Richard Burton, translator of *Arabian Nights* and publisher of the *Kama Sutra* in English. According to Burton, the Sotadic Zone is an area of androgyny, pederasty and generalised perversion lying in the hotter regions to the south of the Alps and the Pyrenees, encompassing Greece, Italy, North Africa, the Iberian Peninsula, much of Asia, and all of the Americas. 'Within the Sotadic Zone', writes Burton, 'the Vice is popular and endemic, held at the worst to be a mere peccadillo, whilst the races to the North and South of the limits here defined practise it only sporadically amid the opprobrium of their fellows who [...] look upon it with the liveliest disgust'.[31] In the first instance, Burton's claim is interesting because it demonstrates the ease with which contemporaneous categories of deviance slipped seamlessly into one another, creating a geographical area around which 'aberrances' of sex, gender, race and nationality were dangerously clustered, aggravated by a hot climate. Just as the categories could not contain the content they supposedly described, so did they blur into one another in mutually empowering ways. Adducing various modes of degeneracy, the hypothesis of the Sotadic Zone emerges as one of the most lucid attempts to naturalise geopolitical and socioeconomic disparities across the globe, since Burton's vast region encompasses both the (post-)colonial nations on which Northern European dominance depended, and the Southern European nations whose relative 'underdevelopment' served to confirm their perceived cultural inferiority.

Whilst the tension between nature and culture remains far from resolved, at the *fin de siècle*, a century of profound social changes brought the conflict to a head, with concerted and systematic attempts to ground social and cultural phenomena — race, sex and gender, even wealth and poverty — in strictly physical terms. The nineteenth century did, after all, witness the rise of industrial society and humanity's assumed position as master of, rather than participant within, 'nature', though at the *fin de siècle*, often it was entire peoples and races that were conceived as controllable elements of the 'natural' world, even if they were considered somehow 'unnatural' in the process. The hypothesis of a deviant Sotadic Zone exemplifies the power of science at the time, which could all too easily be brought into the service of socioeconomic and geopolitical hierarchies. It is noteworthy, in this respect, that Positivist-inspired discourses travelled around the world at the time with such impact, including to countries that were explicitly marginalised by the theories. In one sense, it testifies to the influence that they wielded in their day. But it is a trend that warrants investigation, and indeed already has, particularly in Brazil, where critics of the Naturalist movement have long been receptive to its propensity to denigrate its people.[32] Burton's sweeping claim about the supposed degeneracy of the South could even, perhaps, be considered an invitation to visit the Sotadic Zone and its (presumably perverted) 'scientists' in more detail. This study, then, is dedicated to the Naturalists of Portugal and Brazil and their attempts to adopt, adapt and subvert the pseudoscientific discourses that shaped their respective countries. As we shall see, these were writers that, in different measure and often in dialogue with each other, wrote against naturalising representations of the human that gained special currency at the *fin de siècle*.

## Portugal and Brazil at the *Fin de Siècle*: Naturalism on the Margins

Though formerly coloniser and colonised, by the end of the nineteenth century, and as the theorisation of the Sotadic Zone implies, Portugal and Brazil both found themselves at the margins of the great powers of Northern Europe. Brazil, newly independent in 1822, would retain the practice of slavery for decades to come, with a predominantly agricultural economy that supplied key produce such as rubber, sugar, coffee and cotton to industrial centres in Europe, although from the 1870s its cities began to expand and modernise.[33] Portugal, too, continued to exercise considerable influence on its former colony, where it maintained a visibly exploitative, if diminished, presence through immigration and, often, control of land and property, despite many immigrants being themselves poor.[34] To an extent, the two countries thus continued to share a common socio-economic (and of course linguistic) space, albeit on demonstrably unfair terms. Brazil's sense of economic and cultural marginality was so great that, in 1893, writer and artist Raúl Pompeia, who described Portugal as 'o pérfido Caím' [the perfidious Cain], published a caricature entitled 'O Brasil crucificado entre dois ladrões' [Brazil crucified between two thieves], depicting a Brazilian being sacrificed next to an obese, greedy Portuguese man and an English merchant.[35] Meanwhile, despite its regional dominance, Portugal's imperial heyday had long since passed. A series of colonial losses over previous centuries famously came to a head in the British Ultimatum of 1890, ordering the Portuguese to withdraw from central African areas staked out in the notorious Rose-coloured Map of 1885, presented at the Berlin Treaty to lay claim to a coast-to-coast colony in Southern Africa. The national humiliation was considerable, generating extensive criticism of the ailing monarchy in events that have in retrospect been seen as instrumental in its eventual downfall in 1910.[36] Relatively poor and with little industry, Portugal depended extensively on finance, and indeed military support, from Northern Europe, particularly from Britain. It hence found itself both influential within its dwindling colonial world — continuing to develop its remaining territories in Africa and Asia — and dependent on the centres of global capitalism. This is the conclusion of Boaventura de Sousa Santos in his essay 'Between Prospero and Caliban', in which he argues that Portuguese national identity in the nineteenth century was characterised by the dual experience of marginality and centrality.[37] As Eça de Queirós, whose work I will consider in Chapter 2, himself pointed out, the Portuguese at the time both racially derided Brazilians as 'macacos' [monkeys],[38] and zealously adopted the latest cultural trends from France,[39] tendencies that illustrate rather neatly where all three countries stood within the balance of power in the nineteenth-century world.

No doubt as a consequence, the Positivist discourses of the *fin de siècle* were received with a degree of panic in Portugal and Brazil, where wider concerns about national and cultural decline appeared to resonate with the circumstances of the historical moment. In Portugal, the first group of intellectuals to adopt the principles of Positivism, the *Geração de '70* [Generation of 1870], contemplated no less than the end of the Portuguese nation. Oliveira Martins, for example, argued that the Portuguese were at risk of extinction in competition with 'superior' races,[40] citing their supposed love of indolence, slovenly habits and entrenched syphilis, in a distinctly pathological tone.[41] Another, Antero de Quental, sought to identify the causes of a supposed Iberian *decadência*, a period of cultural decay with its roots in Catholicism and the original colonial project.[42] In the first chapter, on Abel Botelho's *O Barão de Lavos*, I discuss in more detail how contemporaneous concerns about cultural 'degeneration' could be made complicit with Portuguese history to create a pointedly negative portrayal of the nation. The relatively popular, non-canonical position of the novel, meanwhile, demonstrates how the pessimistic reception of Positivist discourse was by no means restricted to the intellectual elite; on the contrary, it reached a growing, if relatively small bourgeois readership, diffusing through society. The *fin de siècle* was also, in Portugal, when the language of degeneracy and pathology entered the realm of journalism, testifying to the increasing 'scientifisation' of everyday life. Three homosexual scandals in particular caused great excitement and scandal in the national press. In August 1881, the Marquês de Valada was caught in flagrante delicto with a soldier on the Travessa da Espera in Bairro Alto, Lisbon, prompting widespread ridicule and a number of compromising caricatures.[43] Meanwhile in 1886, two boys, presumed missing, were found on the Rua do Trombeta, where they had been providing sexual services to a wealthy businessman.[44] Most significantly of all, perhaps, was the Marinho da Cruz case of April 1886, involving the murder of a military cadet by his male lover, this being one of the first instances of contemporaneous psychiatry applied to the Portuguese legal system,[45] with newspapers decrying the murder as the 'sympthoma funesto' [gruesome symptom] of a 'carácter irregular' [irregular character].[46] These examples underline the parallels between Portugal's experience of the *fin de siècle* and, for example, that of Victorian England,[47] with widespread sexual panic and efforts to isolate 'deviant' aspects of society. However, as the historical works of Oliveira Martins testify, Positivists in Portugal often saw the nation's loss of global influence as a *symptom* of some peculiarly national 'decadence' and decline.

If Portuguese intellectuals found the implications of degeneration theory compelling, though difficult to stomach on a national scale, Brazil's experience of the *fin de siècle* witnessed still greater anxiety surrounding the 'viability' of the nation — so much so that the country oversaw a wave of racial-social engineering that in many ways anticipated the eugenics movement in twentieth-century Europe. Concurrent with the *Geração de '70* in Portugal came the *Escola do Recife* [Recife School], a group of Positivist intellectuals encompassing figures such as Tobias Barreto, Araripe Júnior and Sílvio Romero. The last-named, whom I consider in more detail in the third and fourth chapters, used the theories of Jean-Baptiste Lamarck and Herbert Spencer to tackle Brazil's perceived racial inferiority, the troublesome legacy of centuries of slavery. On a visit to Brazil at the turn of the century, for example, British racist James Bryce lamented what he described as the country's 'plight': a huge black and mestizo population.[48] To combat the 'problem' posed by the implications of the European theories, Romero advocated miscegenation to 'whiten', over time, the Brazilian population,[49] an argument that paved the way for the *política de branqueamento* between 1880 and 1920, when immigration rights to Brazil were heavily skewed towards white Europeans.[50] Positivist approaches to race and society thus spurred elaborate plans, by the white ruling elite, for national 'survival' in a present that seemed too dark(-skinned) to contemplate. So too did analogous approaches to sexuality lead to efforts, as in Portugal, at controlling and policing 'deviant' sections of the population in ways that trickled through the social strata. In 1894, Francisco Viveiros de Castro published *Atentados ao pudor: estudos sobre as aberrações do instinto sexual* [*Affronts to Propriety: Studies on the Aberrations of the Sexual Instinct*], an attempt to pathologise sexuality that Green describes as a 'potpourri' of homophobic European theories.[51] A proliferation of new, popular terms emerged to describe homosexuals, such as *bicha, fresco, puto, fanchono* and *viado*,[52] while the main cruising ground of Rio de Janeiro in the nineteenth century, the Largo do Rossio (now Praça Tiradentes) became so notorious that in the 1870s it was closed at midnight to deter what were seen as dangerous liaisons.[53] The Positivist turn in nineteenth-century Brazil thus saw large sections of society targeted for the 'betterment' of the nation, often explicitly and systematically.

Given the evident overlap in the experience of the *fin de siècle* in Portugal and Brazil, whose economic marginality was variously racialised and naturalised, and whose societies remained considerably intertwined, there is considerable merit in studying their cultural output from the period in tandem, an endeavour that has been undertaken in relation to Eça de Queirós and Machado de Assis,[54] for example, but not in the case of the Naturalist movement specifically, despite several book-length studies of Naturalism in Brazil.[55] There has been comparative work undertaken with Abel Botelho and Adolfo Caminha,[56] and indeed Eça and Azevedo,[57] but these studies do not look at the movement in a more global sense and, in the case of Montello at least, seek to elucidate the influence of one (European) author on the other Brazilian one. This book, then, besides its focus on kinship, to which I will turn in the next section, differs in another key sense from previous studies. It aims to analyse Naturalism in Portugal and Brazil as one, if uneven, Lusophone movement, characterised by its tentative resistance to Positivist discourses as conceived in cultural centres of dominance. Botelho, Eça, Azevedo and Caminha are markedly diverse authors where their readerships, literary markets and relation to the canon are concerned, but all grappled with the precarious position of writing in an idiom that pathologised their nations of literary study. In addition, as we shall see, they often deployed (and shared) common techniques and motifs to develop their critiques, establishing a distinctive, at times discursive revision of Lusophone (post-)colonial relations. I therefore aim to demonstrate the ways in which ideas circulated around the Atlantic in mutually productive ways, leading to a transnational questioning of pseudoscience in the Sotadic Zone, where the historic Portuguese colonial project, apparently, was falling victim to its own logic of (re)generation, cultivation and (re)production.

### *Que diabo de trapalhada de parentesco é esta?* Portugal and Brazil: An Uneasy Kinship

Whilst close linguistic, economic and cultural ties in the nineteenth century justify a comparative study of Portuguese and Brazilian Naturalism in their own right, the two countries were brought still closer together in the peculiar circumstances that saw both ruled by the same royal family, the House of Braganza, until 1889. As is widely known, the relocation of the Portuguese court from Lisbon to Rio de Janeiro in 1808, following the Napoleonic invasion of Portugal in the same year, had the unanticipated consequence of stoking the flames of independence in Brazil,[58] a goal achieved in 1822 when Prince Pedro, made Regent of Brazil when the royal court returned to Lisbon, announced his allegiance to the independence cause, declaring himself Emperor. His father Dom João VI, meanwhile, seeing that independence was inevitable, reportedly advised his son to lead the movement so that Brazil might at least be ruled by one and the same family: 'se o Brasil se separar, antes seja para ti, que me hás de respeitar, do que para algum desses aventureiros' [If Brazil breaks away, it had better be to join you, who will respect me, than one of those opportunists].[59] Cordial relations remained in place for a short time; in 1825, the countries signed an alliance described as 'a mais perfeita amizade entre o Império do Brasil, e os Reinos de Portugal e Algarves, com total esquecimento das desavenças passadas entre os Povos respectivos' [the most perfect of friendships between the Empire of Brazil and the Kingdoms of Portugal and the Algarves, forgetting entirely the hostilities felt between their respective peoples] and advocating 'a Paz, Amizade, e boa harmonia entre Povos Irmãos' [peace, friendship and harmony between brother countries].[60] Peace and harmony came to an abrupt end, however, with the *Guerra dos Dois Irmãos* [War of the Two Brothers]. Upon João VI's death in 1826, Pedro, fearing rebellion in Brazil, abdicated his claim to the Portuguese throne in favour of his daughter, Maria II, overseeing the adoption of a liberal constitution in Portugal.[61] In 1828, however, his brother Miguel returned to Portugal on the pretence of marrying his niece, but immediately declared himself king with the support of the absolutists, who rejected the constitution of 1826. The liberals eventually prevailed after Pedro, having also abdicated the Brazilian throne to his son, invaded Portugal to retake the crown, leading to Miguel's exile and the return of Maria II to the throne in 1834. The bitter drama affected Portugal and Brazil for many years, each country experiencing the consequences of their ruling family's wars and marriages.

Given the considerable influence of (monarchic) family ties in Portuguese and Brazilian politics, involving a war of brothers that itself concerned the 'fraternal' ideals of the French Revolution, it is unsurprising, perhaps, that relations between the two countries were often conceived rhetorically in terms of kinship, typified in the first treaty signed between 'Povos Irmãos'. Later in 1880, as relations deteriorated further, Figueiredo Magalhães wrote in *Camões e os Portugueses no Brasil*:

> Então Portugal foi metrópole, o Brasil foi colónia, Portugal descobre e desbrava, dá à luz e cria o Brasil, e fica o ascendente irmão do descendente? Que diabo de trapalhada de parentesco é esta?[62]

> [So Portugal was the metropolis, Brazil its colony, Portugal discovered and tamed it, gave birth to and raised Brazil, and the parent becomes the brother of the child? What the devil is this bungled kinship?]

Decrying the sudden pretence to equality between the two countries in the wake of their historic inequalities, Magalhães, like the diplomats that devised the first Luso-Brazilian alliance before him, deploys a kinship metaphor, though this time for the opposite effect: how can a dominant parent become, post-partum, a dependable brother? His expletive question is rhetorical, though it does have an (unspeakable) answer in intergenerational incest, invoking a non-normative representation of the human to articulate notions of exploitation, an insistent figuration of Luso-Brazilian relations that we will observe in this study. The recourse to kinship metaphors to describe international relations recalls one of the principles of psychoanalysis, whereby familial relationships go on to define those forged as an adult and at a societal level.[63] Indeed, Magalhães's articulation of colonialism, conquest and cultural dependency — Portugal as 'metrópole' — in the language of kinship and its 'unnatural' inversion adduces the same signifying system as Freud: the family as the incarnation of relations of exploitation, dependency and control in society, here imagined as confused and nefarious.

The implication of the family in questions of economic dependency was explored directly in the *fin de siècle*, most notably by Friedrich Engels who, in 1886, related the growth and development of capitalism to the emergence of the patriarchal family.[64] According to Engels, the agricultural revolution precipitated a monumental shift in the West from variously endogamous to strictly exogamous kinship,[65] and the corresponding 'invention of incest'.[66] As families and communities accumulated food, livestock and slaves as surplus property for the first time, inheritance became established through the male line, empowering the position of man — who became head of the family — over woman, in events he describes in characteristically dramatic terms as 'the *world historical defeat of the female sex*'.[67] From this point onwards, family name, capital and bloodline were transmitted through the male heir. The transition from a communal, matriarchal, clan-based form of kinship to the exogamous, patriarchal family concentrated property in smaller social units and slowly established the societal structure with which we are today familiar: '[w]ith the patriarchal family,' as Engels argues, 'we enter the field of written history'.[68] However, the distribution of resources amongst these smaller, tighter units also brought about inequalities with respect to what was once shared, made all the starker by the new-found appetite for slave labour, for which subsistence tribal societies had no use. Hence the dark etymological roots of the word 'family', from Latin *famulus*, a domestic slave:[69] the very terms of the patriarchal family are bound up with questions of ownership, property and dependency. As such, kinship proves a fruitful symbolic realm with which to articulate such notions, perhaps accounting, in part, for the dynamic of power experienced between Portugal and Brazil in the nineteenth century, so often imagined in terms of a (dys)functional family.

The extraordinarily barbed remarks of Figueiredo Magalhães, and the unusual transatlantic, Portuguese dynasty of the time thus form an inspiration for this book, but my decision to focus on kinship in relation to Naturalism in Portugal and Brazil extends beyond the often turbulent relationship of the two countries. Indeed, to consider kinship as a complex signifying system is to return to where I began, the problematic binary of 'nature' and 'culture' implicit in the greater part of Western thought, reaching a high point — or for others, a low point — in the Naturalist aesthetic itself. In a tradition that runs from Freud's *Totem and Taboo*[70] through the works of Claude Lévi-Strauss and social anthropology,[71] kinship has long been considered 'the primal arena for the confrontation of biological nature and cultural nurture', indeed 'the very province of human experience on which this dualism is supposed to be ultimately grounded',[72] constituting the means by which the human species organises into socio-cultural groups. In other words, kinship defines the limits of the natural and the possible in human relationality and subjectivity: as Magalhães's remark attests, one's parent cannot also, in the normative imagination, be one's sibling. The exploration of kinship as a 'precondition of the human' that defines and constrains the subject is the focus of Judith Butler's *Antigone's Claim*, which revisits Sophocles' tragedy to argue that Antigone's struggle to bury her brother's body constitutes, on a figurative level, a fight for recognition within the kinship system.[73] As both daughter and granddaughter of Jocasta, Antigone, the child of incest, 'confounds the language of kinship',[74] being an essentially 'unintelligible' figure exposing the limits of human experience and the symbolic order. Butler then extends the categorical scope of the 'unintelligible' to include non-heterosexual individuals, drawing on Gayle Rubin's insight that the incest taboo, in the capitalist, Western world at least, presupposes a taboo on homosexuality, both being required for the perpetuation of property down the male line.[75] These 'unintelligible' figures represent kinship's 'deformation and displacement',[76] and the taboos that render them unintelligible, supposedly the point of transition from nature to culture, in fact constitute fault lines along which ideas of 'nature', 'culture' and the 'unnatural' are produced. Antigone is 'unnatural' only insofar as her body transgresses a culturally specific taboo on incest, collapsing any viable distinction between nature and culture. To recognise the 'unintelligible', this *trapalhada de parentesco* ['messy' or bungled kinship], is thus to apprehend the cultural forces that delimit 'natural' human experience, performing the inverse of Zola's formula.

By investigating the representation of kinship in Lusophone Naturalist works, then, I mean to problematise the nature–culture binary as implicated in the construction of the patriarchal-capitalist world in the nineteenth century, where the strict social and sexual code that perpetuated the interests of the bourgeoisie was offered an intellectual basis in 'natural' phenomena. Kinship, too, presents a site for tackling in conjunction the evasive categories of 'deviance' of the *fin de siècle*, which moved with ease through questions of gender, sexuality, race and class. Given that race, especially when seen in the context of the miscegenation debate in Brazil, is tied to notions of heritage and bloodline, there is good reason to include it in an analysis of kinship.[77] In this sense, the study sidesteps the thorny debate about how to 'do' the history of homosexuality, for example,[78] by considering its invention and prohibition — *vícios contra a natureza* [vices against nature], according to the Portuguese penal code of 1912[79] — as inextricably bound up with other taboos and 'deviances' from a bourgeois mode of being, desiring and reproducing.[80] Accordingly, although same-sex desire features prominently in my readings of the novels at hand, I will focus on a variety of 'aberrations' of patriarchal kinship, including incest and that other great taboo on the confusion of bloodlines, interracial sex. My aim, in part, is to respond to a passing remark by António Cândido in his now-classic essay, 'De Cortiço a Cortiço', in which he claims that Lusophone Naturalist writers, in supposed contrast to their Northern European counterparts, often preoccupied themselves with same-sex desire.[81] He explains this phenomenon as a 'degradação do enfoque "natural" de Zola' [degradation of Zola's 'natural' focus], as part of his wider argument that the writers adapted the

Naturalist model for an economically 'underdeveloped' context. Since António Carlos Santos has competently called Cândido out on his reproduction of the same marginalising discourse that he so deftly unpicks elsewhere in the essay,[82] my aim is to offer a more nuanced hypothesis: that the preoccupation with kinship across the Lusophone movement, entailing a rewriting of Naturalist literary parameters, can be read as a challenge to the foundations of the patriarchal-capitalist, colonial world that Portugal no longer dominated and Brazil never had, both increasingly represented, in the *fin de siècle*, as 'naturally' inferior. This is the process I would like to call writing 'against nature', which strikes a chord between non-normative kinship and relationality — 'vícios contra a natureza' — and the attempt to deal with the problematic implications of Naturalist discourse.

The term 'contra a natureza' of course chimes with another novel that caused a stir at the *fin de siècle*, Joris-Karl Huysmans's *À Rebours* (1884),[83] often translated as 'Against Nature' and regarded as the beginning of the Decadent movement in France. The story of sensual pleasures and indulgence, said to have inspired Wilde's *The Picture of Dorian Gray*,[84] is a tour de force of *fin-de-siècle* malaise and soon became a cult classic. Degeneracy is foregrounded immediately in the descriptions of its anti-hero Duc-Jean, who suffers from a 'debilitated constitution' and an 'excess of lymph in the blood' traceable through the portraits of his ancestors. However, the novel is equally significant for its rejection of Naturalist aesthetics overall, consisting of a series of recollections and symbols, the most dreamlike and enduring of which is perhaps the gem-studded tortoise, whose shell becomes so heavy that the animal perishes under its weight. So far did Huysmans stray from the predominant narrative conventions of the time that Zola, ever defensive of his movement, reportedly accused the author of 'dealing a terrible blow at Naturalism [...] leading the school astray' and pursuing an aesthetic that would be exhausted by a single novel.[85] Whilst none of the authors discussed in this book could be considered Symbolists, we shall see that at a similar point in the century, before Decadentism reached Portugal and Brazil, the Lusophone Naturalists made their own adjustments to the Naturalist method, often invoking the metaphysical; Azevedo, for example, infuses his first novel with myth and legend. The term 'against nature' therefore alludes to various literary and cultural processes that can be gathered together with the aim of problematising heteronormative, supposedly objective and scientific approaches to literature and the human condition.

If the Lusophone Naturalists often wrote 'against nature', it is important, of course, not to characterise the process as a particularly systematic or concerted one comparable to Huysmans's vocal rejection of the movement. On the contrary, readers should ready themselves for, at times, decidedly forthright depictions of people in physiological terms. When, in Aluísio Azevedo's *O mulato*, the obese Lindoca is described in great detail as akin to a farm animal, 'boleada' [roly-poly] with 'banhas', 'enxúndias' [lard, pork fat] and a 'lombinho' [a piece of loin] for a nose,[86] the author evidently moves towards, not against 'nature' in representation. The uneven and disperse manner of the Lusophone disruption to the Naturalist tradition can thus be conceived in terms of what Marx and Engels referred to as the principle of contradiction,[87] whereby every work of art or literature must, at some level, contain or express ideological values that are not always shared by the author and his social group — hence, in feminist criticism, the now-familiar debate over the degree to which nineteenth-century writers sympathised with their housebound female characters. This principle is similar to the Freudian idea that in speech, latent (unconscious) thoughts are conveyed alongside what was 'meant' to be said. As Cora Kaplan puts it, 'in each speech act the self and the culture speak simultaneously [...] *each time we speak we are also spoken*'.[88] Accordingly, I take as axiomatic the notion that the Lusophone Naturalists both reproduced and criticised the prejudices of the time. Indeed, the criticism is often contained within the reproduction itself. Since Derrida's theorisation of speech as a series of reiterations with no definable origin,[89] each enunciation being a (paradoxically) unique copy as in a game of Chinese whispers, postcolonial criticism has drawn attention to the tendency of marginal literature to adopt cultural trends from centres of dominance only to reiterate them in subversive ways. In 'Nacional por subtração', for example, Roberto Schwarz argues that Brazilian literature should be read in the supplemental space that unfolds at the point of divergence from European cultural models, with the 'national' aspect of cultural production residing precisely in its status as a 'copy'.[90] When the Lusophone Naturalists wrote 'against nature', it was a distortion of a European discourse that they nonetheless, if in different measure, sought to reproduce. My readings thus seek to demonstrate how the texts at hand offer an uncannily different, complementary representation of the nineteenth-century world to those made by the *fin-de-siècle* pseudoscientists of Northern Europe.

The *principle of contradiction*, which implies that works of art can challenge the status quo to a greater or lesser degree, also lies behind my decision to include authors from a range of positions within the literary market and — which is not to imply a causal relationship — the literary canon. One of the most persistent criticisms of Naturalism at the time was that its authors employed a cheap, sordid formula to provoke scandal and sell their books. Botelho's *O Barão de Lavos* suffered this accusation perhaps most of all, though Júlio Ribeiro's *A Carne*, which carries the unfortunate reputation of being the worst novel in the history of Brazilian literature,[91] must run it close. In *Páginas de Sensação*, Alessandra El Far examines this sensationalist aspect of the Lusophone literary market at the time, finding an overlap between censored pornographic novels, titillating low-brow works, and even those now considered centrepieces of the Lusophone novelistic canon, in their capacity to excite a scandalised — and growing — bourgeois readership. Thus when Eça's *O primo Basílio* was published in Brazil, it was given the same euphemistic designation of 'romance para homens' [novel for men] as prohibited pornographic works.[92] That said, Eça's novels have evidently attracted an enduring readership amongst critics that Botelho's have not, despite their popularity during his lifetime; *O Barão de Lavos*, as a case in point, has attracted very little attention from critics. Azevedo's and Caminha's works have fared rather better, but a reluctance to speak of them with critical acclaim persists. By comparing a diverse range of authors, then, I wish to account for how the Naturalist representation of kinship modulates according to the degree to which writers succeeded in gratifying a bourgeois readership that was growing quickly in the urban centres of the Lusophone world. As we shall see, in Portugal for example, the degree to which colonialism — and in the process, the patriarchal family — is called into a question is a key difference between the work of Botelho and Eça.

This book therefore deploys several theoretical perspectives that can, it is hoped, work productively together. On the one hand, the focus on different aspects of the literary market, the kinship structure and the colonial system of economic dependency at the *fin de siècle* owes much to Marxist criticism, itself, of course, born of the social struggles of the nineteenth century. On the other hand, consideration of the aftermath of empire and slavery, and the decision to read the texts in relation to their Northern European models, draws on key principles of postcolonial theory. As part of the investigation into kinship trouble, meanwhile, I deploy psychoanalysis to navigate the complex interplay of desire and identification that makes and unmakes families. The study is also indebted to queer theory insofar as it undertakes an analysis of 'deviant', non-normative relationality — including incest — seeking to move beyond the problematic framework that produces the socially 'abnormal', and that has arisen in different, though interrelated forms since at least the nineteenth century. Indeed, I wish to explore the connection between deviance in being, desiring and reproducing, and deviance in representation — Naturalism against nature — which offers an opportunity to bring together queer and postcolonial theory with the same analytical goal in mind. A particularly helpful definition of 'queerness' in this respect is offered by José Esteban Muñoz: 'an ideality'; 'a mode of desiring that allows us to see beyond the quagmire of the present', and 'the rejection of a here and now and an insistence on potentiality or concrete possibility for another world'.[93] So defined, the 'queer' is loosened from any residual association with 'homosexual' desire to include the more general sense of that which eludes assimilation into the symbolic order of the socio-historical moment, pointing, consequently, to different possible modes of being. Considering that the Brazilian postcolonial critics encourage readers to search for deviances in representation at the margins of the Western world, there are notable points of contact to be established between two disciplines that Murat Aydemir criticises for being 'largely distinct programs' at universities, suggesting an 'apparent need to keep sex and race at some distance from each other'.[94] Running counter to this spirit, I hope to bring the two together productively; for example, as we shall see, the repeated use of allegories of nationhood in the novels — one of a series of formal adaptations to the Naturalist model — can also pressure the established structure of the family such that it becomes sterile, dysfunctional, or otherwise 'unnatural'. Another key supplement to the Naturalist perspective, which I argue is one of the most prominent to circulate around the Lusophone literary space, is the authors' repeated recourse to Greek modes of understanding beauty, desire and the family, drawing on tragedy and Platonic idealism. By teasing out these discursive disruptions to Naturalism, therefore, I hope to expose the 'queer' at the level of the text.

The book is divided into four chapters, each dedicated to a particular author. As such, they become increasingly comparative, drawing out the formal and thematic dialogues between the novels at hand. The first chapter examines Abel Botelho's *O Barão de Lavos*, the story of a 'degenerate' Portuguese aristocrat who falls fatally in love with a scheming, adolescent street urchin. The novel, which was very popular at the time, provides a fitting introduction to the book because its non-canonical status, besides leaving a wealth of material for critics to explore, sheds an illuminating light on the *fin-de-siècle* zeitgeist. However, while I analyse the work to explore degeneration theory in more detail, it becomes evident that the fraught formula of the so-called 'pathological' novel — a medicalised formulation of Naturalism — contains its own dissolution. Indeed, degeneracy proves surprisingly generative, with a series of neologisms and creative wordplay that evoke the intellectual context in exemplary fashion. Broadening the canonical scope, the second chapter moves to the centre of the Lusophone literary tradition to consider Eça de Queirós, whose novels, despite their enduring acclaim, have thus far elicited little attention for their exploration of queer relationality. His *oeuvre* is also complex, marked by a definitive break with Naturalist thought towards the middle of his career. I therefore address his work chronologically to chart his famous path to epistemological disillusionment, drawing on studies of incest in his novels to argue that an indeterminacy in the language of relationality and kinship gradually manifests itself at the level of signification, culminating in his unreliable first-person narrators in later life. His aesthetic trajectory can thus be better understood in relation to his exploration of the limits of the patriarchal order, providing a distinctive contrast with *Lavos*, despite some similarities in form on occasion. Then, in the third and fourth chapters, I turn to the other side of the Atlantic, where I start by considering the novels of Aluísio Azevedo, the most significant figure from the movement in Brazil. I focus on some of his lesser-known works, particularly *O mulato*, which, I argue, has been largely misunderstood and in fact constitutes one of the most significant and influential novels of the Lusophone movement, exploring epistemologies that both draw on and prefigure Eça's work. His novels are perhaps best comprehended in terms of the connections they form with other authors. Taking this insight further, I end with one of the most puzzling works of the Naturalist movement, Adolfo Caminha's *Bom Crioulo*, where intertextuality and 'creolisation' become no less than an organising principle. In many ways a subversive reiteration of *O Barão de Lavos*, the novel brilliantly illustrates the 'corruption' of Naturalism over the course of its global travels, as well as the importance of the movement's propensity for dialogue and literary conversation. Thus in addition to their canonical and geographical range, the novels in this book have also been selected for the themes, motifs and techniques that they share and exchange.[95] Unsurprisingly, race and slavery is a more pressing concern in Brazilian Naturalism, even though it does play an important, if more subtle, role in Eça's work. Nevertheless, as we shall see, the movement on both sides of the Atlantic deploys similar methods to write against the naturalising representations of the human that characterised the *fin de siècle*.

Criticised for being a 'non-aesthetic',[96] inimical to the arts and, later, a vehicle for cementing dangerous cultural prejudices in people's minds,[97] Naturalism has not, perhaps, been received anywhere with the same critical enthusiasm as the aesthetic movements that it preceded and followed.[98] Even the work of Azevedo, the most celebrated Brazilian Naturalist, is described as 'generally mediocre' by António Cândido,[99] while Nelson Sodré, in his broad study of the movement in Brazil, finds no works of any notable creative value.[100] It would take more than one book to address this curious aversion to one of the last literary traditions before Modernism's revolutionary embrace of subjectivity in narration. By investigating Luso-Brazilian Naturalism, however, produced on the margins of Western world in the nineteenth century, it is hoped the book can take a step towards revising the role that the movement played, in its heyday, in understanding the *fin-de-siècle* world, in shaping the Lusophone (post-)colonial space, and in problematising the nature–culture binary that continues to define human experience.

## Notes to the Introduction

1. See Jacques Derrida, '...That Dangerous Supplement...', in *Of Grammatology*, trans. by Gayatri Spivak (Baltimore, MD: Johns Hopkins University Press, 1997), pp. 141–65, for the now-classic deconstruction of the nature–culture binary.

2. Slavoj Žižek, *Less Than Nothing: Hegel and the Shadow of Dialectical Materialism* (London: Verso, 2012), p. 372.

3. Carolyn Merchant, *Reinventing Eden: The Fate of Nature in Western Culture* (London: Routledge, 2003).

4. First theorised by Brazilian sociologist Gilberto Freyre, and later adopted by the *Estado Novo* dictatorship as justification for the Portuguese overseas empire, Lusotropicalism held that a putative Portuguese adaptability to the tropics, and associated capacity for miscegenation, were defining factors in Brazilian growth and development. See Gilberto Freyre, *Integração portuguesa nos trópicos* (Lisbon: Junta de Investigações do Ultramar, 1958).

5. Hilary Owen, *Mother Africa, Father Marx: Women's Writing of Mozambique, 1948–2002* (Lewisburg, PA: Bucknell University Press, 2007), pp. 18–20 (p. 18).

6. Émile Zola, Preface to the first edition of *Thérèse Raquin*, trans. by Andrew Rothwell (Oxford: Oxford University Press, 1992), p. 2.

7. Thus several critics at the time criticised Naturalism for being an 'anti-aesthetic', even 'inimical to the arts'. See Lilian R. Furst and Peter N. Skrine, *Naturalism*, The Critical Idiom, 17 (London: Methuen, 1971), p. 22.

8. For one of the classic treatises of Positivism, see Auguste Comte, *A General View of Positivism*, trans. from the French by J. H. Bridges (Cambridge: Cambridge University Press, 2009). As Comte argues, 'The primary object [...] of Positivism is twofold: to generalise our scientific conceptions, and to systematise the art of social life' (p. 2).

9. See Furst and Skrine, p. 8.

10. This is the distinction drawn by Zola's closest ally, Paul Alexis. See Furst and Skrine, pp. 8–9.

11. Richard Lehan, *Realism and Naturalism: The Novel in an Age of Transition* (Madison: University of Wisconsin Press, 2005), pp. 7–8.

12. Cited by Furst and Skrine, p. 20.

13. Ibid., p. 31.

14. This the conclusion of David Brookshaw, for example, in relation to Naturalist literature in Brazil. See David Brookshaw, *Race and Colour in Brazilian Literature* (London: The Scarecrow Press, 1986), pp. 37–53.

15. Roland Barthes, 'The Reality Effect', in *The Rustle of Language*, trans. by Richard Howard (Berkeley: University of California Press, 1989), pp. 141–48 (p. 148).

16. As Furst and Skrine argue, the tenets of Naturalism are 'impossible'; Zola conceded later that '"a work of art is a segment of nature seen through the eyes of a certain temperament"', thus admitting 'a far greater degree of subjectivity than his theory strictly permits'. See Furst and Skrine, pp. 30–31.

17. A particularly fine example comes from the second novel of Zola's *The Three Cities* trilogy, *Rome*, where, commenting upon the apparent decadence of the city in relation to its industrial sister, Milan, the narrator remarks '[t]he centre of civilisation has been displaced'. Pierre, the protagonist, then seeks a racial explanation for this 'displacement', asking himself 'if the soil were not exhausted [...] if it were not *for ever drained of the sap which makes a race healthy, a nation powerful.*' See Émile Zola, *Rome*, trans. by Ernest Alfred Vizetellt (London: Macmillan, 1901), p. 55 (emphasis added). There are other attempts to find a physical explanation for Rome's 'decline', including 'that other *cause* of mortal languishment, the Campagna — the desert of death which the dead river crossed and which *girdled Rome with sterility*' (p. 54, emphasis added).

18. See, for example, Heike Bauer, 'Measurements of Civilisation', *French Cultural Studies*, 17 (2008), 93–108, for a discussion of the ways in which contemporaneous, pseudoscientific discourses sought to hierarchise different nations and civilisations.

19. See Elaine Showalter, *Sexual Anarchy* (London: Virago, 1992), pp. 24–30. Showalter draws attention to the connotations of commodification and non-conformity implicit in the term 'surplus'.

20. See Showalter, p. 4, and Bauer, pp. 98–99.

21. For an analysis of the various kinds of 'freak' bodies in the *fin de siècle* and their ideological underpinnings, see Elizabeth Stephens, 'Anatomies of Desire', in Sexuallity at the Fin de Siècle, ed. by Cryle and Forth, pp. 25–38.

22. Showalter draws specific comparisons between the *fin de siècle* and the AIDS crisis of the 1980s rather than the environmental crisis I referred to at the beginning; however, since both invoke notions of decadence and decay from an idealised 'natural' and heteronormative, reproductive state, ultimately entailing apocalypse, there are resonances of the *fin-de-siècle* experience in today's debates surrounding natural and cultural 'decline'.

23. Herbert Spencer was one of the first figures to apply Darwin's theory of evolution to society, leaving a considerable legacy on other pseudoscientific disciplines. The sexologist Krafft-Ebing, for example, believed that societies could be hierarchised according to their degree of evolutionary progress, and argued that how they approached sexual relations was a privileged marker for establishing such hierarchies. See Bauer, p. 97.

24. See, for example, Isabella Alston and Kathryn Dixon, *Anatomical Anomalies* (Charlotte, NC: TAJ Books, 2014), p. 4.

25. See Michel Foucault, *The History of Sexuality*, trans. by Robert Hurley, 3 vols (London: Random House, 1979), vol. I: *An Introduction*, p. 43.

26. See Siobhan Somerville, 'Scientific Racism and the Invention of the Homosexual Body,' *Journal of the History of Sexuality*, 5 (2016), 246–66.

27. Michael L. Wilson, 'The Despair of Unhappy Love: Pederasty and Popular Fiction in the Belle Époque', in *Sexuality at the fin-de-siècle*, ed. by Peter Cryle and Christopher E. Forth (Cranbury, NJ: University of Delaware, 2008), pp. 109–22 (pp. 112–13).

28. Stephens, p. 37.

29. In the early 1880s, the syphilis 'crisis' led to talk of 'venereal peril' and the 'syphilisation' of the Western World (Showalter, p. 189). Meanwhile, homosexuality was itself theorised as a 'disease' and moral 'sickness' that threatened to topple society, as it supposedly had Greece and Rome (p. 4).

30. Many theorists distinguished between born 'deviants' (such as criminals and homosexuals) and those who turned to 'vice' through environmental factors. See, for example, Cesare Lombroso, *Criminal Man* [1876], trans. and with intro. by Mary Gibson and Nicole Hahn Rafter (London: Duke University Press, 2006).

31. Richard Burton, 'Terminal Essay', from *The Arabian Nights* (New York: Cosimo Classics, 2008), vol. X, pp. 63–260 (p. 179).

32. Perhaps most notable in this respect is António Cândido's now-classic essay, 'De Cortiço a Cortiço', *Novos Estudos* (CEBRAP), 30 (1991), 111–29, which examines the adaptations to Zola's model in Aluísio Azevedo's *O cortiço*. I will return to this essay shortly.

33. See Nelson Werneck Sodré, *O Naturalismo no Brasil* (Rio de Janeiro: Editora Civilização, 1965), pp. 158–59.

34. See Nelson H. Vieira, *Brasil e Portugal: a imagem recíproca (o mito e a realidade na expressão literária)* (Lisbon: Instituto de Cultura e Língua Portuguesa, 1991), for a discussion of the continuing presence of the Portuguese in post-independence Brazil.

35. Ibid., p. 127.

36. See, for example, Miguel Sanches de Baêna, *Diário de D. Manuel: e estudo sobre o regicídio* (Lisbon: Publicações Alfa, 1990), pp. 55.

37. Boaventura de Sousa Santos, 'Entre Próspero e Caliban: colonialismo, pós-colonialismo e interidentidade', *Novos Estudos*, 66 (July 2003), 23–52.

38. Eça de Queirós, 'O brasileiro', in *Obras de Eça de Queirós* (Porto: Lello e Irmão, 1948), vol. xxv, pp. 397–402 (p. 402).

39. Eça de Queirós, 'O Francesismo,' in *Obras de Eça de Queirós*, vol. ii, pp. 813–27.

40. According to Oliveira Martins, Iberian peoples were in a state of biological decline, with the Teutonic race in comparative ascendency. See Fernando Catroga, 'Raça e História', in 'Historiografia de Oliveira Martins: entre a arte e as ciências sociais', *Revista da Universidade de Coimbra*, 38 (1999), 397–453 (pp. 411–24) for a good summary of his position.

41. Oliveira Martins, *Elementos de antropologia* (Lisbon: Guimarães Editora, 1954), p. 288.

42. Antero de Quental, 'Causas da decadência dos povos peninsulares nos últimos três séculos' (lecture delivered at the Casino de Lisboa, 22 March 1871, available at <http://www.arqnet.pt/portal/discursos/ maio001.html> [accessed 5 May 2017]).

43. One of Portugal's pre-eminent cartoonists, Rafael Bordalo Pinheiro, dedicated an entire issue of his satirical magazine to the scandal on the Travessa da Espera. See Robert Howes, 'Concerning the Eccentricities of the Marquis of Valada: Politics, Culture and Homosexuality in Fin-de-Siècle Portugal, *Sexualities*, 5 (2002), 25–48 (pp. 26–27).

44. Ibid., p. 29.

45. Ibid., p. 32.

46. *Diário Popular*, 24 and 26 April 1886, Biblioteca Nacional de Portugal.

47. Victorian England is the main focus for Showalter's study.

48. In Thomas Skidmore, 'Racial Ideas and Social Policy in Brazil, 1870–1940', in *The Idea of Race in Latin America, 1870–1940*, ed. by Richard Graham (Austin: Texas University Press, 1990), pp. 7–30 (p. 11).

49. See Marshall C. Eakin, 'Race and Identity: Sílvio Romero, Science, and Social Thought in Late 19th Century Brazil,' *Luso-Brazilian Review*, 22 (1985), 151–74 (p. 164).

50. Fabiano Silveira, *Da criminalização do racismo: aspectos jurídicos e sociocriminológicos* (Belo Horizonte: Editora Del Rey, 2007), p. 10.

51. See James N. Green, *Beyond Carnival: Male Homosexuality in Twentieth-Century Brazil* (Chicago, IL: Chicago University Press, 1999), pp. 27–34.

52. Ibid., p. 44.

53. Ibid., p. 25.

54. See, for example, Beatriz Berrini, *Eça e Machado* (São Paulo: FAPESP, 2005).

55. Besides Sodré's study cited earlier, see Dorothy Loos, *The Naturalistic Novel of Brazil* (New York: Hispanic Institute in the United States, 1963), and also Flora Sussekind, *Tal Brasil, qual romance? Uma ideologia estética e sua história: Naturalismo* (Rio de Janeiro: Achiamé, 1984).

56. See, for example, Robert Howes, 'Race and Transgressive Sexuality in Adolfo Caminha's *Bom Crioulo*,' *Luso-Brazilian Review*, 38 (2001), 41–46.

57. See Josué Montello, *Aluísio Azevedo e a polêmica d''O Mulato'* (Rio de Janeiro: José Olympio, 1975).

58. Vieira argues that the movement of the court diminished the importance of Lisbon in Brazil, while the opening of the ports to other nations afforded the colony a greater degree of economic independence, fostering nationalist sentiments. See Vieira, p. 40.

59. Cited by Octávio de Tarquínio de Sousa, *A vida de D. Pedro I* (Rio de Janeiro: José Olympio, 1957), p. 266.

60. Ibid., pp. 72–73.

61. For a helpful timetable of events, see <http://www.arqnet.pt/portal/portugal/liberalismo/lib1826.html> [accessed 9 June 2017].

62. Cited by Vieira, p. 78.

63. This is the overarching argument of Freud's *Civilisation and its Discontents*. See Sigmund Freud, *Civilisation and its Discontents*, trans. by David McLintock (London: Penguin, 2002).

64. Friedrich Engels, *The Origin of the Family, Private Property and the State* (London: Penguin, 1986).

65. Ibid., pp. 83–87.

66. Ibid., p. 65.

67. Ibid., p. 86.

68. Ibid., p. 88.

69. Ibid., p. 86.

70. Freud, for example, like Engels before him, argues that 'primitive man' developed an increasingly strict incest taboo to form the more 'advanced' socio-cultural groups that we recognise today. See Freud, *Totem and Taboo*, trans. by Abraham A. Brill (New York: Cosimo Classics, 2009), pp. 3–25.

71. See Claude Lévi-Strauss, *The Elementary Structures of Kinship*, trans. by James Harle Bell and John Richard von Sturmer (Boston, MA: Beacon Press, 1969).

72. Eduardo Viveiros de Castro, 'The Gift and the Given: Three Nano-essays on Kinship and Magic', in *Kinship and Beyond: The Genealogical Model Reconsidered*, ed. by Sandra Bamford and James Leach (Oxford, NY: Berghahn Books, 2009), pp. 237–68 (p. 237).

73. Judith Butler, *Antigone's Claim: Kinship Between Life and Death* (New York: Columbia University Press, 2000).

74. T. Carver and S. A. Chambers, 'Kinship Trouble: Antigone's Claim and the Politics of Heteronormativity', *Politics and Gender*, 4 (2007), 427–49 (p. 431).

75. See Gayle Rubin, 'The Traffic in Women: Notes on the Political Economy of Sex', in *Towards an Anthropology of Women*, ed. by Rayna Reiter (New York: Monthly Review Press, 1975), pp. 157–210 (p. 180).

76. Butler, p. 24.

77. Gilberto Freyre, for example, implicitly brings together these notions in *Casa-Grande e Senzala* (Rio de Janeiro: Maia & Schmidt, 1933), where he analyses the Brazilian family in terms of its origins in the slave economy.

78. Theorists disagree on whether the invention of the homosexual in the nineteenth century invalidates modern attempts to compare the experience of same-sex desire across history. See, for example, John Boswell, 'Revolutions, Universals, and Sexual Categories', in *Hidden From History: Reclaiming the Gay and Lesbian Past*, ed. by Martin Duberman, Martha Vicinus and George Chauncy (London: Penguin, 1991), pp. 17–36. For the opposite view see David Halperin, 'Sex Before Sexuality: Pederasty, Politics, and Power in Classical Athens', in ibid., pp. 37–53. Although the concept of homosexuality was in any case crystallising at the turn of the century, this study is not directly concerned with its occurrence in the novels at hand, focusing instead on the limits of the language of relationality.

79. See *Diário do Governo*, no. 177 (Lisbon, 20 July 1912), pp. 2714–15 (Biblioteca Nacional de Portugal).

80. Desire, of course, characterised by Eve Sedgwick as 'the glue or force of attachment that binds individuals together', is implicated in the kinship debate insofar as it mobilises social cohesion and division. See Eve Sedgwick, *Between Men: English Literature and Male Homosocial Desire* (New York: Colombia University Press, 1985), p. 2.

81. See Cândido, p. 127.

82. António Carlos Santos, 'O naturalismo sob o olhar modernista: Cândido e a crítica a Aluísio Azevedo', *Crítica Cultural*, 6 (2011), 557–63.

83. Joris-Karl Huysmans, *Against Nature*, trans. by Margaret Mauldon, with intro. by Nicholas White (Oxford: Oxford University Press, 1998).

84. Dorian mentions the novel himself in Chapter 10, whilst Wilde's biographer, Richard Ellman, notes that the author claimed the novel was 'almost' Huysmans's *À Rebours* at his trial for sodomy and gross indecency. See Richard Ellman, *Oscar Wilde* (New York: Random House, 1988), p. 316.

85. See the 1903 Preface to *À Rebours*, available at <http://www.ibiblio.org/eldritch/jkh/rpf.html> [accessed 1 July 2019].

86. Aluísio Azevedo, *O mulato* (São Paulo: Klick Editora, 1999), pp. 79–80.

87. Karl Marx and Friedrich Engels, *On Literature and Art* (New York: International General, 1974).

88. Cora Kaplan, *Sea Changes: Essays on Culture and Feminism* (London: Verso, 1986), p. 73 (emphasis added).

89. See, for example, Jacques Derrida, 'Signature Event Context', in *Limited Inc* (Evanston, IL: Northwestern University Press, 1997), pp. 1–25.

90. Roberto Schwarz, 'Nacional por subtração', in *Que horas são? Ensaios* (São Paulo: Companhia das Letras, 1989), pp. 29–48.

91. Loos, p. 54.

92. Alessandra El Far, *Páginas de sensação* (São Paulo: Companhia das Letras, 2004), p. 195.

93. José Esteban Muñoz, *Cruising Utopia: The Then and There of Queer Futurity* (New York: New York University Press, 2009), p. 1.

94. Murat Aydemir, *Indiscretions: At the Intersection of Queer and Postcolonial Theory* (Haarlem: Colophon, 2011), p. 10. Aydemir offers the 'shared historical origin of strategies of racialisation and sexualisation' as grounds for bringing queer and postcolonial theory closer together.

95. I hope readers will forgive me, in this respect, for not including the novels of Machado de Assis in this book. Although he is undoubtedly an important part of the picture when thinking about Lusophone critiques of nineteenth-century epistemological and literary trends and, I would venture, a prime candidate for further research in this line of inquiry, his aesthetic trajectory circumvents Naturalist methods much more than does Eça's, and has very little, if anything in common with Botelho or Azevedo. There are some interesting parallels with the later work of Eça, but alas, there is only so much ground one can cover in a single study.

96. See Loos, p. 22.

97. Brookshaw, p. 41.

98. Although Eça admittedly constitutes an exception to the rule, perhaps because of his ill-disguised disillusionment with the movement, no other Naturalist writer quite makes it to the centre of the Lusophone canon. Azevedo, Caminha and Botelho, for example, although key figures within the movement itself, are certainly not household names in the same manner as José de Alencar, Almeida Garrett, Oswald de Andrade and Mário de Sá Carneiro.

99. Cândido, p. 112 (my translation).

100. Sodré, p. 225.

# CHAPTER 1

# Abel Botelho

## Introduction

Published in 1891 as part of a series entitled *Patologia Social*,[1] Abel Botelho's *O Barão de Lavos* [*The Baron of Lavos*] is the most renowned so-called 'pathological novel' written in Portuguese, although it seems to have attracted more critical attention for its scandalous subject matter — an aristocrat's ruinous passion for a young *efebo* [ephebe] — than its literary craftsmanship. Indeed, there is very little written about the novel at all in modern times beyond an article-length study by Robert Howes,[2] short entries in so-called 'gay histories',[3] analyses of the Brazilian novel that it inspired, *Bom Crioulo*,[4] and an unpublished Master's thesis by Maria Limão de Andrade.[5] With critics having proven reluctant to regard the novel as part of the established literary canon,[6] instead presenting *Lavos* as a landmark artefact of changing times, 'fatally flawed [...] but nevertheless interesting for being one of the first novels to deal with homosexuality explicitly',[7] there remains an ample space for close reading that has not, arguably, been adequately explored. Howes convincingly sets the novel in the context of several homosexual scandals that appear to have inspired Botelho, including the Marquês de Valada and Rua do Trombeta affairs discussed in the Introduction. He also, importantly, finds moments that are 'almost subversive' to the otherwise pervasive pathological discourse.[8] Participating as it does in the sexual panic of the period, reflected too in the three hundred copies that sold in the week following publication,[9] and containing notable discursive inconsistencies, the novel emerges as a compelling candidate for an analysis of Naturalism 'against nature'.

In the present chapter, then, I would like to build on previous studies in a number of ways. Firstly, within the context of the book as a whole, I would like to introduce the novel as paradigmatic of the 'scientific' approach to literature first imagined by Zola and, in a broader sense, of *fin-de-siècle* sexual panic, exploring how the movement of the narrative parallels contemporaneous patterns of thought. I argue that the novel's many contradictions are largely contingencies of a discourse that attempts to articulate and restrict the evasive concept of sexuality that was increasingly used to buttress the bourgeois family. Paradoxically, however, an explosion of neologisms and pseudo-scientific vocabulary is witnessed in the process with the effect that 'degeneracy' proves surprisingly *generative*. I will then turn to Botelho's equally disruptive recourse to Greek pederasty, which undercuts the 'modern', pathological approach, implicating wider class and gender struggles. As a series of figurative closets are opened over the course of the novel, releasing a contagion of sexual deviance, criminality and working-class culture into the seemingly cloistered bourgeois world, *Lavos* depicts a society deeply preoccupied with the upheavals of the late nineteenth century which, imagined alongside the degeneration of kinship and the nation's 'stock', echo the cries of the racial theorists in Northern Europe. However, I will then consider the allegorical appearance of Dom Sebastião, Portugal's most infamous and possibly homosexual monarch, with which the 'disease' becomes one of national-imperial history. The spectre of Dom Sebastião is characteristically unflattering, but the use of allegory also marks a poetic divergence from the scientific method, a moment in which Botelho writes against nature, and a point of departure for the subsequent readings in this book. As we shall see in the chapters that follow, the novel is important within Lusophone Naturalism as a whole, incorporating many of its key characteristics and directly influencing the movement in Brazil.

*O Barão de Lavos* tells the story of Dom Sebastião de Lavos, a Portuguese aristocrat from an ancient family and last in his line. He is introduced, somewhat improbably perhaps, as the descendant of generations of sodomites reaching far back into the pederastic culture of ancient Greece — in *Lavos*, as I have already indicated, the 'degenerate' can be surprisingly generative. Beginning at the Lisbon circus, where Sebastião scouts for adolescent boys willing to sleep with him for money, the novel depicts the protagonist's gradual descent into moral, social and financial ruin as he develops an uncontrollable passion for a poor, young and handsome *maroto* [rascal], Eugénio. Sebastião maintains Eugénio in an apartment on the Rua da Rosa, hiding him from his social circle. Predictably (*Lavos* is not a novel in which to expect the unexpected), the attachment throws Sebastião's relationship with his wife, Elvira, into turmoil. Increasingly reckless in his precarious double life which, as Howes notes, recalls the lives of several high-profile aristocrats of the time,[10] the Baron starts to invite Eugénio to dine at his Lisbon *palacete* [palace] and educates him as his protégé, introducing him to privileged life at great personal expense. Meanwhile, injured and bored by her husband's inattentions, and after initially despising Eugénio, despite knowing nothing of the affair, Elvira is seduced by the boy herself *às escondidas* [on the sly], initiating a bizarre, intergenerational love triangle that cements Eugénio's growing power. As husband and wife fall hopelessly for the same boy, Eugénio bleeds the family coffers dry whilst playing an impossible game of duplicity. The game is brought to an end when Sebastião, tipped off by a jealous maid, discovers his wife and Eugénio in flagrante delicto, whereupon the family scandal spreads citywide and the Baron flees abroad on the pretext of a 'grand tour'. On his return to Lisbon, the Baron, now almost destitute, experiments with some shady business ventures before resigning himself to a life of poverty and misery. Finally, disfigured by syphilis and prostituting himself to support his precarious existence in a dark basement, Sebastião is brutalised by a group of youths in the Avenida da Liberdade; his dramatic but almost unnoticed death marks the end of the novel. Although *Lavos* is uncompromisingly explicit and caused a stir among critics, it was never prohibited, not even by the repressive Salazar regime,[11] and despite a number of books being banned at the time of publication.[12] As Howes suggests, this was no doubt because of the novel's strongly moralising tone, which led many to believe that *Lavos* was aimed at encouraging the sexually deviant to renounce their 'vices',[13] a hypothesis that will now be put to the test.

## *O Barão de Lavos* and the Pathological Novel

With its predictable plot and focus on one particular 'vice', *Lavos* is a prominent example of literary pathology, a genre that emerged at the end of the nineteenth century and that in many ways intensified the principles of Naturalism, sometimes *ad absurdum*. However, whilst it is the general scientific method that informs Naturalism, social pathology takes the medical sciences as its chief inspiration,[14] with the protagonist developing a 'disease' and typically suffering unto death. The narrator adopts the voice of the doctor, sitting at the 'dramatic convergence of knowledge and power',[15] and drastically foreclosing narrative outcomes such that 'medical power-knowledge [...] comes to be inscribed, in some circumstances, as novelistic fatality'.[16] That Botelho named his most renowned series of novels *Patologia Social* testifies to the enthusiasm with which he brought to Portugal what had started as a French literary trend. His efforts chimed with the ambitions of three prominent Portuguese physicians of the period, Egas Moniz (awarded a Nobel Prize in 1949 for inventing the lobotomy),[17] Sousa Martins, and Miguel Bombarda, who called for the scientific method in all aspects of life,[18] ambitions to an extent shared by the earlier *Geração de '70*, but now invested with an overtly medical thrust. In *Lavos*, Botelho's recourse to the language of medicine leaves the reader in no doubt about the 'disease' in question, although it is never definitively named, being called variously 'pederastia', 'sodomia' and even 'neuropatia' and 'andromania' . Of course, the interchangeability of the Biblical 'sodomia' with contemporaneous scientific terminology demonstrates the ease with which a much older discourse of sin and redemption is supplanted by a pseudo-medical discourse of illness and cure, accounting for *Lavos*'s 'scientifically' justified moralism when really it was a case of the morals justifying the science. As Robert Howes notes, at times the medical language becomes so dense as to detract significantly from reading the story.[19] The penultimate chapter, depicting the Baron's final days of misery, is particularly tortuous; he develops:

> dolorosas sensações de estrangulamento em volta da cinta, no tórax, nos rins, em toda a região intestinal; com sobressaltos de tendões, súbitas alternâncias de frio e calor nas extremidades, formigueiros, cócegas; nevralgias viscerais, violentas crises gástricas, vómitos biliosos; e um sentimento de opressão nos brônquios, sufocações, estases de pulso, dores lombares, tenesmos. (pp. 388–89)

> [painful, strangling sensations around his waist and thorax, in his kidneys and all through his intestinal regions, with jittery tendons, sudden flushes of hot and cold in his extremities, formication, visceral neuralgias, violent, gastric crises, bilious vomit, and a feeling of pressure in his bronchi, of suffocation, loss of pulse, pains in his loins, and tenesmus.]

In this manner, the narrative can become so crowded with medical terminology that it is difficult to tell where the latter ends and the story begins,[20] as though in surrender to the unstoppable forces of 'nature' and physiology. The Baron's grotesque deterioration in symptoms, a medical punishment for a moral sin, renders death the sole possible resolution to the novel.

However, whilst the pathological approach may thus impose considerable limitations on narrative outcomes, suppressing other possible modes of being, it is also self-justifying due to the deterministic assumptions of degeneration theory upon which Botelho draws considerably. As I discussed in the Introduction, degeneration theorists placed human beings at different stages of evolution: at the top of the evolutionary chain stood white, north-western Europeans, and at the bottom were black and African peoples.[21] The categories of analysis were fluid and overlapped: although skin colour appeared to inform the hierarchy, it was then equally argued that the 'inferior' races could be identified by their more liberal attitudes to sexual practices.[22] Havelock Ellis began his analysis of homosexuals by listing their 'race' and 'ancestry',[23] whilst Krafft-Ebing himself speaks of the 'sodomitic idolatry' of Ancient Greece that modern society has supposedly moved 'beyond'.[24] Within this schema, homosexuality — as 'it' had by then been coined, though still not popularly — indicated a 'degenerate', atavistic reversion, doomed to extinction, that could then be medically isolated and purged. The inevitability of the narrative in *Lavos*, casting desire as a terminal illness, thus becomes part of a seizure of power by the narrator, who is given a doctor's authority to marginalise and remove the sexually deviant.

Botelho's close adherence to degeneration theory is further evident in the details of the 'disease'. When Sebastião develops syphilis, for example — named quite candidly in the book, despite being almost unutterable at the time[25] — he develops the physical manifestation of what is initially introduced as a psycho-pathological condition. Syphilis was such a public concern in Europe at the turn of the century that newspapers spoke of 'venereal peril' and the 'syphilisation' of the Western world.[26] As Susan Sontag and others have suggested, the AIDS crisis in the 1980s was akin to the syphilis scare of the *fin de siècle*, in that both saw the physical illnesses semantically undershot with sexual licentiousness.[27] Syphilis was the marker of sexual deviance par excellence (though unlike AIDS, not of sexual orientation), and in *Lavos* it becomes part of the wider search for the deviant, 'homosexual body'.[28] Like illness, race becomes closely bound up with sexuality in the novel when a 'degenerate' black priest appears at a brothel. When Sebastião returns from his grand tour, he pays for sex with another young boy:

> Ao cabo, num desmedido horror de si mesmo, sem poder explicar-se como baixara àquela abjeção suprema, o barão balbuciou:
> — Nunca ninguém te tinha feito isto...?
> Ao que o rapaz, filosofalmente [*sic*], abotoando-se:
> — Ainda ontem... um padre. Era preto. (p. 380)

> [At the end, in sheer horror at himself, unable to explain how he had stooped to such supreme abjection, the Baron stammered:

'Has no one ever done that to you before...?'
To which the boy, philosophically, fastening his buttons, replied:
'Just yesterday... a priest. He was black.']

The rhetorical opposition between 'nunca ninguém' [no one ever] and '*ainda* ontem' [just yesterday] amplifies the perceived threat of social contagion, but the subsequent racial detail quickly distances it from — and comforts — an overwhelmingly white, bourgeois readership. The novel is populated almost exclusively by white, upper- and middle-class *lisboetas*, rendering the priest's blackness unusual and consolidating the perception of degeneracy, both sexual and racial. Nevertheless, the implication that the Catholic Church, a centrepiece of Portuguese society at the time, is 'corrupted', apparently by the very colonial Other that the nation sought to 'civilise' and convert, curiously reintroduces the risk of contagion once more. This is one of the novel's most striking slips, as the colonial past, overwhelmingly presented elsewhere as something lost and to be recovered,[29] is here subtly imagined as a threat to society at large. Indeed, the contagion is never adequately contained in the novel, despite such moments as this where degeneration theory suddenly rears its head with that precise purpose, moulding the narrative to the 'science'. Interestingly, *Bom Crioulo*, which I turn to at the end of this book, recovers race from the 'degenerate' margins to the centre of the story with its black hero and protagonist, leading, in part, to a problematisation of the theory and a much sharper critique of colonialism. The black priest in *Lavos*, by contrast, like the surrender of plot to prognosis, works to confirm the theory; as Howes writes, *O Barão de Lavos* 'is controlled by the tenets of degeneration theory in its most extreme Lombrosian form'.[30]

## Freedom in Madness? The Limits of Literary Pathology

Such moments of structural transparency in the novel, where the theory becomes visible even to the point of pressuring verisimilitude — this latter supposedly cherished by the Naturalists, of course — betray a wider tension between story and theory, freedom and determinism, and indeed 'nature' and 'culture'. Degeneration theory, drawing on Positivist convictions that all phenomena are empirically calculable and that some individuals are born degenerate,[31] leaves little or no wriggle room for agency. Desire becomes disease; failure to comply with the bourgeois sexual code, far from threatening to expose the latter as cultural, is given a 'natural', pathological explanation. When played out in novel form, the pathological approach gives rise to an apparent conflict between, on the one hand, the deterministic theory that dooms the 'diseased' protagonist to worsening illness and death, and, on the other, an attempt to endow him with subjectivity and a plausible inner life. The tension is so great that at times, the narrative questions the entire Positivist epistemological system on which the novel precariously rests. As Howes remarks, 'a careful reader can find a number of different viewpoints in the novel, which makes it more than a simple anti-homosexual diatribe', resulting at times in 'an ambivalence that is almost subversive'.[32] Is there, perhaps, a limit to the narrator's grasp of events, beyond which an alternative voice can be heard?

One such ostensibly 'different viewpoint' in the novel, which Howes himself cites as an example, occurs immediately after the aforementioned episode at the brothel. When the young man reveals to Sebastião that he is one of many pederasts in Lisbon, a remarkable passage of free indirect discourse ensues in which the Baron calls the fundamental tenets of bourgeois morality into question, including its tight restrictions on sexual desire and their newfound justification in a universalising 'science':

> — Como!?... Então não era só ele?... Outros havia também que... E muitos, talvez, quem sabe?... Muitos, sim, provavelmente... Muitos! Bem mais do que ele, do que o mundo imaginava!
> — E porque não?... Que fizera ele de condenável, no fim de contas?... — *na subsequente vibração da insânia, aventurava.* — Quem sabe uma palavra da natureza das coisas? [...] Quem de dizer-lhe onde começa o vício e onde acaba a virtude?... Lérias! Não há ignomínias que se transmutam em glórias?... Cristo, por exemplo! — E tinha um riso cínico. — Nada sobre o caso de ciência certa sabemos. Os nossos modos triviais de pensar e sentir... as nossas predileções, antipatias, jeitos de ver, tendências... as nossas adorações, os nossos ódios, nada têm de racional, de sólido em que se estribem. Nenhum princípio universal e eterno que lhes defina a essência. Pelo contrário, a sua compreensão é ilusória e falível, porque oscila à mercê dos preconceitos... Tal ação é magnânima porque assim vem considerada, por uns tantos homens; tal outra é ignominiosa... porque convém que o seja! Ora adeus!...
> [...]
> E o barão, já na rua, tudo era ainda meditar e bordar atenuantes sobre a extraordinária revelação do rapaz. Alçava com orgulho a cabeça, sentia-se reabilitado, reavia a própria estima. — Isto do bem e do mal, da justiça e da iniquidade, da razão e do desvario, da santidade e do crime, era tudo relativo. Estava por fixar e medir o estalão do vício... E mesmo, afinal, pensando bem, essa ácida gota de linfa que lhe jorrara aos lábios, era uma coisa pura, transcendental, sagrada... era o gérmen misterioso da vida, o líquido fecundo e nobre por excelência... era o divino plasma de todos nós. (pp. 380–81, emphasis added)

> ['What!?... So it wasn't just him?... There were others, too, who... And many, perhaps, who knows?... Many, quite probably... Many! Far more than he or the world would care to imagine!
> 'And why not?... What crime was he guilty of, in the end?...', *he ventured, in the wave of insanity that followed.* 'Who knows anything about the nature of things? [...] Who was anyone to tell him where vice begins and virtue ends?... It was nonsense! Are there not ignominies that become glories?... Christ, for example!', and he laughed cynically. 'We know nothing about exact science. Our trivial modes of thinking and feeling... our predilections, antipathies, ways of seeing, inclinations... our loves, our hates, they are not based on anything rational or solid. No universal, eternal principle defines their essence. On the contrary, their comprehension is illusory and fallible, swaying at the mercy of prejudice... This action is magnanimous because most men consider it so; that one is ignominious... because that's how it was! Away with it all!
> [...]
> And the Baron, on the street now, was still pondering and attenuating the boy's revelation with comforting thoughts. He raised his head with pride, felt

himself rehabilitated, recovered his self-esteem. Good and evil, justice and iniquity, reason and madness, sanctity and crime, they were all relative. The measure of vice was yet to be fixed and defined... And perhaps, in the end, thinking it all through, that acid drop of lymph that rushed to his lips was something pure, transcendental, sacred... It was the mysterious seed of life, the noble and fecund liquid par excellence... it was the divine plasma of us all.] [emphasis added]

These lines bring the chapter to a close, adding weight to the extended free indirect discourse that sits at odds with the condemnatory tone of the doctor. What has elsewhere been described as a gruesome disease becomes the 'divino plasma de todos nós', a corporeal metaphor, but this time one of vitality and even divinity, turning the discourse of sin and pathology on its head. Sebastião goes on to question the fundamental principles of science when applied to 'os nossos modos [...] de sentir' which, as we have seen, overwhelm the narrative elsewhere. 'Quem sabe uma palavra da natureza das coisas? [...] nada tem de racional.' I have added in italics the moment where the doctor's voice returns, ensuring that the scandalous passage is clearly 'diagnosed' as a 'vibração da insânia', the musings of a lunatic. Similarly, the following chapter opens with one of the most chastising passages of the novel:

> O subsequente descrasear desta vida latrinária [sic], as últimas anotações da torpe monografia, hemos de deixá-las apontadas a correr, em fugacíssimas legendas, acossados nesta pressa nauseada e medrosa do viajante que se vê forçado a saltilhar [sic] a deletéria vasa de um pântano.
>
> Porque, de ora avante, a vida do barão arrasta-se, turporosa [sic] e lôbrega, pelas inconfessadas volutas da chatinagem mais sórdida; e resvala às ínfimas degradações do pulhismo, da miséria, da loucura e da infâmia... A loucura em que ele se afundara sem remédio, no momento em que deixou por completo as suas paixões dominarem-no.
>
> Tinha na alma a corrupção do século (p. 382).

> [The subsequent haemorrhaging of this latrinary life, the final words of this obscene monograph, we shall have to write in a hurry, in the briefest of notes, beset as we are with the nauseous and fearful haste of a traveller who finds himself obliged to jump over the treacherous muds of a swamp.
>
> Because from hereon in, the Baron's life dragged itself, torpid and gloomy, through the hidden spirals of the most sordid transactions, sliding through the final degradations of scandal, misery, madness and infamy... the madness in which he had drowned hopelessly since allowing his passions to master him entirely.
>
> He had in his soul the corruption of the century.]

So keen is the narrator to distance himself from identification with Sebastião that he must dismiss his own monograph as 'torpe'. A spate of neologisms to describe the Baron's transgressions, meanwhile, suggests a deficiency in the narrator's ready vocabulary as his object of study begins to fall outside the social order. 'Latrinária' performs a semantic slippage from sexuality to waste and sewage, a discourse sufficiently indecorous to cause any nineteenth-century reader to flush. 'Saltilhar', meanwhile, is of more doubtful origins but might be a mixing of 'saltar' with 'ilhar': a jump into isolation. (Interestingly, it is the narrator who feels this way inclined, even to the point of becoming nauseous in telling Sebastião's story. Is the doctor developing his patient's illness, the 'corrupção do século'? I will return to this possibility later.) Finally, the image of the Baron's life dragging itself down, 'turporosa [sic] e lôbrega', into spiralling misery, suggests an excessive materiality to life, a sluggish immanence, a vision of the soul as body. Momentarily then, Sebastião's desires are given free rein within the text, escaping the prescriptive vocabulary of 'medicine' and the law; however, immediately following his rumination on the arbitrariness of that law, the doctor returns with still greater moralistic force. A barrage of scornful adjectives describes the final years of his sorry life; any prior moments of questioning are quickly snuffed out.

In this sense, the novel sustains a remarkable degree of internal contradiction, mostly played out between the authoritative narrator and the defiant Baron ruminating in free indirect discourse. The very notion of free indirect discourse, as Monika Fludernik describes it, is an 'evocation of subjectivity' within another's subjectivity by means of grammatical cues;[33] Jacob L. Mey argues that the technique can mean the character is apparently 'freed from the constraints of the narrative voice'.[34] The reader is presented with two opposing visions: the insistence on terminal illness that deprives Sebastião of any ability to overcome his plight, and what seems like his defiant agency. The *vaivém* [to-and-fro] of perspectives in the novel thus recalls Mikhail Bakhtin's concept of the monological narrative, in which characters exist only in order to enact and confirm the author's ideology.[35] However, equally for Bakhtin, 'there can be no actual monologue',[36] the underlying 'dialogic imperative' of human language meaning that 'monologistic' writing amounts to a seizure of power attained through the silencing of other voices. In *Lavos*, although Sebastião serves as an object to be marginalised and sacrificed to establish the primacy of bourgeois morality, and his narrated thoughts can end up complying, structurally, with those of the narrator, the degree to which his voice is silenced is questionable. At no point does Sebastião accept or share the narrator's view that he is morally reprehensible, or express regret for his life 'choices'; on the contrary, as we have seen, he often stresses his guiltlessness. Botelho may strive towards monologism, but in the end, as we shall see, the Baron's autonomy is never entirely kept in check, and some degree of polyphony escapes.

The potential for polyphony is confirmed at the end of the penultimate chapter, when the Baron resigns himself to a life of squalor and abjection. Whilst, as we have seen, the narrator revels in the horrors of his 'vida latrinária', Sebastião actively seeks and becomes content with a life of supposed misery. Firstly, whilst the Marquês de Torredeita offers his bankrupt friend 'uma hospedagem generosa e distinta, alojando-o numa das grandes salas senhoriais do andar nobre' [generous and distinguished accommodation, lodging him in one of large, master bedrooms on the first floor], Sebastião opts for 'uma horrível cela do rés-do-chão, mal branqueada a cal, em perene divórcio do sol, escura, salitrosa, com uma janela baixa de grades e porta direta para a rua' [a horrid cell on the ground floor, poorly whitewashed, perennially divorced from the sun, dark, thick with saltpetre, with a low, barred window and a door straight onto the street] (pp. 383–84). This affords him 'a maior soma possível de liberdade, de isolamento e de mistério' [the greatest possible amount of freedom, isolation and mystery]. It is the desire to preserve his freedom, and not necessity, that leads the Baron to live in the squalid, ground-floor cell. Meanwhile, unlike the attics and basements that tend to house nineteenth-century literary 'lunatics', such as the narrator of *Notes from Underground*[37] or the first Mrs Rochester,[38] the ground floor is the most exposed to the street and the outside world. Sebastião and the city have easy access to each other, suggesting a cycle of potential mutual 'corruption' less isolated in society than the reader, or even narrator, might like to think.

Sebastião's choice of furnishing is similarly expressive of his agency:

> Um simples catre de ferro, pintado a preto, quatro cadeiras de palhinha, lavatório de ferro também, com espelho, guarda-fato, uma mesa, e suspenso na parede fronteira ao leito o seu velho Rapto de Ganimedes. — A única joia que do radioso bazar de S. Cristóvão ele havia conservado. Continuava, acima de tudo, adorando-a. Era a melhor, a mais latejante parcela de si mesmo. Era o seu ídolo, o seu talismã, a sua divisa, o seu timbre. Votava-lhe um culto incondicional, uma ardente e religiosa ternura. Delicioso traslado da sua alma... síntese dulceral [*sic*] dos seus desejos, das suas ambições, dos seus ideais, do seu destino. Era o símbolo das perturbações da sua carne, era uma celeste alegoria 'travestindo' em graça as abominações do seu viver.
>
> Nas suas horas mais sentidamente angustiadas, nas frequentes intercadências de dor e de desânimo, o barão, numa súplica, fitava-a... e estava animado, feliz... e estava contente. (p. 384).

> [A simple iron bedstead, painted black, four wicker chairs, an iron washbasin with a mirror, wardrobe, a table, and hanging on the wall opposite his bed, his venerable Rape of Ganymede, the only gem from the radiant bazar of São Cristóvão that he had kept. He continued to adore it above all else. It was the finest, most throbbing part of his being. It was his idol, his talisman, his emblem, his crest. He granted it an unreserved cult, an ardent and religious tenderness. A delightful model for his soul... the sweet synthesis of his desires, of his ambitions, his ideals, his destiny. It was the symbol of the disturbances of his flesh, it was a celestial allegory, graciously 'crossdressing' the abominations of his existence.
>
> In his most heartfelt, anguished moments, in his frequent weaknesses of pain and dispiritedness, the Baron, in prayer, gazed at it... and it raised his spirits, he was happy... he was content.]

The only object that Sebastião retains from his previous life is his most prized possession, the engraving of the Rape of Ganymede. The homoerotic engraving is invested with particular importance in the novel. At the beginning, it is the Baron's fascination and, as Limão de Andrade argues, appears as a corrupting influence.[39] Later, during a dinner party at which Sebastião cautiously (and disastrously) discusses male beauty, he makes reference to the engraving when arguing for the existence of homoeroticism throughout history. Here, at the end of the novel, it becomes the centrepiece of his new life, his talisman and fetish (derived from the Portuguese *feitiço*,[40] something invested with magical powers). The engraving, indeed, charms Sebastião where the narrator only sees 'abominações' (from Latin

*abominatio*, that which is 'shun as an ill omen'),[41] as though it disguises a curse
— curiously metaphysical resonances for a doctor's 'diagnosis'. The similarly
remarkable appearance of the word 'travestindo', equating this false charm to the
deceitful power of crossdressing, exemplifies how the policing of sexuality readily
encroaches into gender norms. But to Sebastião, the engraving is a confirmation of
his individuality and affirmation of independence (for Freud, the fetish is a 'token
of triumph over the threat of castration and a protection against it').[42] Is this the
moment in the dialectic in which the slave recognises himself in his own work?
The Baron's peaceful contemplation of the engraving, a model for his soul, suggests
the pleasure of self-recognition as the doctor strays into the language of charms
and curses, briefly relinquishing his medical authority. Thus although Sebastião's
inner ravings are not always 'subversive' vis-à-vis the narrator's perspective, often
working to confirm the discourse of social pathology, this passage, like the ground-
floor flat or indeed the narrator's nausea in telling his tale, does seem to mark a
moment in which the novel escapes the echo chamber of degeneration theory,
allowing other voices and even epistemologies to be heard.

### *O Barão de Lavos* and Social Context: Whose 'Pathology'?

*O Barão de Lavos* thus deploys an array of methods to exert power over the sexually
'deviant', although this power seems constantly to be slipping away. The exchange
of opposing perspectives reflects the context of sexual panic in which the novel was
written and the insufficiency of a universalising 'science' that fails to circumscribe
its object; 'nature' can never quite be pinned down. On this note, and before I
turn more precisely to the representation of the Portuguese family, I would like to
dwell briefly on the novel's position within the socio-cultural landscape to draw
out its dialogue with other discourses from the period. The reference to a number
of *fin-de-siècle* scandals in particular marks a tentative shift in focus from individual
to national pathology, with which the threat of contagion surfaces once more.

As I suggested in the Introduction, the arrival of the principles of Positivism
and degeneration theory in Portugal inflected the discourse with acutely national
concerns. The nation's extensive imperial losses and the humiliating British
Ultimatum of 1890 seemed to lend historical weight to, for example, theories of the
Sotadic Zone that cast Southern European nations as racially inferior to France and
Britain, where these theories were conceived.[43] Indeed, at this point in the century,
the notion of Iberian 'decadence' and 'decay' was well established, introduced
earlier by the *Geração de '70* and then widely accepted by the leading intellectuals of
the age. Botelho thus echoes the work of others in his pathological approach, even
when considering more critical (and canonical) voices, as we shall see in the case of
Eça de Queirós in the following chapter. Even the nineteenth-century stalwart of
Portuguese Romanticism, Camilo Castelo Branco, raises the spectre of degeneration
theory in *A Brasileira de Prazins* (1882), in which the daughters of the disgraced
Honorata are regarded by local people as condemned to lunacy and debauchery on
account of their transgressive mother and mad grandmother. 'Má mulher [...] de má
árvore, ruim fruto' [A bad woman [...] from a bad tree, a rotten fruit],[44] ventures

Tia Maria de Vilalva. As the popular Portuguese saying dictates, *os pecados dos nossos avós fizeram-nos eles, pagamo-los nós* [the sins of our grandfathers were committed by them and paid for by us].[45] Interestingly, according to the *Diário Popular*, Camilo also congratulated Judge Thomás Ribeiro for using scientific principles to absolve Marinho de Cruz of his crime in 1888.[46] This scandal in particular, which followed those of the Marquês de Valada (1881) and the Rua do Trombeta (1886), added to the panic surrounding the disintegration of the family and empire; Cruz was, after all, a student at the Escola Militar that trained the nation's (assumedly heterosexual) brothers in arms. All three public scandals appear to have served as an inspiration for *Lavos* and as a reminder that the 'corrupção do século', along with the 'scientific' discourses that scrutinised it, had reached all levels of society.

Further comment is warranted on the Marinho de Cruz case as it is especially revealing of the extent to which Positivist and medical discourses had permeated the public sphere. The newspaper coverage of the story is vast and detailed, following the initial trial for weeks on end and, two years later, the retrial in which Marinho de Cruz was convicted, stripping him of his military honours and leading to his imprisonment in front of a huge crowd.[47] When the story initially broke on 24 April 1886, the *Diário Popular* devoted about a third of its total space to the incident. The language used in the newspapers is revealingly similar to that of the narrative voice in *Lavos*:

> N'um caracter tão irregular como o de Marinho da Cruz parece que todos estes factos causaram uma terrivel impressão... Havia tempos que o alferes Marinho da Cruz se sentia dominado por alguma idéa sinistra ou por alguma preoccupação que não podia vencer. Como em certos casos de loucura o enfermo tem a previsão do accesso proximo, parece que Marinho da Cruz havia tempos que receiava não ter a força de vontade suficiente para resistir a uma tendência funesta.[48]

> [In a character as irregular as that of Marinho da Cruz, it seems as though these events had a terrible effect... For a while Marinho da Cruz had felt dominated by some sinister idea or worry that he was powerless to stop. As in certain cases of madness in which the patient foresees an impending attack, it seems as though Marinho da Cruz had long feared not having the strength of will to resist a fatal tendency.]

The 'tendência funesta', a sense of hereditary inevitability thwarting any attempts at self-control, finds an echo in the deterministic narrative of *Lavos* five years later. Similarly, the controversy of the initial court case, which as we have seen was one of the first of its kind in acquitting the accused on the grounds of being mentally ill and therefore legally irresponsible, bears the same ideological fault lines as the novel. As one commentator argued on 26 April 1886:

> O assasinato perpetrado pelo alferes Marinho da Cruz é um sympthoma funesto de que o positivismo contemporaneo não tem um papel mais efficaz de moralisador do que o anathematisa do sentimentalismo romantico. As circunstancias asquerosas que o precedem e que o revestem estão recommendando este crime á curiosidade doentia dos naturalistas.[49]

[The assassination committed by Second Lieutenant Marinho da Cruz is a fatal symptom of the fact that today's Positivism is no greater moralising force than its anathema, Romantic sentimentalism. The grotesque circumstances that led to it and surround it owe themselves to the sickly curiosity of the Naturalists.]

The prosecution, which was largely making the moral argument to push for a prison sentence, reviled the potential for the medicalised, deterministic argument to absolve criminals of all culpability. On the one hand, the scandal was so unpalatable as to require a whole new order of discourse to isolate and describe it. On the other, that same discourse deprived the sexually deviant of such a degree of autonomy that they could no longer be held responsible for their actions, affording them the dubious freedom in madness sought by the Baron of Lavos. In this sense, the problematic debates that simmer in the 1891 novel were widespread in society, from the courtroom to the newspapers and high- and low-brow fiction, Botelho having drawn upon them considerably. Ironically, even the above commentator who condemns the 'curiosidade doentia dos naturalistas' slips into the language of degeneracy in the process, presenting the 'crime' as a direct consequence — more, a 'symphthoma funesto' — of Positivism itself.

## The Pederastic Love Triangle: Class Struggles and the Demise of the Portuguese Family

Sickness, symptoms and 'perturbações' [disturbances] were thus the order of the day, the discourse of degeneracy proving diffuse and reaching its most powerful, if also contradictory, moment when concerned with sexuality. It is no surprise that of Botelho's series *Patologia Social, O Barão de Lavos* is the most widely, if not necessarily fondly, remembered, being the only instalment to deal primarily with the 'vice' of same-sex desire,[50] though the contagion threatens to spill over into the national community as a whole. With this in mind, I would now like to focus more closely on the different amorous attachments in *Lavos*, drawing on my assertions in the Introduction that the policing of sexuality works to consolidate the accepted structure of kinship and inheritance under patriarchal capitalism. As we shall see, the broken Portuguese family becomes a 'symptom' of wider social changes, particularly surrounding class, precipitating a slippage of signifiers from deviant sexuality into myriad other transgressions as an individual's pathology spreads through society in many guises.

Considering that Sebastião's love for Eugénio is never in fact named as 'homosexual', instead denoted by a host of terms from 'inversão sexual' [sexual inversion] to 'pederastia' and 'neuropatia', it is clear that the relationship is non-normative in multifaceted ways and not easily reducible to same-sex desire. Whilst this is inevitably a part, perhaps even the crux, of the transgressions, finer tools of analysis are required to capture the wider dynamic of knowledge and power at play. To begin with, the Baron is around twice the age of Eugénio, is the exclusive penetrative partner,[51] and is repeatedly described as a 'pederasta' (Limão de Andrade argues that it and 'sodomita' are the most insistent terms).[52] He is primarily attracted to adolescent boys, though also to women, again rendering inappropriate the term 'homosexual', which typically denotes exclusive attraction to the same sex. Indeed, the pederastic relationship in *Lavos* is described as heralding from the 'efebismo [*sic*] da antiga Grécia' [the ephebism of Ancient Greece] via the Baron's ancestors (p. 27). The term *efebo* [ephebe], denoting an adolescent boy, dates from classical antiquity and is often used by the doctor-narrator to describe Eugénio, while the two other cases of same-sex desire in the novel, involving the Coronel Militão and the nameless black priest, are also pederastic, raising the prospect that Botelho chiefly takes Greek pederasty, and not necessarily contemporaneous studies of the newly invented 'homosexuality', as his paradigm.[53] That Sebastião adores his engraving of Michelangelo's Rape of Ganymede, on one occasion justifying homoeroticism based on its prevalence in Ancient Greece, suggests that it is also his guiding star. This 'reversion' to Greek understandings of male relations is itself curious, undermining as it does the novel's attempts to define the Baron's malady as the 'corrupção do século' [corruption of the century] and, perhaps obliquely, the authority and reach of contemporaneous medical thought.

If pederasty is taken to be the organising principle of Sebastião's relationship with Eugénio, a dynamic that, as I have indicated, we will see at work across the Lusophone Naturalist movement, a host of interrelated practices are uncovered that upset the social order. Greek pederasty was closely associated with pedagogy (indeed, both derive from *paedos*, meaning 'boy'). According to Pausanias in Plato's *Symposium*, two kinds of love derive from Aphrodite, each heralding from different parental lineages ascribed to her in Greek mythology. As daughter of Zeus and Dione, offspring of love between a man and a woman, Aphrodite represents the common love of the body. However, this love is less 'pure' than that represented by Aphrodite, daughter of Uranus which, by contrast, is the love of youths, reason and the soul.[54] Love of youths is thus of a higher order and inseparable from the search for, and transmission of, knowledge. As we shall see, the educative aspect of pederasty features prominently in *Lavos*, infusing the central love triangle with class struggles that almost rival sexuality for the panic they generate in society. The corruption of the family (literally 'uma família [...] a desfazer-se' [a family [...] undoing itself] [p. 92]) is imagined as the breakdown of the patriarchal-capitalist order.

The central love triangle in *Lavos* contains members from each of the three social classes: Sebastião de Noronha, the aristocrat; Elvira, his wife, an 'alma lisa de burguesa' [a simple bourgeois soul]; and Eugénio, the working-class orphan who comes to Lisbon in search of a better life. Since the *Guerra dos Dois Irmãos* in the 1830s, the Portuguese aristocracy had lost considerable influence, a decline that continued through the decades leading up to the 1908 regicide, in contrast to the correspondingly ascendent bourgeoisie. Accordingly in *Lavos*, with each pillar of society represented, the ensuing affair becomes a miniaturised, allegorical upheaval of the class structure. At the beginning, the old order remains in place, with the Baron seemingly firmly in control of events, bribing Eugénio to accept his advances. Paradoxically, indeed, it is the accumulation of wealth in one family, through generations of (normative) patriarchal marriage, that affords the Baron the privilege to pursue *non*-normative desires, ultimately leading to the loss of the family fortune. His pederastic desire to educate Eugénio — which also belies a fetishisation of his working-class background[55] — gradually leads to the erosion of his powerful position. At first, Sebastião's financial control over Eugénio allows him to transform the latter into a narcissistic extension of self:

> D. Sebastião fê-lo vestir e calçar de novo. Ele próprio o acompanhava, no princípio, aos estabelecimentos, onde lhe abriu crédito e onde presidia à escolha dos artigos — tudo do melhor! — , normalizando-lhe o gosto, incutindo-lhe regras de asseio, de apuro, de elegância. O falar ia-lho igualmente corrigindo. Não que o barão não gostasse de ouvir silvar os plebeísmos na boca acerejada do amante. Encantava-o até a propriedade flagrante e o sabor acanalhado de muitas dessas fórmulas da rua, que resumem tanta vez uma filosofia inteira. Mas entrara de flutuar-lhe na alma, inconfessado, tímido, o desejo de se apropriar, de tornar inseparável da sua aquela existência imprescindível... Por isso queria desbastá-lo, afiná-lo, fazê-lo correto, dândi, na previsão de ter de apresentá-lo um dia — que diabo tinha! — às pessoas das suas relações. (p. 99)

> [Dom Sebastião again made him try on new clothes and shoes. He himself accompanied him, at first, to the establishments, where he opened an account for him and presided over his choice of articles — only the finest! — normalising his taste, teaching him the rules of neatness, perfection and elegance. He also went about correcting his speech. Not that the Baron was impartial to hearing his lover's cherry-like mouth whistle colloquialisms. He was enchanted by the flagrancy and coarse taste of those street words, which so often capture an entire philosophy. But a desire, timid and unconfessed, to make that indispensable being his own, inseparable from him, had begun to stir in his soul... And so he wanted to civilise him, refine him, correct him, turn him into a dandy, in the hope of presenting him one day — for God knows he had to! — to his acquaintances.]

The Baron takes evident delight in dressing Eugénio as he pleases, in fancy clothes, so that he might one day be presented to his social circle as a fashionable accessory. Sebastião is not unlike Pygmalion falling in love with his sculpture, a myth that gained renewed popularity in the nineteenth century.[56] The phrase 'normalizando-lhe o gosto' according to 'regras' suggests a correction of taste, reminiscent of the Foucauldian examination, in which disciplinary power is enforced by the regular measuring of subjects according to a norm.[57] Furthermore and most symbolically, Sebastião teaches Eugénio to speak the language of his social class, free of slang or 'plebeísmos'. As we shall see, the command of language becomes central too in Eugénio's subsequent affair with Elvira. The Baron's economic power in the opening chapters allows him to control the *efebo* through his appearance and language, recoding him as a member of his class.

However, as Eugénio accumulates luxurious presents and greater familiarity with high society, he begins to assert his independence, often ignoring the Baron and missing rendezvous. On one such occasion, Eugénio disappears for more than a day with a younger woman, greatly angering Sebastião. When the boy seduces Elvira, now dejected and bored to tears, he gains de facto control over the household.

Showered with gifts from husband and wife, coming and going to the *palacete* in the knowledge that Sebastião, who in marital acrimony sleeps elsewhere, will not learn of his infidelity, Eugénio extracts every *tostão* from the family fortune. Just as Sebastião uses his wealth to follow unspeakable passions, so does Eugénio entertain these passions to accumulate wealth. The ability of sex to transcend and upset class boundaries was of course crystallised in the Naturalist imagination with works such as Zola's *Nana* (1880), in which the protagonist rises from the slums to join the finest society in Paris.[58] However, in *Lavos*, the educative, pederastic relationship results in a particularly intense reversal of fortunes as the pupil goes on to outwit the teacher. At the end, the class inversions reach their conclusion, Sebastião dying destitute on the street at the hands of urchins, and Eugénio found to be a rising star at the Teatro da Trindade, a more reputable venue than the circus, where he goes on to bankrupt another aristocrat. In *Lavos*, the violation of the patriarchal sexual code, which is itself paradoxically facilitated by the great disparities of wealth that it creates and works to sustain, is always imagined as a ruinous space in which class relations are dangerously renegotiated.

In this manner, over the course of her affair with Eugénio, Elvira unwittingly comes to assimilate the *efebo*'s working-class idiom. Sebastião is shocked to find his wife's use of vulgar names for coins, such as 'camisa lavada' [washed shirt], 'coroa mulata' [mulatto crown] and 'penteado' [hairdo] (p. 303). As the narrator continues:

> O caso era que a fraseologia de calão vinha agora aos lábios da baronesa com uma insistência, uma predileção e uma propriedade, que as suas simples relações de sociedade com o efebo não podiam explicar bastantemente. Seria latitudinar [*sic*] demasiado o instinto da imitação. — Ela como que se revia, se comprazia no termo chulo. A cada instante. Essa vasconça aravia da escumalha parecia ser a que melhor lhe dizia às plebeias condições do temperamento e às tacanhas solicitações do espírito. (p. 304).

> [The truth was that the phraseology of slang was now escaping the lips of the Baroness with an insistence, a predilection and mastery that her simple social relations with the ephebe could not sufficiently explain. It would be overestimating the instinct to imitate. How she delighted, how she took pleasure in the word 'scrounger'. At every opportunity. That double Dutch, Arabesque nonsense from the gutter seemed to be the language that best suited the plebeian condition of her temperament and the base desires of her spirit.]

The 'predileção' indicates an unconscious (and therefore more profound) linguistic contagion, whereby words highly unsuited to the bourgeois home involuntarily find their way in, reaching the supposed bastion of bourgeois domestic propriety (and property), the Baroness herself. The neologism 'latitudinar' (a broadening, or amplification) is particularly noteworthy, as the narrator appears to require an expanded vocabulary himself to describe the linguistic contagion before him — perhaps another moment where he tastes his own medicine. He appears irritated with Elvira's obsession with the word 'chulo', suggested by the repetitive syntax in the phrase 'como que se revia, se comprazia'. Is the doctor losing his empirical cool? That 'chulo' is Elvira's slang word of choice, meanwhile — meaning both something vulgar and an 'individual who takes advantage of someone and lives at their expense'[59] — is intriguing in itself. Elvira does not appear to notice that her lover is in fact the 'chulo' and that she is supporting his lifestyle. As she assimilates Eugénio's speech (described remarkably as Basque-Arab-like nonsense from the dregs of society),[60] she takes on more than she can handle, foreshadowing the impending catastrophe; the linguistic contagion thus accompanies the process by which Eugénio seizes control of the bourgeois sphere. It should be stressed that Elvira's relationship with Eugénio is highly non-normative in itself. The scandalous age difference between the Baroness, who is in her thirties, and the teenage *efebo*, coupled with the adultery and class disparities that lead to Elvira paying to keep Eugénio, flout the patriarchal code in multiple ways. That Eugénio's language, having once been 'corrected' by Sebastião, has now, in symmetrical fashion, returned to 'corrupt' the heart of the household, testifies to growing power of the working-class *efebo*, an inversion of fortunes brought about by the violation of the sexual code.

As a consequence of Eugénio's 'intrusion', Sebastião and Elvira's marriage, although founded on a degree of mutual affection at the start, steadily falls to pieces. Elvira, whose great expectations for her future with the Baron are shattered as he spends ever less time at home, begins to rebel. Already in the third chapter, the Baron's patronising tone after refusing to accompany her on an outing provokes a defiant response:

> — Supões-me mais idiota do que sou.
> — Ó filha, não é isso! — afagou o barão com a mais afetuosa bonomia. [...]
> — Bem! não faltava mais nada. Agora chamas-me criança! — explodiu ela com vivacidade, enquanto arrastava para longe, num sacão de arremesso, a chávena de cujo chá bebia os últimos goles.
>    Desta vez o barão, posto em prova, afastou da mesa o tronco, alto e direito, e cravou na mulher um severo olhar de reprimenda. Mas ela, de cotovelo fincado sobre a toalha, franzir desdenhoso nos lábios, a mão cocegando a ponta da barba num jeitinho impertinente e raivoso, pôs-se a fitar com altiva insolência uma das rosetas do teto e a fustigar o parquet num bater de pé provocante. Uma trepidação elástica e felina corria-lhe o colo, os seios e a face rija e redonda, em cujas vénulas engrossadas se via a fremir e a subir um sangue roxo, irritado.
>    De repente, abate sobre o marido as pupilas, crispantes de desafio:
> — Preciso sair hoje... Não me acompanhas?
> — Logo vi!... ou eu não tivesse que fazer!... — respondeu com ímpeto o barão.
> — Que marido tão condescendente, tão amável que eu tenho, Santo Deus!... Nem de encomenda! — E depois de uma pausa, numa irritação crescente: — Para que me foi tirar a casa dos meus pais? (pp. 40–41)

> ['You suppose I am an idiot.'
> 'My dear girl, far from it!' wooed the Baron, feigning affection. [...]
> 'Well well! That's all I needed. Now you're calling me a child!' she burst out spiritedly, pushing away the teacup from which she'd taken her last sips with a sudden thrust.
>    This time the Baron, put to the test, moved away from the table, standing tall and straight, and cast his wife a grievous, reprimanding look. But she, with her elbow resting on the tablecloth, a disdainful scowl on her lips, and her hand stroking her chin in a vexed and impertinent manner, sat staring with haughty

insolence at one of the rosettes on the ceiling and tapping her feet provocatively on the parquet floor. An elastic and feline shudder ran through her lap, her breasts and her round, firm face, the veins of which could be seen filling with purple, irritated blood.

Suddenly, she turned her eyes towards the Baron, squinting in defiance:

'I need to go out today... Will you not accompany me?'

'Of course you dooo!... As if I had nothing to do myself!...' replied the Baron forcefully.

'What a forgiving, loving husband I have, good God!... You couldn't make it up!' And after a pause, in growing irritation, she said, 'why did you take me from my parents' home?']

Sebastião, treating his wife like a daughter and with no regard for her needs and desires, finds his patriarchal authority suddenly threatened as she questions his decision to marry her. Her gesture of indifference, resting her elbow and gazing the ceiling, accompanied by a sexualised shudder and sudden flush of blood, foreshadows her future 'misbehaviour' and adulterous relationship with Eugénio. Indeed, her increasing rebelliousness — and dominance — reaches a climax when she effectively cuckolds her husband and steals his lover in the same move:

Porque no [...] espírito [do barão] a noção da mulher, da esposa desaparecera, para só ver nela, em rodilhões de ciúme, um trambolho, um rival, um estorvo odiado, um empecilho irritante, um competidor terrível, que assim vinha, traiçoeiro e impudente, tomar-lhe o passo — com que direito? — roubar-lhe o amor do efebo — que era só dele! — destorvá-lo [sic], desbancá-lo, atravessar-se... impedir a sua regalada e solta fruição da vida! (p. 307)

[For in the [...] Baron's spirit, the notion of a woman, of a wife, had disappeared, such that all he saw in her, through spiralling jealousy, was an obstacle, a rival, a hateful impediment, an irritating hindrance, a terrible competitor who had come, treacherous and impudent, to beat him at his game — with what right? — to steal his love for the ephebe — who was his alone! — and surpass him, ambush him... and put a halt to his indulgent and boundless enjoyment of life!]

Elvira has remarkably become not only a rival, but is repeatedly articulated grammatically in the masculine, with a lengthy display asyndeton that suggests the Baron's shock as much as it does Elvira's growing power. Here, Botelho radically reassembles the nineteenth-century love triangle, leaving Sebastião 'cuckolded' twice over by his wife and lover. The 'classic' nineteenth-century love triangle, as discussed in René Girard's *Deceit, Desire and the Novel*, establishes a bond of rivalry between two men over one woman, which Eve Sedgwick analyses as 'homosocial', being disrupted by the denial of any potential for homoerotic desire.[61] The effect was to maintain the position of women as 'currency' in the (re)production of heirs to transmit name, capital and bloodline, women being tacitly passed between men in patriarchal power games.[62] In *Lavos*, by contrast, the violation of normative heterosexuality allows the triangle to do the full loop, Elvira being seduced by another man (worse, a boy), and taking her husband's lover at the same time, elevating her to the status of (masculine) rival. The repositioning of the woman in this manner constitutes another semantic slippage from pederasty into gender trouble and female empowerment which, as we have seen, were key concerns at the *fin de siècle*, when talk of a 'surplus' of women was rife, owing to the perceived threat of their growing economic independence.[63] As we shall see in subsequent chapters, the reimagining of the nineteenth-century love triangle, often rendered sterile and always proving ruinous, is a key strategy with which the Lusophone Naturalists problematise their world. Indeed, however horrified Botelho may appear by the demise of the patriarchal family, it is striking that even he implicates the social inequalities that it produces in its eventual undoing, again shifting the focus from individual to societal malaise.

In *Lavos*, therefore, the patriarchal family, consolidated through heterosexual marriage and a privileged male space of brotherly rivalry, is turned on its head, signalling, too, an inversion of economic bonds in society. As Howes comments in reference to Eugénio's ruinous appearance in the Baron's domestic life, '[h]omo-sexuality is seen as a threat to the family, and in particular the family as incarnation of property'.[64] Paradoxically, however, it is precisely wealth and property that facilitates the pursuit of destructive, forbidden passions in the novel, another moment where the dominant ideology is implicated in the very 'symptom' that it sets out to cure. The recourse to Greek pederasty, which subtly challenges the universality of 'science', is instrumental in this respect, allowing class and gender struggles to creep into the picture and decimate the family fortune, spreading the pathology beyond the Baron's body. A wider contagion is thus released into society, prising open the doctor's flood gates that seek to protect the 'natural' family from its 'unnatural' counterpart.

## From Private to Public: Opening the Urban Closet

Since the violation of the sexual code in *Lavos* entails other tensions surrounding race, gender and class, it seems pertinent to include an analysis of the urban environment in the novel, a space that becomes gradually more chaotic as the scandal unfolds, and that again leads to moments in which the contagion escapes the cure. Urbanisation in the nineteenth century changed the face of cities beyond recognition: Lisbon's population more than doubled between 1849 and 1900,[65] giving rise to several unprecedented urban projects, most famously the Avenida da Liberdade, which supplanted the old Passeio Público. The novel has already been identified by critics as illuminative of queer life in *fin-de-siècle* Lisbon;[66] Howes ventures that Botelho develops a tension between the 'sanctity and security' of the Baron's house and the 'social and sexual promiscuity' of the street, whose boundaries become porous as the Baron introduces the *efebo* into his home.[67] I will largely depart from this insight, arguing that an initially divided and hierarchical city, in which bourgeois *lisboetas* are shielded from the realities of working-class life, falls into disarray, with an epidemic of disease, sexual deviance, criminality and prostitution — all facets of the same 'degenerate' peril — spreading through society. In a sense, the chaos resembles an urban 'closet', or series of closets, being opened. Eve Sedgwick defines the closet as 'the relations of the known and the unknown, the explicit and the inexplicit around the homo/heterosexual definition'.[68] Given the lack of established homo/heterosexual binary at the *fin de siècle* and, on the contrary, the dissolution of deviant sexuality into other modes of deviance, I will be using Sedgwick's model to describe a range of practices that coalesce around the undoing of the normative family, these being initially 'closeted' insofar as they are contained within the urban environment, far from the bourgeoisie, before being slowly released into the wider world as the Baron's secret is divulged. The resulting class and sexual turmoil in the capital of the empire, Lisbon, which in the language of pathology figures as a public health problem, further threatens the supremacy of the doctor's perspective.

Already at the beginning of the novel, urban spaces of ambiguous meaning serve as a harbinger of what follows. Botelho sets the opening chapter in the circus on the Rua do Salitre, which links upper-class Rato to the newly built Avenida da Liberdade, where Sebastião cruises for adolescent boys. The circus, although not an invention of the nineteenth century, witnessed a huge surge in popularity in the 1800s,[69] and represents the triumph of the new social classes, most especially the working class and the petit bourgeoisie. Furthermore, as Howes notes, the circus in *Lavos* recalls one of the acrobat boys involved in the Rua do Trombeta scandal.[70] It is also the site of corporeal spectacle par excellence, not only prefiguring the series of social performances that the Baron will be coerced into to fasten the closet doors, but also calling to mind the bodily 'aberrations' of the freak shows that typically featured at the nineteenth-century circus, gaining enormous popularity in the *fin de siècle*,[71] age of the Elephant Man and the 'original' Siamese twins. As Alston and Dixon argue, the controlled exhibition of the exotic at the circus serves to regulate the seductive temptation of the other,[72] thus reflecting a growing, if implicit, tension between bourgeois ideology and the new elements of society that at once generated fear and fascination. In this way, the beginning of the novel sits at the point of conflict between the new and the old, the permitted and the prohibited, the known and the unknown, the 'normal' and the 'deviant'; indeed, an array of divisions and exclusions that, in their regulated showcasing, serve to consolidate bourgeois identity at the same time that the need to contain and police them already implies that this identity is in potential danger. The ambivalent space of the circus introduces the fault lines in the social fabric that will gradually open as the novel progresses.

For a time after the ominous opening, the Baron's affair is enacted strictly behind closed doors. His ancestral *palacete* is located on the Largo de São Cristóvão, one of the oldest and most noble centres of the city. Lavishly decorated and with panoramic views over Lisbon, it is here that he lives with his wife and entertains his guests. However, he enacts his affair with Eugénio in his apartment on the Rua da Rosa, Bairro Alto, a notorious neighbourhood of fishwives, 'vice' and prostitution, described by the narrator as filled with 'haréns carimbados' [disreputable harems] (p. 283). The Bairro Alto was also where the Marquês de Valada was caught with a soldier in 1881, on the nearby Travessa da Espera, again suggesting an engagement with contemporary events. The dingy apartment has the purpose of hiding the

Baron's relationship with Eugénio, which at this point remains confined to the private sphere in a particular part of the city, far from the bourgeoisie. Thus where Howes describes the clandestine apartment as something of a 'half-way house between the illicit sexuality of the street and the world of domestic respectability',[73] it might also be said to resemble a closet facilitating the precarious separation of these two worlds, not dissimilar to the regulation of 'exotic' and 'abnormal' bodies at the circus.

It is only when Sebastião decides to introduce Eugénio to life at the *palacete* that the relations of the permitted and the prohibited begin to break down. Dressed as a dandy and now 'muito bem ensaiado' [very well rehearsed], Eugénio has the veneer of refinement whilst fulfilling perfectly the degeneration theorists' conviction that nurture could only go so far towards altering nature. On his first visit he is stunned at the luxury of the Baron's household:

> Eugénio pasmava, considerava com um espanto que era quase desconfiança aquela colónia de maravilhas. Ele não lhes media o valor; não podia sentir o que havia de superiormente belo, de fascinador, de requintadamente bom e confortante naquele entesourar de raridades, naquele ardente rebuscar de harmonias plásticas, naquela seleção de cores, naquela coabitação de obras primas. A voluptuosidade artística não a tinha; não lhe davam para isso a grosseria do temperamento nem os rudimentos da educação: mas uma noção vaga de prazer e de respeito fazia-o aplaudir. (p. 162)

> [Eugénio was astounded and suspected that that colony of wonders was not to be trusted. He didn't weigh up their value; he was unable to grasp what was so especially beautiful and fascinating, so fine and comfortable about that treasure trove of rarities, that zealous quest for harmonies of form, that selection of colours, that cohabitation of masterpieces. He had no artistic sensitivity; his rough temperament and simple manners afforded him none, but a vague notion of pleasure and respect made him applaud.]

Eugénio's lower-class habits render the luxury of the *palacete* entirely other to him, so much so that he contemplates the strangely exoticised '*colónia* de maravilhas' with distrust. Thus whilst Sebastião's privilege affords him free and secret passage between spheres, giving substance to the public fascination with aristocrats living Jekyll-and-Hyde double lives, Eugénio's access to privilege remains regulated by the Baron. Merely masquerading as a member of high society, he cannot lead a double life but must assimilate and simulate upper-class behaviour, setting the stage for the series of contagions that ensue upon his arrival in the domestic sphere: a wolf disguised as grandma, but a wolf nevertheless. Indeed, the mask slips on Eugénio's first visit, with his rehearsed praise for the 'café magnífico' [magnificent coffee] quickly becoming embarrassing as he compares it to the coffee of an establishment named 'O Refilão' [The Grouch] (p. 159). The Baroness, in shock, replies, 'O Refilão!... Que vem a ser?' [The Grouch!... What on earth is that?] The word is something of a shibboleth, described by Derrida as that which both includes and excludes, a 'password, a mark of belonging'[74] (or not-belonging) allowing us to 'recognize and be recognized by one's own, for better or for worse.'[75] Indeed, Elvira later muses, 'Era esquisito!... Como podia um rapaz inteligente e educado, como este era sem dúvida, falar daquele modo?... Ou não era realmente inteligente, ou era muitíssimo grosseiro, ou tivera uma péssima educação' [It was strange! How could a clever and well-mannered boy, as this one doubtless was, speak in that way?... Either he wasn't really intelligent, or he was extremely rude, or he'd had a dreadful upbringing] (p. 170). She evidently perceives the incommensurability of his language and etiquette, although it is not enough to prevent her from assimilating his idiom later in the novel. On the contrary, the inability to tame Eugénio's apparently 'incorrigible' working-class 'nature' implies that it will always return to exert a threatening influence: his 'colonisation' of the heartlands of the bourgeoisie can only prove troublesome. His very language, branded improper, in fact disarticulates the normative speech of the upper classes. If the circus functions as a space in which relations with the exotic can be sold, consumed and regulated, working to suppress any degree of reciprocity, Eugénio's appearance in the family home as a working-class imposter testifies to the unpredictability and perceived danger of the encounter with the other that arises when two separate, strictly policed spheres come into contact.

It is, indeed, the Baron's decision to introduce Eugénio into his home and the public sphere, and not the relationship per se, that brings about the unravelling of his precarious life. Once Eugénio's assimilation of bourgeois culture allows him to exploit the situation and destroy the family home, culminating in its mortgage and sale, Sebastião is forced to renounce his double life for a lower social status in order to pursue his transgressions. This process spreads the contagion, formerly limited to the home, to the remainder of the city. He invests in a disreputable atelier producing pornographic photographs of models, these chiefly adolescent boys whom he finds 'pelos vários cantos de miséria e crápula da cidade' [in the many miserable and abject corners of the city] and then brings to the atelier, situated deliberately in Bairro Alto as the 'ponto central da cidade' [central point of the city] (pp. 363–65). The subsequent horror of the passing bourgeois families is described in detail:

> De sorte que então aconteceu, não raro, uma ou outra família burguesa defrontar, horrorizada, na galeria, no toilette, na sala de espera, com vultos suspeitos de mulheres de xale e lenço, carmim na face e saia engomada, as quais se enrolavam nos fauteuils, de cabeça baixa, como gatas, ou, tapando o rosto, cosiam-se com os cantos. E aqui e ali, a esmo, cuias, andrajos, ligas, aventais, farrapos, fitas ensebadas; e pelo ar gordo um cheiro nauseante, misto aziumado de lupanar e de taberna.
>
> Por tudo isto, breve um denso véu de descrédito se correu sobre o famoso atelier. (p. 368)

> [And so it was that, not uncommonly, some or other bourgeois family would find themselves in the gallery, in the dressing room and the waiting room, horrified by the shady figures of women wearing shawls and handkerchiefs, with crimson on their cheeks and starched skirts that rolled onto the *fauteuils*, their heads down like cats, shielding their faces, covering themselves with the seams. And here and there were scattered wigs, rags, garters, aprons, scraps, greasy ribbons; and the fatty air carried a nauseating smell, an acid mix of brothel and tavern.
>
> As a result, before long, a thick veil of discredit shrouded the famous atelier.]

The nauseating smell and greasy accessories add to the sense of a sickness brought to the city centre. Eventually, a sex scandal engulfs the establishment, reaching the papers, involving 'os mais graúdos frascários da arte e da finança' [the greatest libertines of art and finance] (p. 368), and the atelier, shunned and debt-ridden, is forced to close. Sebastião's financial situation worsens further, his reputation all but destroyed. As he is 'outed', the closeted areas of the city become increasingly visible. Rather fittingly, this social and urban disturbance is brought about by a photography business. As Elizabeth Stephens argues, the photograph, after its invention and popularisation in the nineteenth century, constituted:

> a new technology that both reflected and participated in the rapidly changing assumptions about the nature and purpose of the body... [understood as] a pure and unmediated form of representation, promising to make visible the 'reality' of the body.[76]

Seen in this context, the atelier becomes all the more scandalous, documenting and flaunting the bodies of individuals paid to strip for a photograph, providing 'proof' of homoeroticism in the heart of the city with the privileged authority of the new technology. Here one wonders, however, whether the doctor is again administered a dose of his own medicine, since the Baron's supposedly perverse, 'scandalous' new technology seems uncomfortably close to the narrative technique that promises to articulate his pathological 'truth'. Either way, just as the novelty of photography and pathology seemed to contribute to their authority, here they also reinforce the sense that class and sexual turmoil are a modern, and thus more urgent problem, despite the references to Ancient Greece.

After the disaster of the atelier, the dramatic reversal of class roles in *Lavos* concludes with Sebastião taking up life in some of the most disreputable areas of the city. Though it should be stressed once more that Sebastião chooses to renounce the upper-class sphere, refusing the offer of a noble salon in his friend's home, he does so to maximise his sexual freedom, confirming the sense that his 'aberrations' can only be accommodated in the abject corners of the urban environment, if not quite in the attic, avoided by the bourgeoisie although now made visible by the perverse narration, the photographs, the new avenues; in short, by modernisation. The Baron's decision to occupy the cramped basement is also a resignation to losing the privilege of moving between social strata. From this point on, his body carries various physical markers of transgression. No longer cruising the circus to pay for sex, he wanders the most notorious alleyways in the city, Calçada do Garcia and Beco do Forno, behind Rossio square:

> Aí, no mistério dos antros defumados a alfazema e candeias de petróleo, o sinistro andromaníaco sofria os mais aviltadores exercícios, prestava-se às mais secretas exações, às mais infames promiscuidades. E assim, nesta vesânia circular em volta às mesmas abjeções e aos mesmos vícios, teimava esbodegando a dignidade e a vida — amarrado agora à cancela das casas suspeitas, logo rompendo a tragar mais uma gota de vitríolo na última baiuca ainda aberta, espojado depois nas enxergas dos alcouces — pelos ínfimos bosteiros da cidade solto e doido completando o ciclo prostibular do seu destino. (p. 397)

[There, in the mystery of the caverns filled with the smoke of lavender and oil lamps, the sinister andromaniac suffered the most degrading of acts, involved himself in the most secret of transactions, in the most scandalous of promiscuities. And thus, in this circle of insanity surrounding the same abjections and the same vices, he feared squandering his life and dignity — finding himself tied to the gates of disreputable houses one minute, drinking a drop of vitriol in the last tavern still serving the next, only to slump onto the beds of the brothels — wandering the basest dungheaps of the city, alone and crazed, completing the whorish cycle of his destiny.]

Sebastião seems to blend into his environment, merely another incidence of 'sickness', decay and vice, doomed by nature to extinction. Interestingly, he forms part of the 'mistério' of this part of the city (from Latin *mysterium*, meaning something secret)[77] as though he and his dark, smoky surroundings somehow escape signification — particularly fitting for a narrative object that can never quite be brought under control. Is the doctor reaching the limits of his perspective? The pseudoscientific term 'andromaníaco' attempts to reassert medical authority, but it is noteworthy that the doctor then segues to the Baron's alcoholism: defining 'andromania' results in a deferral to other non-normative 'symptoms'. Meanwhile, 'antros' connotes an (atavistic) regression to the state of nature, the primitive darkness of the cave. The Baron's apparent transition from being an active to a passive sexual partner here, becoming himself a prostitute in the process, inverts the state of affairs at the beginning of the novel, where he assumes the other side of the transaction. His life is described as a 'vagabundagem' and he is driven to theft, including from his old friends, the Paradelas. Crime, vice, prostitution and illness become interchangeable, both in the characterisation of the Baron and of the area of the city to which he is confined.

Even when with the Paradelas, the only friends of the Baron who still invite him to their house, his difference from them is made abundantly clear. The virginal daughter of the family is physically disgusted by his presence:

Natural que à filhita dos Paradelas a presença do barão não agradasse. Nutria por ele uma invencível repulsão física; arrepiava-a de nojo e de terror aquela afrontosa e senil leprosidade [*sic*]. [...] Era uma repugnância absoluta, essencial, inteiramente rebelde ao domínio da vontade. (p. 402)

[Of course, for the Paradelas's little girl, the Baron's presence was unpleasant. She harboured an invincible physical repulsion to him; she shivered in disgust at that outrageous and senile leprosity. [...] It was an absolute repugnance, essential and entirely immune to her strength of will.]

The encounter between the Baron and the Paradelas's daughter completes the novel's gradual disintegration of the closet safeguarding the licit from the illicit. Whereas once the two had conversed as equals, free of suspicions surrounding the Baron's sexuality, his unspeakable secret is now visible and inscribed onto his body in the form of disease and poverty. His sexual 'disease' figures as 'senil leprosidade', leprosy being not only a Biblical curse[78] but also, for Foucault, the original 'othering' sickness that provided the model for modern psychiatry.[79] Interestingly in *Lavos*, the 'psychiatric' discourse of 'andromania' gets re-inscribed (atavistically?) as the 'original' malady, one even older than the pederasty of Ancient Greece, branding Sebastião as cursed — again rather metaphysical terms, perhaps, for a doctor to deploy. Perennially excluded from the bourgeois sphere, the Baron owes any contact with his former friends to charity, with the Paradelas, for example, deliberately leaving a coin for him to 'pinch' upon entry. Indeed, when once the Baron crossed urban spheres effortlessly, moving between his *palacete* and the Rua da Rosa, now his visit to the Paradelas, strictly at their invitation, only confirms his position as debarred from the bourgeois world and all its privileges, not least the coveted attention of its young brides-to-be, which constitute one half of the bourgeois social economy that has now been irrevocably rejected.

However, as we have seen, the narrative of *Lavos* never keeps the closet doors open to the bourgeoisie for long. The doctor's voice returns to pathologise and purge transgressive behaviour, and at this point in the epidemic, the only fate that can restore the *cordon sanitaire* is the Baron's death, almost eliminating the 'disease' from the city, although not entirely, as Eugénio lives on, as we have seen, to 'corrupt' the lives of the wealthy. The closing lines of the novel, in which his corpse is found by a policeman, remove Sebastião from the social order:

> Lobrigando o velho estendido, foi um polícia acudir. Empurra com o pé, brada, ameaça. Por fim, perante aquela absoluta imobilidade, sério, debruçou-se. — As duas pernas e um braço, partidos... o negro charco em que a face nadava, não era vinho, era sangue. — Imaginara um bêbado, defrontou um cadáver. (p. 415)

> [Noticing the old man lying down, a policeman went over to help. He pushed him with his foot, shouted and made threats. Finally, faced with such motionlessness and growing more serious, he bent over. Two legs and an arm were broken... The black swamp engulfing his face was not wine; it was blood. He had presumed to find a drunkard but stood before a corpse.]

The switching of perspective to that of an anonymous policeman has the effect of depriving Sebastião of his name and identity, which the unusual verb 'lobrigando', to see obscurely, fades into the surroundings. Sebastião becomes a faceless 'cadáver', swimming in blood for gory effect. Furthermore, the appearance of the policeman, who now finds and 'diagnoses' the Baron himself, demonstrates the complicity of medical and criminal discourses, the doctor's gaze being seamlessly exchanged for that of the policeman. Desire becomes disease; disease becomes poverty; poverty becomes crime; all these lead to death. With renewed confidence in the ability of the Positivist disciplines to 'treat' transgression, illustrated by the policeman's examination of the Baron's body, prudish readers ought at last to rest assured that order has returned. Interestingly, the policeman first appears to see wine before perceiving it to be blood. Is this another Biblical reference, in which an unholy sacrament comes horribly to fruition? There is the suggestion that Baron's death is sacrificial, purging the world of its sins, these now reimagined as sicknesses that can be eradicated to cleanse the bourgeoisie.

Botelho's choice of location for Sebastião's death provides a final twist to sweeten his readers. Sebastião dies at the hands of street urchins on the Avenida da

Liberdade, the new avenue replacing the old Passeio Público, built in Parisian style, and amid much controversy, between 1879 and 1886. The Avenida was a triumph of Liberalism in Portugal, reminiscent of Haussmann's regeneration of Paris and bringing a new artery of commerce and luxury housing to the centre of Lisbon.[80] In *Lavos*, the last representative of one of the oldest houses in the country thus dies in its newest development, one that epitomised the ascendency of middle-class *lisboetas* at the time. Mercilessly beaten and left to die on the altar of the bourgeoisie, Sebastião, in his final moments, also breathes the last allegorical breaths of his entire social class, an ancient aristocracy fading amid the urbanisation and mercantilisation of the nineteenth century. Just seventeen years after the publication of *Lavos*, Dom Carlos I of Portugal was assassinated in the Terreiro do Paço, leading to the nation's precarious First Republic. The chief beneficiary of this century of transformations was, of course, the bourgeoisie, and the sense of societal 'cure' following Sebastião's death in the novel was thus surely all the more keenly felt by a middle-class readership that was, in general, quietly willing to observe the decline of the old nobility, who at the end of the novel remain vulnerable to Eugénio's influence. No doubt it was at least in part this comforting ending to a sensationalist text that led to the widespread criticism, at the time of the novel's publication, that Botelho was chiefly writing for money.[81] Certainly, he speaks chiefly to and for the dominant classes, naturalising their ideology with 'science'. That said, the working classes (represented by Eugénio) do appear to be going places at the end of the novel; there is no static resolution to the bourgeois ascendency, just as its justification in 'science' seems slippery throughout, occasionally capturing its own 'perversion' in a lewd photograph.

Analysing the configuration of urban space in the novel, therefore, besides revealing much about sexual life in *fin-de-siècle* Lisbon, helps us to position it within the class structure of the period, as well as pick apart the *cordon sanitaire* with which it seeks to excite, delight, and occasionally terrify its readership. The gradual spread of the 'sickness' through an initially segregated city is witnessed through the lens of a new 'science' of pathology and criminology, eventually handing victory to the bourgeoisie as the aristocracy suffers a terminal diagnosis. However, although Botelho provides the reader with the illusion of good health in the midst of the epidemic, there are moments in which the cure fails and the contagion, like the Baron's agency, escapes unscathed. These moments, such as the mysterious appearance of the city's dark cruising grounds, or the re-inscription of illness as curse, would appear to work against nature, in that they gesture towards limits in the reach of social pathology when contemplating the demise of the patriarchal family. As we shall see, it is a process that is echoed in the novel's equally noteworthy use of imperial allegory.

### Allegories Against Nature: Dom Sebastião, Kinship Trouble and the End of Empire

For scholars seeking to address the role heteronormativity has played in Portuguese history, the figure of Dom Sebastião (1554–1578) has presented a particular draw: a boy king who inherited the world's most powerful throne, but whose failure to leave an heir, sparking rumours of homosexuality, brought Portugal under the crown of Castile after his disappearance in the disastrous battle of Alcácer-Quibir. That his body was never found led to a widespread belief that he would yet return to restore the Portuguese empire, so much so that various false pretenders appeared in the years following, and an island in Maranhão was specifically designated for his use in case of shipwreck.[82] An occasionally fierce debate has arisen surrounding the king's alleged homosexuality,[83] much of which revolves around contemporary assertions that 'elRey de nenhuma maneira pode ver molher [sic]' [the King will not see women under any circumstances],[84] though Johnson finds further evidence that the king sought illicit encounters near his palace in Sintra.[85] Although I have no desire to wade into the historical debate, I do find the speculation significant, not least since it has a long history, as the characterisation of Sebastião in *Lavos* suggests. In Botelho's novel, clear parallels are developed between the protagonist and the king, adding an allegorical dimension to the novel that serves to shape the pathological discourse with national concerns. However, as we shall see, although there is a movement towards naturalising the nation's ills, there is also a disruptive countermovement, since the poetic recourse to allegory supplements and enriches the pathological method.

Botelho's reference to the 'failed' Portuguese monarch, besides his protagonist's name, which is often accompanied by the title *Dom*, is carefully constructed. As in the sixteenth century, the destruction of an ancient household follows the violation of the patriarchal code demanding normative heterosexuality and the need for progeny to perpetuate name, bloodline and property. The Baron, whose lineage, 'duplamente bastarda' [doubly bastard] (p. 23), is meticulously traced through the illegitimate children of the Portuguese and Spanish royalty, already carries the atavistic blood[86] that mixes pederasty and the corruption of family lines with the pernicious approximation of Portugal and Spain. Like the king, too, Sebastião dies physically on the new frontier of the Empire, alone and unidentified, having turned his back on home, bringing an end to his ancient line and leaving the future of the nation in doubt. The pathological language strengthens the sense that the Baron is at least an atavistic, if not necessarily messianic, revenant of the king: a regression, a compulsion to repeat a much older national trauma. Botelho's intriguing conflation of individual and national demise, of course, comes just a year after the British ultimatum that all but destroyed the monarchy's reputation.

Through the figure of Dom Sebastião, therefore, the discourse of degeneracy reaches a national pitch that blends novelistic fatality with the end of empire. The doctor's voice comes to confirm the diagnosis of such public intellectuals as Oliveira Martins who, in accordance with the tenets of northern European degeneration theory, prophesied the slow extinction of Portugal and other 'lesser' races. Conversely, Portuguese imperial decline is also used to confirm degeneration theory in the novel, despite the aforementioned slip of the black priest, a complicity of history and theory that invests 'deviance' and kinship trouble with the chilling prospect of national apocalypse. The result is an alarming cultural pessimism in *Lavos* that seemingly embraces the theories of northern Europe, catastrophic as they were for countries such as Portugal, adding pathological substance to the perception that the nation was suffering the consequences of its 'degenerate' sons and daughters. The allegorical leap from individual to national degeneracy almost casts sexual panic as an ethno-racial problem in an apparent indictment of Portuguese blood. Thus although the bourgeois reader is saved from immediate 'infection' when Sebastião dies, more pervasive questions about the future viability of the nation and its bloodline remain unanswered. Dom Sebastião returns as the myth promises, but instead of restoring imperial greatness, he is atavistically compelled to repeat the 'mistakes' of the past.

Botelho's naturalisation of Portuguese imperial 'decline' in his novel, then, reintroduces the risk of contagion to the bourgeoisie that elsewhere he seeks to protect. However, his recourse to allegory in the process constitutes a particularly intriguing structural decision, since although there are many moments elsewhere in the novel where the theory encounters its own limits, here, the doctor seeks a different register. Allegory, indeed, stands strikingly at odds with the fundamentals of the Naturalist method. Characterised by Paul de Man as a dialectical movement between symbol and allegory, each producing the other's meaning in the absence of any 'asserted superiority' of one over the other,[87] the technique mystifies that layer of meaning that in the Realist-Naturalist model, as explored so compellingly by Barthes, is designed to denote reality itself.[88] The spectre of Dom Sebastião returns to pressure the representation of an individual 'pathology' by subtly reinstating it as a national 'disease'. Here the novel would appear to reveal its position in the literary space of the Western world at the time. So pathologised was the nation of study in contemporary discourses that Botelho could conflate 'degenerate' individual and nation in allegory, a move that constitutes an unexpected supplement to the arrival of literary pathology in Portugal and which, although used to confirm the imported theories, also quietly writes against their method by introducing another, more figurative field of meaning and interpretation. Although, as we shall see, such allegories are repeated more disruptively, and with greater critical insight, in the work of the other authors considered in this book, *Lavos* is nevertheless notable for its refocusing of 'science' to foreground the marginal cultural context, a distinctive feature of Naturalism in Portuguese.

## Concluding Remarks

With its erratic narrative, tortured contradictions and fatalistic plot, *O Barão de Lavos* bears all the fault lines of *fin-de-siècle* discourse, testifying to an age of profound social unease. As fascinated by deviant desire as it is horrified, the doctor-narrator deploys degeneration theory to isolate and remove the 'diseased', only to produce their 'pathology' in the process. The novel plays out the contemporaneous proliferation of epistemological categories in fictional form. Thus the attempt to isolate sexuality as a site of 'deviance' precipitates a slippage of signifiers into gender, class, race and illness. The central pederastic relationship in particular, with its educational imbalance, sets the stage for a reversal of class and gender roles that accompanies the violation of the patriarchal code. Meanwhile, as city and domestic sphere are ripped apart by the 'epidemic', encompassing crime and poverty, licentiousness and disease, all imagined as part of the same malady, the focus shifts from 'deviant' desire to the worrying state of the nation, haunted by the grandiose memory of a colonial past that cannot be recovered, mired in the upheavals of the century. And although the Baron's death surely testifies to the demise of the aristocracy in Portugal — to the perverse delight, no doubt, of a comforted bourgeois readership — his resemblance to Dom Sebastião belies an extreme cultural pessimism that no citizen can easily ignore.

The bleak implications of *Lavos* testify to the disturbing extent to which degeneration theory had circulated in Portugal and Europe as a 'natural' explanation for what were little more than economic and socio-cultural disparities. Botelho's quest to ground deviance in physiological phenomena leads to the location of Portuguese imperial decline in its 'degenerate' bloodline; cultural despondency is translated into ethno-racial inevitability. It would take more critical voices than Abel Botelho, as we shall see in the case of Eça de Queirós in the following chapter, to challenge the principles of the new 'sciences' and explore kinship trouble as a potential site for national renewal. Nevertheless, against all the odds, Botelho does write 'against nature' at times; the contagion is never adequately contained, mysterious limits emerge in the medical gaze, and the doctor on more than one occasion catches his patient's 'disease'. Two techniques in particular stand out that recur again and again in Lusophone Naturalist works, confirming the novel's importance within the movement as a whole. Firstly, his recourse to Greek ideas about male relationality supplements the contemporaneous, pathological approach, undercutting hyperbolic claims that the Baron's illness is a 'corrupção' of the nineteenth century and implicitly limiting the discourse of medicine. Secondly, his use of allegory expands the Naturalist perspective, pressuring the 'reality effect' to conflate individual and national 'pathology'. Is *Lavos*, to return to Howes's words, 'fatally flawed'? If so, its fatality is also remarkably creative, its obsession with degeneracy surprisingly generative. Its paroxysm of neologisms and shrewd, if slippery, use of metaphor warrant a level of close reading that critics have generally been unwilling to engage with, and the novel should at least be brought back from the brink of canonical oblivion for the insights it offers into the *fin-de-siècle* world, both in Portugal and beyond. Indeed, despite its overwhelmingly moralising-medicalising tone, there are many moments in which the reader glimpses an alternate morality — and even epistemology — to the one that defines the narration. This, perhaps, is the 'corrupção do século' that the doctor *seems* to condemn throughout, but which he is, no less, determined to contemplate.

## Notes to Chapter 1

1. Abel Botelho, *O Barão de Lavos* (Porto: Lello & Irmão, 1982). All page references are to this edition.

2. Robert Howes, 'Concerning the Eccentricities of the Marquis of Valada: Politics, Culture and Homosexuality in Fin-de-Siècle Portugal', *Sexualities*, 5 (2002), 25–48.

3. See e.g. Robert Howes's entry, 'Abel Botelho', in *Who's Who in Gay and Lesbian History from Antiquity to World War II*, ed. by Robert Aldrich and Garry Wotherspoon (London: Routledge, 2001), pp. 73–78.

4. See e.g. Leonardo Mendes, *O retrato do Imperador: negociação, sexualidade e romance naturalista no Brasil* (Porto Alegre: Edipucrs), p. 193.

5. Maria Raquel Limão de Andrade, 'A homossexualidade no masculino e no feminino: para uma abordagem sociológica dos romances de Abel Botelho, *O Barão de Lavos* e *O livro de Alda*' (unpublished master's thesis, Universidade Lusófona, 2003; held at Biblioteca Nacional de Portugal).

6. As Aubrey Bell wrote in 1922, 'This may be magnificent pathology, but it is not art or literature.' See Howes, *Who's Who...*, p. 64.

7. Robert Howes, *Who's Who...*, p. 64.

8. Robert Howes, 'Concerning the Eccentricities...', p. 39.

9. Ibid., p. 33.

10. See Howes, 'Concerning the Eccentricities...'.

11. Howes, 'Concerning the Eccentricities...', p. 34.

12. Alessandra El Far, *Páginas de sensação* (São Paulo: Companhia das Letras, 2004), p. 62.

13. Howes, 'Concerning the Eccentricities...', p. 33.

14. See Peter Cryle, 'Foretelling Pathology: The Poetics of Prognosis', *French Cultural Studies*, 17 (2006), 107–22.

15. Ibid, p. 113.

16. Ibid, p. 114.

17. Burton Feldman, *The Nobel Prize: A History of Genius, Controversy, and Prestige* (New York: Arcade Publishing, 2013), p. 286.

18. Limão de Andrade, 12.

19. Howes, *Who's Who...*, p. 63.

20. Cryle, p. 109.

21. See e.g. Arthur Balfour, *Decadence* (Cambridge: Cambridge University Press, 1908) for an archetypal treatise on degeneration. Available at <https://archive.org/stream/decadencehenryso1baltgoog#page/n6/mode/2up> [accessed 9 September 2019].

22. Heike Bauer, 'Measurements of Civilisation', *French Cultural Studies*, 17 (2008), 93–108 (p. 97).

23. Siobhan Somerville, 'Scientific Racism and the Invention of the Homosexual Body,' *Journal of the History of Sexuality*, 5 (1994), 246–66 (p. 249).

24. Richard von Krafft-Ebing, *Psychopathia Sexualis: The Classic Study of Deviant Sex*, trans. by Franklin S. Klaf with intro. by Joseph LoPicclo (New York: Arcade Publishing, 1965), no pagination.

25. Elaine Showalter, *Sexual Anarchy: Gender and Culture at the Fin de Siècle* (London: Virago, 1992), p. 200.

26. Ibid, p. 189.

27. Susan Sontag, *Aids and its Metaphors* (New York: Farrar, Straus and Giroux, 1988), p. 48.

28. See Diana Seitler, 'Queer Physiognomies; Or, How Many Ways Can We Do the History of Sexuality?', *Criticism*, 46 (2004), 71–102 (p. 77).

29. This is the argument I will develop in relation to the novel's aforementioned Sebastianic allegory.

30. Robert Howes, 'Race and Transgressive Sexuality in Adolfo Caminha's *Bom-Crioulo*', *Luso-Brazilian Review*, 38 (2001), 41–62 (p. 52).

31. See Cesare Lombroso, *Criminal Man*, trans. by Gibson and Rafter (London: Duke University Press, 2006) for the classic articulation of this view. Lombroso divides individuals into 'born' and 'occasional' criminals.

32. Robert Howes, 'Concerning the Eccentricities...', pp. 39–40.

33. Monika Fludernik, *The Fictions of Language and the Languages of Fiction: The Linguistic Representation of Speech and Consciousness* (London: Routledge, 1993), p. 363.

34. Jacob L. Mey, *When Voices Clash: A Study in Literary Pragmatics* (Berlin: Mouton de Gruyter, 1999), p. 74.

35. See Phyllis Margaret Paryas, 'Monologism' in *Encyclopedia of Contemporary Literary Theory: Approaches, Scholars, Terms*, ed. by Irena R. Makaryk (London: University of Toronto Press, 1993), p. 596.

36. See glossary to Mikhail Bakhtin, *The Dialogic Imagination*, ed. by Michael Holquist and trans. by Caryl Emerson and Michael Holquist (London: University of Texas Press, 1982), p. 426.

37. Fyodor Dostoevsky, *Notes from Underground*, trans. by Richard Pevear and Larissa Volokhonsky (London: Vintage Classics, 1994).

38. Charlotte Brontë, *Jane Eyre* (London: Penguin, 2006).

39. Limão de Andrade, p. 32.

40. <http://www.etymonline.com/index.php?term=fetish> [accessed 5 March 2016].

41. <http://www.etymonline.com/index.php?term=abomination> [accessed 5 March 2016].

42. Freud, 'Fetishism,' in *The Standard Edition of the Complete Psychological Works of Sigmund Freud*, trans. by James Strachey in collaboration with Anna Freud (London: Hogarth Press, 1961), vol. XXI, pp. 152–59 (p. 154).

43. Richard Burton, 'Terminal Essay', from *The Arabian Nights* (New York: Cosimo Classics, 2008), vol. X, pp. 63–260.

44. Camilo Castelo Branco, *A brasileira de Prazins* (Lisbon: Ulisseia, 1994).

45. I am indebted to Limão de Andrade (p. 13) for this proverb.

46. *Diário Popular*, 5 August 1888, Biblioteca Nacional de Portugal.

47. *Diário de Notícias*, 6 September 1888, Biblioteca Nacional de Portugal.

48. *Diário Popular*, 24 April 1886, Biblioteca Nacional de Portugal.

49. Ibid.

50. Botelho's *O Livro de Alda* (Porto: Lello, 1982) contains a brief episode of Lesbian desire, but it is not the chief focus of the story.

51. 'Ele tinha por enquanto junto do efebo os mesmos apetites de penetração e de posse que o homem sente de ordinário para com a mulher' [He had when he was next to the ephebe, the same appetite for penetration and possession that a man ordinarily feels for a woman] (p. 92).

52. Limão de Andrade, p. 27.

53. Robert Howes also notes that *Lavos* was published at the 'mid-point in the development of 19th-century sexology', and speculates that Botelho owes more to French medical writers such as Charcot, who were 'heavily influenced by contemporary theories of degeneration'. See Howes, 'Concerning the Eccentricities...', pp. 38–39.

54. Plato, *Symposium*, trans. by Benjamin Jowett (Rockville, MD: Serenity Publishers, 2009), p. 52.

55. Elaine Showalter discusses the widespread fetishisation of the working class amongst wealthy, *fin-de-siècle* homosexuals. See Showalter, p. 111. As Howes notes, Sebastião and Elvira are both titillated by Eugénio's working-class idiom. See Howes, 'Concerning the Eccentricities...', p. 40.

56. See Annegrete Dinter, *Der Pygmalion-Stoff in der europäischen Literatur: Rezeptionsgeschichte einer Ovid-Fabel*, in *Studien zum Fortwirken der Antike*, vol. XI (Heidelberg: Carl Winter Universitätsverlag, 1979).

57. See Michel Foucault, *Discipline and Punish*, trans. by Alan Sheridan (London: Penguin, 1991), pp. 170–94.

58. Émile Zola, *Nana* (Paris: Ligaran, 2015).

59. <http://www.priberam.pt/dlpo/chulo> [accessed 5 March 2016, my translation].

60. 'Double Dutch' has been offered as a translation of 'vasconça', but the bizarre addition of 'aravia' emphasises even further the foreignness (and heresy?) of Elvira's speech *vis-à-vis* the bourgeois reader. As Susan Sontag notes, disease is often articulated as a foreign problem (hence the English describing syphilis as 'French pox'). See Sontag, p. 48.

61. See Eve Sedgwick, *Between Men: English Literature and Male Homosocial Desire* (New York: Columbia University Press, 1985), pp. 22–27.

62. See Luce Irigaray, *This Sex Which is Not One*, trans. by Catherine Porter and Catherine Burke (Ithaca, NY: Cornell University Press, 1985), p. 72.

63. Showalter, pp. 24–30.

64. Howes, 'Concerning the Eccentricities...', p. 40.

65. Miriam Halpern Pereira, 'Demografia e desenvolvimento em Portugal na segunda metade do século XIX', *Revista do Instituto de Ciências Sociais da Universidade de Lisboa*, 7 (1969), 85–117 (p. 92).

66. See Howes, *Who's Who...*, p. 63, and David Higgs in *Queer Sites: Gay Urban Histories Since 1600*, ed. by David Higgs (London: Routledge, 2002), pp. 128–32.

67. Howes, 'Concerning the Eccentricities...', p. 40.

68. Eve Kosofsky Sedgwick, *The Epistemology of the Closet* (London: Harvester Wheatsheaf, 1999), p. 3.

69. Paul Bouissac, *Semiotics at the Circus* (Berlin: Walter de Gruyter, 2010), p. 71.

70. Howes, 'Concerning the Eccentricities...', p. 33.

71. Isabella Alston and Kathryn Dixon, *Anatomical Anomalies* (Charlotte, NC: TAJ Books, 2014), p. 4.

72. Ibid, p. 71.

73. Howes, 'Concerning the Eccentricities...', p. 40.

74. Jacques Derrida, 'From *Shibboleth*', in *Acts of Literature*, ed. by Derek Attridge (London: Routledge, 1992), pp. 370–413 (p. 396).

75. Cited by John D. Caputo in *The Prayers and Tears of Jacques Derrida: Religion Without Religion* (Bloomington: Indiana University Press, 1997), p. 251.

76. Elizabeth Stephens, 'Anatomies of Desire' in *Sexuality at the fin-de-siècle*, ed. by Peter Cryle and Christopher E. Forth (Cranbury, NJ: University of Delaware, 2008), pp. 25–38 (pp. 26–27).

77. <http://www.etymonline.com/index.php?term=mystery.> [accessed 7 March 2016].

78. In the second Book of Kings, Elisha curses Gehazi with Naaman's leprosy as a punishment for abusing his authority. 'Naaman's leprosy will cling to you and to your descendants forever.' II Kings 5. 27.

79. See Foucault, Michel, *Madness and Civilization: A History of Insanity in the Age of Reason* (New York: Vintage, 1965) for a discussion of the development of the mental asylum from medieval leper colonies.

80. See Martin Wynn, *Planning and Urban Growth in Southern Europe* (London: Manswell, 1994), p. 81.

81. Howes, 'Concerning the Eccentricities...', p. 33.

82. See Pedro Braga, *O touro encantado da Ilha dos Lençóis: o sebastianismo no Maranhão* (Petrópolis: Editora Vozes, 2001).

83. Johnson, for example, uncompromisingly accuses certain Portuguese historians of 'ignorance' and an 'unconscious abhorrence' of homosexuality, which he claims has led them to suppress knowledge of the king's sexuality. See Harold Johnson, 'A Pedophile in the Palace', (2004), available at <http://people.virginia.edu/~hbj8n/ pedophile.pdf> [accessed 28 April 2014].

84. Pero Roiz Soares, cited by Joaquim Veríssimo Serrão, *História de Portugal* (Lisbon: Verbo, 1978), vol. III, p. 69.

85. Johnson, p. 14.

86. Concerning the Baron's sixth great-grandfather: 'O atavismo fez explodir neste com rábida energia todos os vícios constitucionais que bacilavam no sangue da sua raça' [Atavism brought about an explosion inside him of all the constitutional vices mixed into the blood of his race] (p. 26).

87. Paul de Man, *Blindness and Insight: Essays in the Rhetoric of Contemporary Criticism* (Abingdon: Routledge, 1983), p. 208.

88. Roland Barthes, 'The Reality Effect', in *The Rustle of Language*, trans. by Richard Howard (Berkeley: University of California Press, 1989), pp. 141–48.

# CHAPTER 2

# Eça de Queirós

## Introduction

— Vem tu cá abaixo! Posso perfeitamente conversar na água!

[Reinaldo] saiu, berrando por William, o seu criado inglês.

Quando Basílio desceu ao banho, Reinaldo estirado com voluptuosidade na tina, donde saía um forte cheiro de água de Lubin, exclamou, deleitando-se no seu conforto:

— Então cartinha apanhada nos papéis sujos!

— Não, Reinaldo, mas francamente estou embaraçado. Que achas tu que eu faça?

— As malas, menino!

E sentado na tina, ensaboando devagar o seu corpo magro:

— Aí está o que é fazer amor às primas da Patriarcal Queimada!

— Oh! — fez Basílio, impaciente.

— Oh, quê? — E, coberto de flocos de espuma, com as mãos apoiadas ao rebordo de mármore na tina: — Pois tu achas isso decente [...] Uma mulher que, como tu mesmo disseste, usa meias de tear!

[...]

Basílio deu logo provas: descreveu belezas do corpo da Luísa; citou episódios lascivos.

O tecto e os tabiques envernizados de branco reflectiam a luz, com tons macios de leite; a exalação da água tépida aumentava o calor morno; e um cheiro fresco de sabão e água de Lubin adoçava o ar.

[...]

E tomando a esponja, [Reinaldo] deixava cair grandes golpes de água pela cabeça, pelos ombros, soprando, regalado na frescura aromática. [...]

— E partimos amanhã? — gritou Reinaldo.

— Amanhã.

— Por Madrid?

— Por Madrid.

— *Salero!* — Pôs-se de pé, na tina, entusiasmado...[1]

['Come down here! I can easily talk to you from the water!'

Reinaldo left, shouting for William, his English manservant.

When Basílio went down to the bathhouse, Reinaldo, stretched out voluptuously in the bathtub, which was filling the room with the scent of Lubin perfume, exclaimed, basking in comfort:

'So, a letter fished out of the waste paper!'

'Honestly Reinaldo, I really am embarrassed. What do you think I should do?'

'Pack your bags, my boy!'
And sitting in the tub, slowly lathering his thin body:
'Well that's what comes of making love to your cousins from the Patriarcal Queimada!'
'Oh!' groaned Basílio impatiently.
'Oh, what?' And, covered in flecks of foam, resting his hands on the tub's marble rim: 'Come now, do you really think it's decent [...]! A woman who, as you yourself have said, wears stockings made on a loom!' [...]
Basílio tried to justify himself: he described the charms of Luísa's body, citing lascivious episodes.
The ceiling and partitions, varnished in white, reflected the light in soft milky tones; the steaming warm water added to the gentle heat, and a fresh scent of soap and Lubin perfume sweetened the air. [...]
And taking up the sponge, [Reinaldo] let the water cascade over his head, over his shoulders, sighing, wallowing in the aromatic freshness. [...]
'And we're leaving tomorrow?' shouted Reinaldo.
'Tomorrow.'
'For Madrid?'
'For Madrid.'
'*Salero!*' He stood up in the bathtub, excited.']

In this striking passage from *O primo Basílio* (1878), two long-standing companions, Basílio and Reinaldo, converse while the latter lies (and later stands) naked in the bathtub. As Reinaldo rubs soap and water over his body, covered in flecks of foam, the pair discuss their travelling plans and love interests. The conversation, which restricts bawdy talk to women alone, makes for exemplary homosocial camaraderie. However, to the reader — or at least this reader — the scene exudes an erotic excess that undermines the pair's efforts to contain it. The rhythmic asyndeton of 'pela cabeça, pelos ombros' deflects our attention, like the water, onto Reinaldo's naked body. And yet Basílio's attention seems to be elsewhere. Indeed, put more accurately, the scene exudes both eroticism and its conspicuous absence, leaving the quality of the friends' desire fundamentally indeterminate.[2] The contrast with Botelho's prose is immediate: whilst the latter restlessly seeks to identify and contain eroticism, here Eça leaves it considerably more difficult to pin down and open to interpretation.

Indeed, the apparent confusion surrounding desire, social and sexual relationships in Eça's work, which is a central concern of the present chapter, evidently sits at odds with the pathologising tone of Botelho, whose most (in)famous novel makes a strange prelude, perhaps, to the work of one of Portugal's most celebrated novelists. Besides the authors' positions at opposite poles of the literary canon, an analysis of Eça's work is further complicated by his efforts to distance himself from the Naturalist movement over the course of his life. Despite Machado de Assis's famous description of Eça as 'um fiel e aspérrimo discípulo do realismo propagado pelo autor do *Assommoir*' [a faithful and coarse disciple of realism propagated by the author of *L'Assommoir*],[3] critics have long drawn attention to his lack of confidence in the epistemological and transformative potential of Naturalism that its first proponents had promised,[4] his style shifting considerably from a darker and more Zola-esque tone to an apparently more optimistic one,[5] while two of his major works, *A relíquia* and *O mandarim*, include elements of the supernatural and fantastical, not to mention unreliable first-person narrators. It is possible only to speculate how a man often reduced to caricature, with his cranelike figure and discerning monocle, would have reacted to that drawn by Raphael Bordalo Pinheiro, depicting his funeral in 1900, in which Abel Botelho appears with 'Eça' written across his chest, as though heir to the Portuguese Naturalist crown.[6] Eça had, after all, caricatured himself twelve years earlier in the form of João da Ega, a dilettante from the *esquerda caviar* [champagne socialist] elite of *Os Maias* who professes to be writing a novel called *Memórias de um átomo*, narrated by an atom, that ten years later remains unfinished, surely a rather damning indictment of the Naturalist movement in general. It is perhaps more likely that Bordalo Pinheiro was mocking not Eça but Botelho, who in the drawing walks alongside some of the former's most memorably piteous characters, such as the pompous Conselheiro Acácio from *O primo Basílio*. Either way, the caricature illustrates the degree of overlap, if not continuity, between Eça's ideas and those of Botelho in the popular imaginary, however far posterity has since prised them apart.

Eça's immediate association with Naturalism in Portugal doubtless stems from his vigorous public support for the movement as a young writer. His speech given at the Casino Lisbonense in June 1871, arguing, in line with Zola, that 'O Realismo deve proceder pela experiência, pela fisiologia, ciência dos temperamentos' [Realism ought to proceed from experience, from physiology and the science of the temperaments], envisions literature as a scientific experiment, as 'a análise com o fito na verdade absoluta' [analysis with the aim of absolute truth],[7] a radical gesture that cemented his position within the reformist *Geração de '70*, alongside his Coimbra peers. The reference to physiology, of course, suggests an overlap with the vocabulary and techniques of Botelho. His much-cited ambition while writing *O primo Basílio*, seven years later, was to 'pintar a sociedade portuguesa [...] e mostrar-lhe, *como num espelho*, que triste país eles formam' [paint Portuguese society [...] and confront it, as in a mirror, with the sad country that its people form],[8] again reiterating his vision of literature as an exercise in precision, even if, as the above passage suggests, the theory was never quite put into practice, at least not necessarily as intended. In any case, his thought became ostensibly more nuanced, and in 1893 he cheered the symbolist and spiritualist turn, arguing, in Hegelian fashion, that the burgeoning reaction against Positivism would be 'benéfico',[9] and conceding that imagination and idealism play a worthy role in the arts. 'Nunca mais ninguém, com medo da ciência e das repreensões da fisiologia, duvidará em ir respirar, pela imaginação, e se for possível colher, as rosas brotadas do sangue do santo incomparável' [never again will anyone, fearing science and the chastisements of physiology, cast doubt on the need to breathe, explore our imagination, and if possible gather the roses budding from the blood of the holiest saint], he writes, two years after the publication of *O Barão de Lavos*. The intellectual divergence of Eça from the likes of Botelho, therefore, and arguably from his younger self, presents two key opportunities for an analysis of desire and kinship in his work. The first is to chart his growing disillusionment with the movement at the level of the text, a sentiment which entails, as I shall argue, an increasing confusion surrounding social, familial and sexual relationships, culminating in the troubled first-person narrators that characterise his later novels. The second, in light of my reading of *Lavos*, is to consider the degree to which the representation of relationships modulates according to the popularity, insight and canonical longevity of the texts concerned. Was Bordalo Pinheiro in any way justified in reincarnating Botelho as Eça — do their techniques overlap — or are their approaches essentially unrecognisable? As we shall see, despite very significant differences in their work, there may be ways in which both authors, in a recognisably Lusophone fashion, write against Naturalism and its claims to absolute truth.

It is curious to note that whilst Eça's novels have attracted far more attention from critics than those of Botelho, very little has been from a queer perspective, to the extent that *Lavos* has probably garnered more interest in this regard. Whether this imbalance testifies to the more subtle exploration of relationality in Eça's work, the assumptions of many readers, or both, is hard to say. With a few more recent and notable exceptions, the body of scholarship on Eça's work has overwhelmingly taken an implicit heteronormative view of erotic relations, appearing to assume that desire operates exclusively on a heterosexual axis. The vast tome by João Gaspar Simões, for example, *Vida e obra de Eça de Queirós*, describes sexual desire in Eça as an 'espada de fogo apertando o macho da fêmea' [blade of fire attracting male to female].[10] Beatriz Berrini identifies Teodorico's lively interest in women in *A relíquia*, but not in his childhood sweetheart Crispim or the 'formoso Manassés' [beautiful Manassés] who visits him in his dreams.[11] Saraiva speaks of the 'encontro de príncipes' [meeting of princes] in *Os Maias* as a relationship of esteem and admiration,[12] arguably overlooking the erotic potential of the 'belo príncipe' [handsome prince] (as I will argue, a recurring figure across Eça's work). Nor does Alexander Coleman in his discussion of such a relationship in *A cidade e as serras*,[13] which Carlos Reis, too, describes as 'amizade fraternal' [brotherly friendship].[14] As we shall see, such readings might underestimate the disruption to the language of desire and indeed Naturalism itself, as well as the extent to which the troubling of kinship figures at the heart, rather than at the surface, of the author's concerns surrounding cultural centrality, marginality and decline — that 'triste país' that he sought to mirror in *O primo Basílio*.

Indeed, maintaining a heteronormative perspective of Eça's work risks reading the discourse of degeneration at face value. Although degeneration theory does not govern Eça's writing to the extent that it does Botelho's, it nevertheless features prominently: the author himself described Portugal as 'uma sociedade podre' [a rotten society] which he was preparing for its ruin,[15] echoing the 'national degeneration' theories of Herbert Spencer that other members of the *Geração de '70*, such as Oliveira Martins, took particularly seriously.[16] Eça was acutely aware of his country's infatuation with England and France, describing it, in a famous essay entitled 'O francesismo', as 'um país traduzido do francês em vernáculo' [a country translated from French into slang],[17] a characteristically apposite metaphor for what today might be termed cultural dependency. He was also personally familiar with both countries, having worked as a diplomat in Newcastle, Bristol and Paris, where he penned many of his most famous novels. However, for all the attention that incestuous (and occasionally 'homosexual') desire in his work has received, critics have tended to read both as symptomatic of this 'sociedade podre', a result and reflection of the nation in decline,[18] materially so where the question of empire was concerned, and assumedly so according to contemporaneous theories of degeneration. Happily, more recent work has parted considerably with this thesis. Maria Manuel Lisboa in particular has read the central incestuous relationship in *Os Maias* as gesturing towards a new beginning rather than symbolising the end of the nation, heralding (if only briefly and unsuccessfully) the end of patriarchal capitalism.[19] In a similar vein, I want to argue that, unlike in *Lavos*, the disruption to kinship and erotic desire in Eça might be read as a yearning for a new social structure rather than as a lament for the demise of an old one. Going a step further, I propose that the revelation of an insufficiency in the language of desire entails a radical questioning of Naturalist principles, which find their discursive limits at the movement's cultural periphery. By implicating normative kinship in the production and understanding of 'truth', most especially in *A relíquia*, the entire system of representation is called into question. Eça's aesthetic trajectory might thus be said to reach a highpoint in the Lusophone tradition of writing 'against nature', an undoing of Naturalism as implicated in the consolidation of a socio-economic system that (re)produced geopolitical hierarchies.

The recent work of a number of scholars provides a departure point for a series of readings that, at the textual level, seek to tease out the ambiguous nature of erotic desire in Eça. Firstly, Ana Paula Ferreira has analysed the perplexing short story 'José Matias', in which she identifies a 'will to know' on the part of the narrator in relation to his feminised subject that echoes the 'homosexual panic' of the *fin de siècle*.[20] She also raises the possibility of other such characters in Eça's novels,[21] and I will return to 'José Matias' later in light of these. A highly original article by José Carlos Barcellos, meanwhile, identifies a series of relationships in Eça's novels in which there is a 'continuidade básica' [basic continuity] between homosociability and homoeroticism.[22] However, Barcellos then restores a distinction between 'homosexuals' and 'heterosexuals' in his analysis, which can prove problematic when trying to capture the ambiguities in the texts. Meanwhile, Phillip Rothwell and Anna Klobucka have addressed the issue from a different perspective. Klobucka studies the figure of Libaninho in *O crime do Padre Amaro*, a clerk and later sacristan who is caught in the act with a local sergeant,[23] and to whom I will return in due course. Rothwell, who draws on Lacanian theory to argue that Eça's male characters are notable for their 'weak paternity', explores the homoerotic implications of the 'belo príncipe' in *A cidade e as serras*, whereby the narrator is 'besotted'[24] with his friend Jacinto, a Portuguese aristocrat seeking identification as a father. In many ways, the present chapter builds on Barcellos's work, analysing relationships across a range of Eça's novels in which the nature of erotic desire is ambiguous, and assessing their significance in relation to the author's critique of Naturalism and patriarchal capitalism. However, I will also be extending Rothwell's study of weak paternity and *sebastianismo* in Eça, bringing it into play with Lisboa's work on the radical implications of incestuous desire. With the aforementioned aim of charting Eça's ideological shifts across time, I follow a roughly chronological structure, beginning with *O primo Basílio* and ending with his later works, with the caveat that *A relíquia* is considered after *Os Maias*, despite being published a year earlier. This is justified by the novel's narrative similarities with (for example) *A cidade e as serras*, as well as the fact that *A relíquia* was written at the same time as *Os Maias*. As we shall see, the gradual move away from third-person narrative is prefigured by characterisation and classical influences in his early work.

## *As primeiras sensações, e as mais intensas* [the first feelings, and the most intense]: Platonic Love, Oedipal Trouble and Colonial Mistakes in *O primo Basílio*

Published in 1878, *O primo Basílio* tells the story of Luísa and Jorge, a petit-bourgeois couple living in the (appropriately named, as it transpires) Patriarcal Queimada neighbourhood of Lisbon.[25] Whilst her husband is away on business in the Alentejo, Luísa begins an adulterous affair with her cousin and first love, Basílio. Basílio eventually deserts Luísa, continuing to Madrid, as we have seen, with his friend Reinaldo, but in events that, like in *O Barão de Lavos*, implicate class disparities, Luísa's covetous maid recovers a discarded love letter and blackmails her mistress to obtain ever more luxuries, eventually becoming de facto mistress of the house. Learning of his wife's secret much later, when Basílio sends her another letter from Paris, Jorge confronts Luísa, precipitating her gruesome death from shock and delirium. Although narrated in the third person in a tone that on occasion treads a fine line between objectivism and condescension,[26] as we shall see, the novel anticipates and incorporates many of the ideological concerns that would prove pivotal in the conception of his later, first-person narratives.

   *Basílio* was criticised at the outset for being a plagiarism of *Madame Bovary*, a hypothesis that has since been expertly challenged by Silviano Santiago who, focusing on Eça's clever addition of Ernestinho's play (the unfolding plot of which parallels the novel itself) instead reads the work as a lucid reflection on cultural marginality and the perceived need to adopt trends from centres of dominance.[27] In this respect, it seems reasonable to propose another crucial difference with Flaubert's story of adultery: the friendship between Jorge and Sebastião, which is well developed and, I believe, central to the novel's meaning, even if it might appear peripheral in relation to Luísa's dramatic fall from bourgeois grace. Jorge and Sebastião live together both before and after the former's calamitous marriage, a cyclical turn of events that, within the narrative, frames the heterosexual union as transient and episodic. Discussing their grand plans for the future as young men, the pair christen themselves the 'Sociedade Sebastião e Jorge' [the Jorge and Sebastião society] (p. 120), a term that undercuts the sense of a business partnership — which typically calls for surnames — with the intimacy of marriage. Indeed, before Jorge meets Luísa, there is a honeymoon-like phase in their relationship in which they imagine a future together: 'pensaram mesmo em viver juntos; habitariam a casa de Sebastião, mais larga e que tinha quintal; Jorge queria comprar um cavalo' [They even thought about living together; they would live in Sebastião's house, which was larger and had a garden; Jorge wanted to buy a horse]. Although marriage disrupts these plans, Sebastião remains Jorge's most loyal friend and companion in life. Upon his first appearance in the novel, he is described in the following terms:

> Era ele, Sebastião, o grande Sebastião, o Sebastiarrão, o Sebastião *tronco de árvore*, — o íntimo, o camarada, o *inseparável* de Jorge, desde o latim, na aula de Frei Libório, aos Paulistas. (p. 53)

> [It was he, Sebastião, the great Sebastião, Sebastiarrão, Sebastião the tree trunk — Jorge's intimate, *inseparable* comrade, ever since Latin lessons, in Brother Libório's class, at the Paulists.]

He is named in seven different ways, while the asyndeton evokes a sense of breathlessness and inability to recall an adequate superlative. Interestingly, he is identified as a 'camarada', but the italicised '*inseparável*' again undercuts this term by suggesting dependency, as though Sebastião is Jorge's perfect other half, or indeed his brother.[28]

Comrades and male friendships are not, of course, unusual in nineteenth-century novels; on the contrary, they are the order of the day, as René Girard and Eve Sedgwick in particular have convincingly argued. In the previous chapter, however, we saw how the archetypal love triangle of the nineteenth-century novel, where a bond of rivalry between men secures their societal dominance, is recast and eventually blown apart by pederasty, events that are also bound up with an upheaval in the social class structure. In *Basílio*, at least where Jorge and Sebastião are concerned, the Girardian triangle does not appear to apply. Sebastião, a timid but kindly character, and the only one described by Eça himself as a 'bom rapaz' [good boy],[29] extends his friendship to Luísa during Jorge's absence, defending her against Juliana and never exhibiting the least suggestion of adulterous or ulterior motives. There is no rivalry to be observed between the two friends, and unlike in the case of most other male relations in Eça, Luísa is not introduced to one friend by the other. Instead, the *Sociedade Sebastião e Jorge* is a model of male companionship, and may in fact bear greater resemblance to older modes of friendship than the triangulated framework typical of the nineteenth-century novel:

> Já então os dois rapazes vizinhos, Jorge e Sebastião, eram íntimos. Jorge mais inventivo, dominava-o. No quintal, a brincar, Sebastião era sempre nas imitações da diligência, o vencido nas guerras. Era Sebastião que carregava os pesos, que oferecia o dorso para Jorge trepar; nas merendas comia igual, deixava a Jorge toda a fruta. Cresceram. E aquela amizade sempre amuos, tornou-se na vida de ambos um interesse essencial e permanente. (pp. 119–20)

> [By this point the two neighbouring boys, Jorge and Sebastião, were intimate. Jorge, who was more inventive, dominated him. When they played in the garden at being soldiers, Sebastião was always defeated in war. It was Sebastião who carried the weights, who offered himself for Jorge to piggyback; at lunch

he was much the same, leaving Jorge all the fruit. They grew up. And that
unaltered friendship became an essential and permanent feature of their lives.]

The narrator's digression here, detailing the friends' childhood games, develops an
unusual dynamic of dominance and submission. How much significance can be
attached to the piggybacking is difficult to say, but in the context of their idealised
relationship as a whole, it seems reasonable to postulate an influence from Platonic
ideas about male companionship, not dissimilar to those we saw at work in *O Barão
de Lavos*, although here its function within the critique of the bourgeois family
is many times more radical. As we have seen, Pausanias valorises the pederastic
relationship (characterised by dominance and submission) above heterosexual love,
believing it to be more conducive to love of the soul over the body.[30] Montaigne
makes a similar argument in the sixteenth century, although ostensibly without the
pederasty, idealising male love as a union of souls, in contrast to love for women
which he saw as 'fickle', subject to change and untrustworthy.[31] The similarities
with classical approaches to friendship gain traction when we consider the enduring
nature of the pair's relationship and their resolution to live together again at the end.
Thus despite the lack of scandal that surrounds Jorge and Sebastião and the relative
nuance and subtlety of their interaction, the central male relationship in the novel
has more in common with that of *Lavos* than might meet the eye, since both are
better understood by returning to Greek modes of love and friendship than they are
by bonds of rivalry for which the nineteenth-century novel is so renowned.

The current of Platonic idealism that works its way into the narrative fabric of
*Basílio*, alongside the metafictional digression of Ernestinho's play, distinguishes the
novel from *Madame Bovary* formally but also in its critical scope, giving a striking
contrast to the seemingly central story of adultery, and clearly contextualising the
latter as a whimsical product of the historical moment. Thus Jorge's courtship with
Luísa, despite the reference to passion, is penned in notably passionless terms:

> Conheceu Luísa, no Verão, à noite, no Passeio. Apaixonou-se pelos seus cabelos
> louros, pela sua maneira de andar, pelos seus olhos castanhos muito grandes. No
> Inverno seguinte foi despachado, e casou. (p. 21)

> [He met Luísa in summer, at night, in the park. He fell in love with her blond
> hair, her gait, and her very large brown eyes. The following winter he was
> offered a job, and married.]

In contrast to the detailed development of Jorge's friendship with Sebastião, Luísa's
attributes are listed drily in three sentences, being clearly rooted in conventional
notions of beauty and femininity, as though she happens to fulfil an expected
social role. As Lisboa argues, the couple love each other 'mediocremente'[32] and
are thus destined for 'traições desastrosas' [disastrous betrayals][33] from the outset.
Luísa's infatuation with Basílio is similarly mimetic, a futile re-enactment of the
Romantic novels she reads that ends in abandonment and death. Set against the
looming backdrop of the novel's first and most lasting relationship, the *Sociedade
Sebastião e Jorge*, the romantic attachments in *Basílio* appear shallow, vain and
ultimately destructive. The supposedly Realist 'mirror' that Eça holds to society
in the novel thus sits in an unflattering frame of idealism, pitting the status quo

against meaningful relationships that hark back to another age. There is evidently a critique of vacuous bourgeois values at work here, commensurate with the novel's concern with fashion, consumption and the urban middle classes that grew in the wake of the Liberal Wars of the 1830s. The greed and materialism of Juliana, who rises from poverty to rest her feet while Luísa cleans the house, only to jaundice and die when caught trying to sell her love letter — itself transformed into a commodity — provides a secondary cyclical plot motif that again condemns the futility of contemporaneous domestic and social values. Therefore, although the recourse to idealism is perhaps surprising given the author's own comments about his novel, it is nonetheless noteworthy that his apparent critique of the social economy — with marriage at its centre — is developed through the depiction of a redemptive counterpoint, one involving alternative modes of loving and relating in society, indifferent to the desideratum of (re)production. The near-opposing functions of Greek idealism in Eça and Botelho are laid bare here, the latter re-inscribing it as pathology, the former elevating it above the futility of Jorge's attempts to marry and have children.

The influence of classical approaches to love and friendship in Eça is discussed extensively by Lisboa, who argues that the principles of Greek tragedy in particular work to disrupt and undermine the Naturalist method. Reading Carlos's incestuous relationship with his sister in *Os Maias* as a Freudian re-enactment of desire for his lost mother, who abandons him as an infant, Lisboa explores how an ancient discourse of fate and predestination contradicts Carlos's attempts to regenerate his country and, by extension, the Naturalist belief in a logical and rational approach to society.[34] Crucially, the pair decide to terminate their relationship upon realising its incestuous nature, capitulating to the taboo on endogamous relationships in patriarchal society and thus symbolically turning down the opportunity to build a different social economy. Much like in *Basílio*, then, though in this case drawing on Sophocles, Greek epistemologies are deployed to problematise and provide a counterpoint to the banality of relationships in nineteenth-century Portuguese society, constrained by the perceived need to expand the family and its fortunes. Like Carlos, Jorge's dreams of fathering a 'pequerrucho' (p. 61) to continue his name are never realised and refuge is sought in the comforting presence of Sebastião. The return to the Greek classics in *Basílio* thus already anticipates its comparable function in *Os Maias*, even if the theme of incest itself is explored only obliquely in the 'incestozinho' of cousins Basílio and Luísa.

In fact, the influence of Sophocles can also be detected in *Basílio*, adding another facet to the novel's critique of patriarchal capitalism. To begin with, Jorge's 'love' for Luísa seems to be triggered by the death of his mother, as though one replaces the other, anticipating the logic that Freud would later term the Oedipus complex, in reference, of course, to Sophocles' play. 'Quando sua mãe morreu, porém, começou a achar-se só [...]. Decidiu casar' [when his mother died, however, he began to feel lonely [...]. He decided to marry] (p. 21). As we know, for Freud, young boys typically identify with their fathers as they come to terms with the loss of the mother, seeking another woman in her image as an adult. Fearing punishment under the father's law — castration anxiety — the boy opts to become like the father, attaining a privileged social position that compensates for the loss of the mother.[35] Accordingly, Jorge's marriage to Luísa provokes paternal attitudes in him, much like with the Baron of Lavos; his bride is more of a daughter to him than a wife, described repeatedly in the diminutive as 'A Luísa, a Luisinha [...], um passarinho, como um passarinho amiga do ninho [...]. [E] aquele serzinho louro e meigo veio dar à sua casa um encanto sério' [Luísa, little Luísa [...], like a little bird, a little bird tending to the nest [...]. And that blonde and meek little being brought great charm to his house] (p. 22). Luísa is thus mother, daughter, wife and piece of decor all in one. Significantly for this reading, Jorge tries to prevent Luísa from seeing her childhood friend and sweetheart, the brash and tactless Leopoldina, with whom she shares 'as primeiras sensações, e as mais intensas' [the first feelings, and the most intense] (p. 162), not to mention her first kiss, in school. The curious reference to Lesbian desire here, which parallels the physical intimacy of Jorge and Sebastião in their formative school years, is interpreted as a clear threat to the domestic order. '[d]i questo no parlaremo piú, o donna mia! À sopa!' [Of that we shall speak no more, my lady! To the soup!] (p. 41), cries Jorge at dinner, banishing Leopoldina from the house and asserting his paternal authority over his daughter-wife.

Nevertheless, as for Oedipus, cracks become visible in Jorge's quest to become a patriarch. Interestingly, he articulates his law in Italian, a performative gesture that recalls the bourgeois fascination with Italian opera.[36] Just as Verdi's 'La donna è mobile' paradoxically codifies a woman's inconstancy to render it constant, so do Jorge's words universalise 'questo', or Luísa's relationship with the transgressive Leopoldina, speaking them beyond the household even as he sets out to silence them, foreshadowing the growing fragility of his patriarchal rule. Luísa proves to be a wayward child, enacting an adulterous affair with her cousin and childhood sweetheart, Basílio, an affair that is also incestuous, or at least constitutes, as we have seen, an 'incestozinho' (p. 251). According to the old Portuguese adage, quanto mais prima, mais se lhe arrima [the closer the cousin, the closer the bond]. Jorge cannot wield his law successfully; in the end, his 'donna mia' slips from his control. Leopoldina, for example, is never really banished from the house, returning while Jorge is away in the Alentejo like the tiger who came to tea, exciting Luísa with stories of her romances and in part inspiring her to copy her behaviour. His mother's imposing portrait, in the apparent absence of his father's, looms ominously over the household throughout the novel, as though overshadowing his attempts to identify as an authoritative father by choosing a daughter for a wife. The portrait seems to bring his mother back from the dead, or indeed keeps her undead, disrupting his 'replacement' of her with Luísa. Her death at the end leaves him lost for words: 'que fiz eu?' [what did I do?] (p. 413), he stutters, relinquishing himself of all responsibility. Weakened and distraught, Jorge's consolation is to move back in with Sebastião, this time indefinitely. His inability to possess his mother-daughter-wife and impose his own law leaves him widowed and childless, his line destined to end with him, his attempts at paternal identification lying in tatters. The apparently inauthentic, mimetic nature of relations in the novel, and their disastrous outcomes that contrast with the idealised friendship of Jorge and Sebastião, thus chime with the questioning of normative kinship performed by Engels in his contemporaneous, genealogical study of the development of patriarchal-capitalist society, and which I addressed in the introduction: the body politic is organised in accordance with the economic system of (re)production and inheritance,[37] at the expense of rewarding personal relationships. Moreover, it is through a recourse to classical epistemologies that Eça contextualises and makes visible the hegemonic mode of relating in his day.

The question of same-sex desire in the novel, therefore, is an interesting one if Jorge's marriage is read as a failed attempt at paternal identification that echoes Sophocles and anticipates Freud, not least since the latter's position on the subject is complex and navigates the same contours and contradictions of the patriarchal family in nineteenth-century Europe. On the one hand, as Michael Warner notes, the Oedipus complex assumes that identification and sexual desire move along different gendered axes and are rendered mutually exclusive, the mother, later her image, figuring as the object of desire and the father as the subject with whom one identifies. The schema is thus based upon an assumption of gender difference as absolute alterity and a homo/heterosexual system of oppositional desires, further normalised by Freud's assertions elsewhere that homosexuality is the result of an 'inversion' of the Oedipus complex.[38] Nevertheless, Freud also stresses that:

> [p]sycho-analytic research is most decidedly opposed to any attempt at separating off homosexuals from the rest of mankind as a group of a special character [...] all human beings are capable of making a homosexual object choice and have in fact made one in their unconscious. Indeed, libidinal attachments to persons of the same sex play no less a part as factors in normal mental life.[39]

Curiously, then, Freud undercuts his own developmental matrix of oppositional desires with the assertion that all individuals experience, at some level, its 'normal' and 'inverted' forms. This suggestion is, in fact, central to his claim that desire for the father works to mobilise a boy's identification with him, his image serving as an ego ideal upon which to model himself.[40] Such a teleological view of sexual development, whereby an early homosexuality makes way for 'normal' sexual behaviours as an adult, finds an echo in homophobic discourses that assert homosexuality to be the result of adolescent 'confusion' or a 'passing phase' on a journey towards (re)productive relationships in patriarchal society. It is interesting that in *Basílio*, the school years of Jorge, Sebastião, Luísa and Leopoldina all feature same-sex relationships of intense emotional and physical proximity. For the latter two, there is a clear, mutual acknowledgement of a childhood physical attraction. 'Que agonia de ciúmes! Que delíria de reconciliações! E os beijos furtados! E os olhares! E os bilhetinhos, e todas as palpitações do coração, as primeiras da vida!' [the agonies of jealousy! The ecstasy of reconciliation! And the stolen kisses! And the looks! And the little notes, and all the flutters of the heart, the first in life!] (p. 162). The free indirect discourse here, in which Leopoldina recalls her 'saudades' for her formative years, paints their relationship as a lost moment of happiness from the past, not dissimilar from the *Sociedade Sebastião e Jorge*, which again features as a phase superseded by the expectations of adult life. Confining intimate, same-sex relationships to the past, the characters privilege the same teleological and productive view of sexuality that Freud, perhaps inadvertently, reiterated in his formulation of child sexual development later in the century. These affectionate childhood relationships, ultimately scorned in favour of normative adult relations, recall the words of E. M. Forster: 'feelings of beauty and tenderness [...] like plants that are all leaves and show no sign of flower'.[41]

That the author rejects a linear approach to sexual development becomes clear upon consideration of the novel's peculiar narrative movements, which already anticipate those of his mature work. To begin with, as we have seen, Jorge's attempts at paternal identification bear no fruit, and at the end, he resumes the convivial arrangement with Sebastião that was once the dream of his youth. The breakdown of his marriage, precipitated by a purloined letter analogous to the handkerchief of Desdemona, bears the hallmarks of predestination and *hamartia* characteristic of Greek tragedy, a narrative turn antithetical to notions of linearity and progress, and not missed by Lisboa, who argues that the novel already anticipates the disillusionment and despondency of *Os Maias*.[42] As much as characters try to assume expected sexual and social roles, the narrative appears to foreclose the possibility of progressive and ultimately stable development. Another motif worthy of mention in this respect, and one that we saw at work in the previous chapter, is the allegory of empire and nationhood that arises through subtle references to colonialism and, in particular, the brief and calamitous reign of Dom Sebastião, a figure drawn upon by Botelho in his 1895 novel. The *Geração de '70* identified him early on as pivotal in a putative Portuguese cultural *decadência*, holding him responsible for burying the last hopes of the nation in the battle of Alcácer-Quibir.[43] As usual, his appearance sits at the crossroads of kinship trouble, national degenerescence and the limits of Naturalist discourse but, as we shall see, the function of the allegory in Basílio is to question the age-old logic of (re)production that inspired his crusade and that Botelho seeks to reinforce through the abjection of his protagonist.

The explicit reference to Dom Sebastião in *Basílio* is brief but significant. Besides sharing his name with the king — like the Baron of Lavos — Sebastião also names his magnificent rose collection 'rosas D. Sebastião' (p. 102, author's italics). The blooms appear on several occasions, being gathered for Jorge's courtship with Luísa 'com cuidados devotos, sem espinhos' [with devout care, thorns removed] (p. 120) and gifted repeatedly to her during her husband's absence, acting as a symbolic investment in the marriage and its fortunes. The importance attached to the 'rosas D. Sebastião' (and by extension, Jorge's marriage) parallels the hope placed in the sixteenth-century monarch to secure the future of the Empire by providing an heir, a future dreamed, and perhaps also doubted, by Camões in his closing address to the King himself.[44] The allegory of Dom Sebastião in *Basílio* is strengthened by the intense companionship of the two friends in youth, recalling the longstanding anxieties surrounding the boy king's suitability for rule owing to his preference for male company and alleged misogyny. Indeed, the figure of the king in *Basílio* is evoked by both Sebastião and Jorge, the former apparently spurning the obligation to wed and father children, demonstrating no interest in women, and the latter leaving Lisbon and the family home to expand its fortunes further south, albeit in the Alentejo rather than Morocco.[45] Drawing on the insight of postcolonial theory that overseas territory is often imagined as a feminine body to be exploited,[46] a vision crystallised in the Portuguese literary canon with the bountiful rewards of the Ilha dos Amores,[47] the novel can be read, as we shall see, as an allegorical reassessment of the myth of Dom Sebastião, detaching the concept of national prowess from the development of heterosexuality under patriarchy.

By likening both male characters to Dom Sebastião in different ways — Jorge, the heirless conquistador, and Sebastião, the king who remains at home to tend to his rose garden — Eça fractures the myth, allowing it to be reworked to present an alternative history, in contrast to its function in *Lavos*, for example, where the inscription of the king into one 'degenerate' character reaffirms its normative assumptions. Thus while Jorge pays the price for failing to 'correct' Dom Sebastião's 'mistake' — a fruitless tale of marriage and business ventures that leaves his house with no heir — Sebastião's story in the novel offers a different, less destructive path. The only character to present any degree of consistency in his relations with others, and seemingly uninterested in marriage, Sebastião is left largely unharmed by the novel's events and recovers his formally inseparable comrade at the end, whose comparably miserable fate is thrown into relief. Lisboa, drawing on the hostility of the *Geração de '70* towards the ongoing Portuguese colonial project, argues that, in *Os Maias*, the central incestuous relationship prompts us to think whether 'talvez tivesse sido melhor ter ficado ibericamente em casa' [perhaps it would have been better to stay Iberianly at home],[48] again finding a national allegory in the unconscious desire to return to the family home through endogamy. There are surely traces of this sentiment when we see the consequences that Jorge suffers for his actions following the death of his mother, which appears to unleash his futile Oedipal journey towards a (re)productive paternal identity formalised, and in part normalised, by Freud in subsequent decades. What the Old Man of Restelo deemed to be 'vaidade' and 'vã cobiça' in a poem prophetically dedicated to Dom Sebastião himself[49] finds an echo in Jorge's vain pursuit of bourgeois ideals allegorised as the original colonial 'mistake'. As such, although the ghost of Dom Sebastião in *Basílio* may not provide an ostensibly generative solution to the problematic myth — both Sebastião and Jorge end the story childless — it does invite the reader to contemplate whether, like Sebastião, the nation would have been better off had it not been for the expectation, produced by the ruling classes, to leave the domestic and national nest in search of an ultimately deceitful fecundity. This transhistorical allegory is in keeping with the recurrent criticism of the *Geração de '70* that the Portugal that emerged from the *Guerra dos Dois Irmãos* had largely replaced the former absolutist regime with the empty (and just as exploitative, considering the figure of Juliana) values of the ascendent bourgeoisie. If we follow this argument, it is the idealised bond between Sebastião and Jorge, interrupted by a mundane bourgeois marriage, that signals the return to the home(land) that was always, in the end, desired.

Thus whilst in *Lavos* and the Sebastianic myth, normative desire is offered as the only way to rescue the nation (the Baron attempts to rekindle his relationship with his wife as a 'remedy' for his ruinous passion for Eugénio), in *Basílio*, it in fact mobilises the 'mistake' that precipitates the demise of the family, calling into question the historic logic of marriage, patriarchy and colonialism. This apparent criticism, of course, arises in the context of the redoubling of Portuguese colonial pursuits in the nineteenth century post Brazilian independence, these now focused on Africa, the destination for which Gonçalo claims to depart in *A ilustre casa de Ramires*.[50] Eça described the remaining territories in Africa and Asia as 'velhas salvas de família postas a um canto num armário' [old pieces of the family silverware stowed away in the corner of a cupboard], calling for their sale before what he saw to be their inevitable loss to northern Europe.[51] Accordingly, in *Basílio*, he questions a mode of desire and conquest perhaps first criticised by Gil Vicente in *Auto da Índia*, now tragically repeated in the bourgeois family home.[52] Like Vicente, Eça allegorises Portuguese colonial history as a story of adultery, adding another layer of meaning to his self-described 'mirror' of bourgeois society. Indeed, despite the comparative radicalism of Eça's novel, the author nevertheless shapes his 'study' with similar tools to Botelho. The figure of Sebastião introduces a national allegory that supplements the story of *Madame Bovary* to explore Portugal's imperial decline and possible domestic regeneration. One might argue that by problematising, like Sophocles before him, the process of identification in patriarchal society, as well as casting it as a historical mistake, the novel becomes a meditation on the patrilinear, expansionist logic of Western history written from its oldest and then-crumbling overseas empire. Eça thus works in the opposite direction to Botelho, rewriting rather than reinforcing the notion of a glorious but forever-lost past, and suggesting alternative epistemologies and relationships to those that continued to haunt Portuguese history. Already as a young writer, moreover, Eça appears to place little faith in the transformative potential of Naturalism, foreclosing the possibility of social progress and even drawing on the ancient logic of predestination.[53] The representation of relationships that work against the hegemonic mode of being and desiring is key to the movement of the narrative in the novel, which weaves together *Madame Bovary* with Platonic idealism and national allegory to contemplate Portugal's complex global position at the time. As we shall see, *Os Maias* and the later novels would further develop the author's concern with sexuality and the family, propelling his trajectory towards disillusionment with Naturalism and, in his later years, overhauling his prose and style.

## Queer Kinship, Tragedy and the Economics of Love in *Os Maias*

*Os Maias* (1888) is the story of the demise of the ancient Maia family.[54] Spanning four generations, the novel focuses on the life of Carlos, the last of the Maias, who is raised by his grandfather Afonso. When Carlos was a baby, his father Pedro had committed suicide after his wife, Maria Monforte, eloped with a minor Italian aristocrat, taking Carlos's sister, Maria Eduarda, away with her. Assumed dead, Maria Eduarda has disappeared from the lives of Carlos and Afonso and is rarely spoken of again; however, when the family returns to Lisbon in the 1870s, Carlos unwittingly begins a passionate affair with her, believing her initially to be the wife of a Brazilian businessman, Castro Gomes. The incestuous nature of what seems like their perfect love for each other is finally revealed at the end of the novel, and the two sibling-lovers separate forever, Carlos remaining unmarried and seemingly unable, like Jorge in *Basílio*, to provide an heir to the family. Often regarded as marking the apex of Eça's disillusionment with his country and the Naturalist tradition more generally, his longest and most celebrated work is also the one that most explicitly deals with the question of kinship although, as aforementioned, the incest has traditionally been read, in terms reminiscent of Botelho, as a symptom of Portuguese imperial and cultural decline. In what follows, on the contrary, I will draw on Lisboa's analysis of the relationship as gesturing towards a different familial and societal structure, a reading that echoes the questioning of patriarchal society already evident in *Basílio*, and entails another Oedipal tragedy working to interrupt Naturalist dreams of social progress. Indeed, this reading will attempt to elicit how the troubling of kinship in the novel plays out in male friendships, a close examination of which reveals an insufficiency in the language of desire and relationality similar to that described by Butler in her analysis of Sophocles' *Antigone*.[55] As we shall see, the limitations of the social economy make themselves visible in language throughout the narrative and are implicated in the novel's tragic conclusion, foreclosing the possibility of societal change. Revelling in the uncertainties and contradictions of the language of patriarchy, *Os Maias* thus becomes pivotal in Eça's lifelong dismantling of Naturalist aesthetics and the naive epistemological claims of Positivism.

The quotation from *Basílio* at the start of this chapter, where the presence and perception of eroticism is ambiguous, thus introduces a theme that is developed further in *Os Maias*, where relations between men are often idealised or eroticised, and almost always misunderstood. Like Jacinto in *A cidade e as serras*,[56] Carlos da Maia is frequently described as a 'belo príncipe' by his peers. Indeed, 'beautiful princes' are prevalent across Eça's work, where they function as figures that obscure the limits of friendship and question the logic of identification. Although Carlos is admired throughout Lisbon, his sycophant par excellence is surely Dâmaso Salcede, who declares everything Carlos owns, does and says to be 'podre de chique' [filthy chic], a decidedly vernacular compliment that betrays his lower social class. Lisboa describes their relationship as idolatrous, Carlos being 'fanaticamente admirado',[57] the model for Dâmaso's ego ideals. Dâmaso regularly copies Carlos's behaviour and appearance, such as his beard, 'que havia meses deixara crescer para imitar Carlos' [which for months he had been growing to imitate Carlos] (p. 350), a performative imitation designed to codify him, like Eugénio in *Lavos*, as a fashionable member of the social elite. Barcellos is reluctant to attribute more to Dâmaso's attachment than a 'sentimento de emulação' [feeling of emulation]; however, he describes Dâmaso as one of the novel's several 'heterossexuais',[58] perhaps leading him to overlook the extent to which idolatry may entail libidinal or physically covetous tendencies. As Kaja Silverman notes in relation to Freudian theory, there is no good reason why identification should end the possibility of libidinal desire, the object of identification thus remaining 'susceptible to sexualisation; eros is never far away'.[59] Barcellos, for example, identifies the portrait of Carlos on horseback, kept by Dâmaso in his rooms, as a marker of idolatry,[60] yet the portrait verges uncomfortably on the romantic, with its 'vistoso caixilho de flores em faiança' [showy frame of faience flowers] (p. 518), a garish, rosy display of his sentiments for Carlos. Furthermore, the accompanying silk slipper, purchased upon Carlos's recommendation that the room contain a 'relíquia de amor' [relic of love] is wonderfully ironic: is it far more a relic of his 'love' for Carlos than it is any woman.

The quality of Dâmaso's attachment is further complicated by his first sighting of Carlos. After the two are introduced, the narrator remarks that Dâmaso 'não despregava os olhos de Carlos' [did not take his eyes off Carlos] (p. 148); 'continuava a admirar Carlos' [continued to admire Carlos] (p. 151). Transfixed by Carlos's presence and never averting his gaze, there is the hint of physical attraction. At the end of the novel, when the former friends encounter each other upon Carlos's visit to Lisbon, the attraction seems to be rekindled:

> — Adeus, rapazes. Tu estás bom, Carlos, estás com boa cara!
> — É dos teus olhos, Dâmaso.
> E nos olhos do Dâmaso, com efeito, parecia reviver a antiga admiração, arregalados, acompanhando Carlos (p. 657).

> ['Goodbye, boys. You look good Carlos, you look well!'
> 'It must be your eyes, Dâmaso.'
> And in Dâmaso's eyes, indeed — filled with desire, following Carlos — the old admiration seemed to come to life once more.]

*É dos teus olhos, Dâmaso*: beauty is truly in the eye of the beholder. Dâmaso's body language, too, regularly reflects his fascination with Carlos; when they are first introduced, 'aproximou-se do Maia, banhado num sorriso' [he approached Carlos, grinning from ear to ear] (p. 148). At the Cohens' dinner, he is found to be 'todo debruçado sobre Carlos' [leaning all over Carlos] (p. 161), describing his friend as 'a melhor coisa que há em Lisboa [...] acredite [...] que isto é do coração!' [the best thing Lisbon has to offer [...] believe me [...] this comes from the heart!] (p. 166) — the heart, as Dr. Gouveia says in *O crime do Padre Amaro*, being a polite allusion to another part of the body.[61] Dâmaso soon becomes inseparable from him, achieving an 'intimidade de rosas' [rosy intimacy] (p. 179). Nominally a friend, then, Dâmaso in fact appears to harbour a libidinal interest in his 'belo príncipe' that, even if not erotic, is so strong as to risk exceeding the parameters of friendship, or at the least to question where they lie.

Dâmaso's infatuation with Carlos is prefigured in the previous generation by Pedro's admiration for the handsome Neapolitan nobleman, Tancredo, who elopes with Maria Monforte, Carlos's mother. This is a parallel to which I will return later, although at this stage it is worth noting the repetition and resurfacing of the same confused terms of friendship across the generations, which points to the instrumentality of the patriarchal family in reproducing the social order. Tancredo is variously described by Pedro — who begins an intimate friendship with him almost overnight — as 'um herói' [a hero], 'belo rapaz' [handsome boy], 'rapaz adorável' [adorable boy], 'o príncipe' [the prince] (pp. 37–38) and by the narrator as 'um homem esplêndido, feito como um Apolo, de uma palidez de mármore rico [...], uma fisionomia de belo Cristo' [a splendid man, formed like an Apollo, pale as fine marble [...], with the physiognomy of a handsome Christ] (p. 39). The references to classical notions of beauty in the figure of Apollo, the athletic god of truth and poetry, resonate with those in Botelho's *O Barão de Lavos*, where the Baron's fascination with his *efebo* recalls older modes of male relationality. Similarly, when the narrator of *A correspondência de Fradique Mendes* describes his intellectual idol as having 'a forma [...] de um mármore divino' [the form of a divine statue] and dazzling 'pele láctea' [milky skin],[62] we glimpse the erotic potential of the subject of identification, again articulated through a return to Greek understandings of masculinity. However, despite his invocation of Apollonian beauty, Pedro, a Romantic man of the moment, describes his relationship with Tancredo as one of exemplary friendship: 'somos como dois irmãos de armas' [we're like two brothers in arms] (p. 40). In this manner, friendships have the potential to become invested with the erotic when they are identified in terms of a brotherly camaraderie recalling the modern Republican ideals of equality and fraternity. Again reminiscent Montaigne's characterisation of desire for the body as fickle and untrustworthy,[63] Tancredo, proves to be a treacherous brother-friend, while Carlos and Dâmaso grow to loathe each other, so much so that Carlos vows to kill him on account of an injurious newspaper article, suggesting there is very little, if any, reciprocity to these relationships. Instead, the pattern of identification, infatuation and then hatred following betrayal recalls the primary narcissistic pleasure that the child feels upon (mis)recognising himself in the mirror, any threat to which induces rage. That Dâmaso and Pedro both believe these to be, on the contrary, great friendships, examples of brotherly love, demonstrates the inadequacy of the terms used to articulate friendship and brotherhood, even as they are reproduced problematically across time. The return to an eroticised classical discourse in particular comes to pressure the modern, republican terms of male friendship as 'natural'.

Even Carlos and João da Ega, his best friend, a pair whom Lisboa has described as having a purely asexual relationship without the least insinuation of sexual desire,[64] appear to push the boundaries at times. On two extraordinary occasions, Ega seems to treat Carlos as a lover while inebriated. The first time is in Coimbra:

> [Carlos] teve de o arrastar à casa das Seixas, despi-lo, aturar-lhe os beijos e a ternura borracha, até que o deixou abraçado ao travesseiro, babando-se (p. 172).

> [[Carlos] had to drag him to the Seixas's house, undress him, endure his kisses and drunken tenderness, before leaving him hugged to the pillow, drooling.]

The second such occurrence arises when Ega is taken to Craft's house after a disastrous night at the Cohens' fancy-dress party:

> [...] apanharam João da Ega. E enquanto o levavam para o quarto dos hóspedes e lhe despiam o fato de Satanás, não cessou de choramingar, dando beijos babosos pelas mãos de Carlos, balbuciando:
> — Raquelzinha!... Racaquê, minha Raquelzinha! Gostas do teu bibichinho?... (p. 262).

[[...] they took hold of João da Ega. And as they led him to the guest room and took off his Satan costume, he would not stop whimpering, covering Carlos's hands with slobbery kisses, stammering:
'My poor Raquel!... Racaquê, my dear little Raquel! Do you like your coochie coo?']

*In vino veritas*? Ega's drunken effusiveness here may have a significance beyond comic effect. In *As máscaras do desengano*, Isabel Pires de Lima identifies a series of discomfiting analogies in *Os Maias* that testify to an age of profound moral ambiguity. Ega and Carlos, for example, initially heralded as 'espíritos superiores' [superior beings], turn out to be uncomfortably like their ostensible inferiors.[65] Dâmaso's obsession with Carlos would be risible if it were not so akin to Carlos's admiration for Craft,[66] an Englishman who rivals Carlos in his reputation for refined taste. Ega's demonstrations of affection towards Carlos — and Carlos's timely undressing of Ega's Satanic costume — might constitute just such an awkward analogy: by confusing man for woman, friend for lover, when inhibitions are lowered, Eça suggests that, in the end, a friend may never be 'simply' a friend.

The lack of qualitative difference between friend and lover, a concern that in the West goes back to Greco-Roman antiquity, is confirmed when, at the end of *Os Maias*, Carlos and Ega, described twice as 'como irmãos' [like brothers],[67] do not in fact turn out to be lifetime companions. Ega asks Carlos if he will ever return to Lisbon:

Então Ega perguntou, do fundo do sofá onde se enterrara, se, nesses últimos anos, ele não tivera a ideia, o vago desejo de voltar para Portugal... (p. 672)

[And so Ega asked, from the depths of the sofa into which he had buried himself whether, in these latter years, he hadn't had the idea, the vague desire to return to Portugal...]

The ellipsis here connotes a palpable longing for his friend and 'brother',[68] but Carlos replies that he will remain in Paris, thus deserting him much in the manner that he deserts his lover-*sister*, Maria Eduarda: sibling love of any kind could never be. Furthermore, seemingly unable to pursue intimate relationships following his incestuous relationship, Carlos equally cannot return to the old days of the Ramalhete, where he and Ega lived together for long periods. He becomes estranged from both 'siblings', that is, friend-sibling and lover-sibling, completing the sense that both social and sexual love, both figurative and physical love, are subject to the same constraints, and may indeed be at some level indistinguishable.

A potential inability to distinguish friend from lover is at least the implied conclusion of Montaigne when he speculates that a union of bodies as well as souls could result in the most perfect loving relationship between men.[69] Some of the most enduring and harmonious male friendships in Eça — Jorge and Sebastião and, as we shall see, Jacinto and Zé Fernandes — are those in which genuine reciprocity (as opposed to Dâmaso's unreciprocated, hierarchical idolatry) is accompanied by desire of a confused or indeterminate physical nature, as though they could or might be lovers. That Carlos ends *Os Maias* physically separated from both Ega and Maria Eduarda, formerly the perfect friend and the perfect lover respectively, is the effect not of a perceived inviability in ambiguous, potentially incestuous desire but, on the contrary, of the restoration of kinship certainties after Maria Monforte's letter confirming the lovers' consanguinity is fatefully handed to Ega. His decision to inform the family initiates a return to normative kinship and transparency in relationships, suspending Carlos's most important ones indefinitely.

Perhaps the most overt manifestation of the imputation of sexual desire into friendship and fraternity in Eça is in *O crime do Padre Amaro* when Libaninho, a devout office clerk — 'o beato mais activo de Leiria' [the most active churchgoer of Leiria] (p. 47) who though a layman claims to be in God's service, spreading His word at the local barracks (p. 447) — is caught in flagrante delicto with a sergeant. Whether brothers in arms or brothers of the church, the necessity for asexual camaraderie in such institutions is made apparent precisely through the possibility of breaking the rule: the establishment of an asexual imperative paradoxically implies a potential for sexuality to surface. 'Brother' thus implicitly carries with it that which it purports to exclude, surely highlighted by the chilling parallel to which Carlos draws attention in *Os Maias*, realising that he and Maria Eduarda, having shared a bed as adults, once shared a cradle as infants (p. 584). Indeed, when a brother can be so many things, the words of Padre Natário in *O crime* ring true in a particularly ironic sense: 'todos somos irmãos! Todos somos irmãos!' [we are all brothers!] (p. 177). The sexual relations between Libaninho and the sergeant, which are also symbolically incestuous as a love between 'brothers', confuse and disrupt the terms friend, brother and lover. The foundations of the Church and the army — the mainstays of the nation — collapse if the terms of kinship are rendered inadequate, the discourse of republican 'fraternity' finding its unspeakable limit. The resulting scandal is inevitable: as Anna Klobucka notes, Libaninho is swiftly relegated to 'the bottom of [the] hierarchy', losing his job at the office, and the fact that he later obtains a professional role at the cathedral probably says more about the Church's hypocrisy than it suggests any scope for a more flexible structure in such institutions.[70]

If, as Gayle Rubin and others have argued,[71] normative kinship presupposes exogamous heterosexuality, the inadequacy of kinship terms in Eça can be read as revealing rather than concealing these presuppositions. Whilst *Lavos*, for example, naturalises normative kinship by pathologising and restricting 'deviant' relations, Eça effectively writes against the naturalised language of relationality by pointing to its excesses and insufficiencies. Thus terms such as friend, lover and brother threaten to become porous and mobile, merging into each other. A friend's love may be physical and covetous. A friend can be a brother only to be (mis)taken for a lover. A lover, meanwhile, can be (mis)taken for a brother, as Basílio in *O primo Basílio* understands when he describes his rendezvous with Luísa as 'um passeio de amigos, de irmãos' [a friendly, brotherly stroll] (p. 129). And of course, in the case of Carlos, a brother can *be* a lover. As we have seen, critical work on Eça has often read the incestuous relationship at the heart of *Os Maias* as symptomatic of the 'situação estagnada de Portugal' [Portugal's stagnated situation] precipitated by *fin-de-siècle* decadence.[72] Maria Manuel Lisboa's reading parts with this thesis, arguing instead that the 'amor perfeito' [perfect love][73] between Carlos and Maria is in fact a gesture towards 'um novo começo' [a new beginning],[74] an 'antídote' to,[75] rather than a symptom of, the status quo that enforces a taboo on their perfect love. It is, indeed, their eventual decision to end their relationship that quashes this remedial gesture and constitutes the true marker of resignation and decadence in the novel. In a similar vein, the troubling of kinship in Eça through queer and erotically indeterminate desires can be read as a problematisation of the status quo, whereby the restrictions imposed on desire are rendered insufficient, producing what they purport to exclude.

There is evidently a disruption to the discourse of republicanism — *liberté, égalité, fraternité* — at play here, particularly since the variously eroticised, idolatrous relationships entail a social pecking order that undercuts suggestions of equality, the pretence to fraternity amongst the dominant classes disguising a governing dynamic of hierarchy and competition. Already in *Basílio*, the critique of the values of the ruling classes is well developed, anticipating what Pires de Lima, drawing on Marx and Lucien Goldmann, identifies in *Os Maias*: the pre-eminence of exchange value over use value in social relationships:

> [...] na socialidade capitalista, aquela onde o romance nasceu, o valor de troca ameaça e penetra toda e qualquer relação autêntica. O *valor de uso*, que preside às relações naturais e sãs entre homens e bens, é mascarado, torna-se implícito e degrada-se.[76]

> [[...] in capitalist society, which gave birth to the novel, exchange value threatens and penetrates every authentic relationship. Use value, which governs natural and healthy relations between men and commodities, is disguised, becoming implicit and degraded.]

In *Os Maias*, the importance of exchange value shapes human relations and precipitates a crisis of 'ambiguidade moral', entailing a distortion of the value of things, and sending characters along a path from *ilusão* to *desilusão*.[77] It is this trajectory towards disillusionment that characterises the *vencidos da vida* [defeated by life], the feeling of hopelessness amongst Eça and his contemporaries after the perceived failure of the grand ambitions of the *Geração de '70*, thwarted by Portugal's embrace of free-market economics following the promising victory of Dom Pedro in the *Guerra dos Dois Irmãos*. Pires de Lima thus establishes a link between the emergence of a modern capitalist order and the supposed melancholic spirit of Eça's generation that no longer believed in its capacity to effect change. Maria Manuel Lisboa, meanwhile, draws on Lévi-Strauss, René Girard and Eve Sedgwick to demonstrate how, in Eça, 'homosocial' bonds between men are consolidated through the exchange of women in a patrilinear, capitalist order,[78] a dynamic we glimpsed in the opening of this chapter, where any potential for homoeroticism at the bathhouse is seemingly disavowed in the bawdy talk between Basílio and Reinaldo. In *Os Maias*, women become valuable instruments through which men conduct power games between each other. As Irigaray reminds us, 'in order for a product — a woman? — to have value, two men, at least, have to invest (in) her'.[79] I wish to enter the debate by addressing what might be termed the 'repression of the homosexual into the homosocial'[80] in the novel which, as we shall see, becomes implicated in its tragedy, unleashing a calamitous return of the repressed, and urging a reconsideration of the laws of relationality. Returning to my initial question of Eça's midlife pivot away from Naturalism, I hope to show how the vanquished spirit of the *vencidos da vida* allowed non-normative desire to gesture towards a way of being and knowing uncorrupted by the incursion of exchange value, only for it, too, to be stifled.

One quite candid reference to queer behaviour in *Os Maias*, which Fernando Curopos mentions in his study of the emergence of homosexuality in nineteenth-century Portuguese literature,[81] demonstrates neatly how exchange value governs and shapes sexual desire. After a cash-strapped Ega dismisses his domestic staff from his opulent, if garish love nest, the *Vila Balzac*, he is accused of employing a manservant for sex. The mother of one of the maids arrives with her lover to demand money from Ega, angered that her daughter has eloped with the manservant. Ega initially refuses, though he soon concedes under pressure:

> Ega recusou-se a atender as reclamações da matrona. Que diabo tinha ele com essas torpezas?
>
> Então o amante da criatura interveio, ameaçadoramente. Era um polícia, um esteio da ordem: e deu a entender que lhe seria fácil provar como na Vila Balzac se passavam 'coisas contra a Natureza', e que o pajem não era só para servir à mesa... Nauseado até à morte, Ega pactuou com a intrujice. (pp. 271–72)

> [Ega refused to hear the matron's grievances. What the devil did he have to do with such filth?
>
> And so the creature's lover made a threatening intervention. He was a policemen, a pillar of order, and made it clear that it would be easy to prove that the *Vila Balzac* was host to 'acts against nature', and that the manservant wasn't just there to serve at table... Sickened to the core, Ega made a pact with the fibster.]

The allusion to sodomy in the phrase 'coisas contra a natureza' — incidentally, the exact phrasing of Portugal's anti-sodomy clause from 1912, appropriated strategically in this book — leaves Ega sickened and mortified. He pays off the policeman handsomely, landing himself in significant debt. Lisboa argues that the women in *Os Maias* function in Irigarayan terms as a 'moeda corrente' [currency],[82] Ega later offering Carlos the possibility of an affair with the Condessa de Gouvarinho in a tacitly acknowledged exchange for money to alleviate financial difficulties. This is the second half of the story, however, since Ega is only in such dire financial straits at this point because of the unexpected costs of leaving the *Vila Balzac*. Whilst relations with women offer men capital gains, 'coisas contra a natureza' signal the opposite.

Earlier, I referred to a parallel between Carlos's relationship with Dâmaso and Pedro's with Tancredo in *Os Maias*. Pedro, in idolising (and perhaps eroticising) Tancredo is likened to Dâmaso, who admires Carlos in a similar manner. The relations can of course be considered triangular, involving 'mimetic' desire as theorised by René Girard in *Deceit, Desire and the Novel*, a schema that we saw disrupted in *O Barão de Lavos*, in which Elvira herself becomes the rival. In *Os*

*Maias*, Pedro and Tancredo are placed in rivalry over Maria Monforte, and Carlos and Dâmaso over her daughter, Maria Eduarda. In this case, the triangulation is disrupted by the unacknowledged, excess desire that spills over into the nominally social bond between the men. I infer a parallel between these triangles because father and son (Pedro and Carlos) both fall victim to the corruption of male friendship, even when occupying opposing positions of power. Pedro da Maia is likened not to Carlos but to Dâmaso who, like Cohen, Gouvarinho and countless others, lets himself be used by a rival whom he perceives to be a friend. As we have seen, Pedro considers Tancredo to be an 'irmão de armas', having invited him into his home to convalesce. He is evidently motivated in part by a desire for Tancredo's company. But Tancredo has quite different ideas, eloping with Maria Monforte and leaving Pedro alone in Lisbon with (baby) Carlos. By 'losing' the game of the erotic triangle, in which patriarchal power is negotiated through the exchange of women, Pedro sets in motion the demise of his family line. To begin with, he spends too much time with Tancredo, neglecting his wife:

> Agora logo de manhã, [Pedro] subia para o quarto do príncipe, de *robe-de-chambre* e cachimbo na boca, e passava lá horas numa camaradagem, fazendo grogues quentes [...]. Maria sentia-lhe por cima as risadas. Às vezes tocava-se viola. [...]
>
> [...] Maria, por fim, perguntou a Pedro, muito séria, se além de todos os amigos da casa, duas enfermeiras, dois escudeiros, o papá e ele Pedro — era necessária também constantemente a sua própria criada no quarto de Sua Alteza!
>
> Não era. Mas Pedro riu muito à ideia de que a arlesiana se tivesse namorado do príncipe. Nesse caso Vénus era-lhe propícia! O napolitano também a achava picante: *un très joli brin de femme*, tinha ele dito.
>
> A bela face de Maria empalideceu de cólera. Julgava tudo isso de mau gosto, grosseiro, impudente! (pp. 38–39)

> [Now, first thing in the morning, [Pedro] would go up to the prince's bedroom in his *robe-de-chambre*, pipe in his mouth, and spend hours there in camaraderie, drinking hot toddy [...]. Maria could hear the peals of laughter above her. Sometimes they played the guitar. [...]
>
> [...] Finally, Maria asked Pedro very seriously whether, besides all the family friends, two nurses, two servants, papa, and Pedro himself, her own maid's presence was constantly required in the room of His Highness?
>
> It was not. But Pedro laughed considerably at the idea that the girl from Arles had fallen in love with the prince. In that case Venus was on her side! The Neapolitan also thought she was piquant: *un très joli brin de femme*, he had said.
>
> Maria's pretty face turned pale with rage. She thought it all in bad taste, crude, impudent!]

Maria's exclusion and loneliness are all the more pronounced when she hears the jovialities in the rooms above her. Pedro, besotted with Tancredo and spending long hours drinking with him in his pyjamas, ignores his wife's needs, enraging her. Her carefully worded, pointed jibe of 'Sua Alteza', which she asks 'muito séria' but not without exasperation, suggests she has brooded considerably on her husband's devotion to his 'belo príncipe'. It is little wonder, perhaps, that she elopes with him. Pedro's 'mistake' is to cultivate a bond with Tancredo so strong that it is no longer recognisably 'homosocial', no longer negotiated through a woman, allowing Tancredo to poach his wife before his eyes. Tancredo, for his part, plays the game much more effectively, his attachment to Pedro only ever serving him insofar as it affords him access to Maria Monforte. As soon as he has conquered her favour, the two depart, never to be seen again in Lisbon. In other words, his bond with Pedro is matched and measured by a heterosexual attachment to Maria, creating an asymmetry with his 'camarada', who allows his infatuation with Tancredo to go unchecked. He is thus outmanoeuvred by his 'friend', leading to his suicide and the eventual dwindling of the Maia line. In a society that markets women as objects of exchange in order to establish (re)productive bonds of competition and camaraderie between men, desire between men must be measured in accordance with sexual desire for women. When eroticism and idolatry creep into the ostensibly 'homosocial', the power structure that holds two men in a position of rivalry becomes asymmetrical and destined for treacheries.

A generation later, Carlos appears to find himself in the reverse role to his father. Indeed, as Pires de Lima notes, Carlos has been educated in the latest ideas and appears, at least upon his arrival in Lisbon, as 'um ser de excepção no meio português, mesmo dentro da classe a que pertence' [an exceptional being in the Portuguese milieu, even amongst his own social class].[83] He seems to be the perfect antidote to his weak and mollycoddled father: strong, virile, with his celebrated good looks, good sense and good taste, 'tudo parece perfeito: formação excepcional — vontade de agir' [everything seems perfect: an exceptional education and a desire to act].[84] He is something of a Sebastianic figure himself,[85] returning to Lisbon to restore the viability of family and nation, with all his grand plans for cultural expansion, a kind of Pessoan Fifth Empire *avant la lettre*. Upon the Maias' return to Lisbon after years of Afonso's self-exile in Santa Olávia, he appears to have overcome his father's 'weaknesses', proving adept at playing the love triangle through his adventures first in Coimbra and later, back in Lisbon, with the Viscondessa de Gouvarinho, which Ega, and to a lesser extent Carlos, orchestrate to make a fool of her husband.[86] His conquest of Maria Eduarda, who at the time is believed to be Madame Castro Gomes and involved with Dâmaso, is equally successful. Carlos plainly uses his acquaintance to gain access to her, a tactic seen already at their first meeting, in which Dâmaso, having fixed his eyes longingly on Carlos, boasts of his intimacy with Maria and her 'husband':

> — Bem sei! Os Castro Gomes... Conheço-os muito... Vim com eles de Bordéus... Uma gente muito chique que vive em Paris.
> Carlos voltou-se, reparou mais nele, perguntou-lhe, afável e interessando-se:
> — O Sr. Salcede chegou agora de Bordéus?
> Estas palavras pareceram deleitar Dâmaso como um favor celeste (p. 148)

> ['Ah, I know just who you mean! The Castro Gomes... I know them very well. I came with them down from Bordeaux... A very chic pair who live in Paris.'
> Carlos, intrigued, turned around and took more notice of him, asking affably:

'Have you just arrived from Bordeaux?'
These words seemed to delight Dâmaso like a celestial gift.]

Carlos only notices Dâmaso, becomes 'afável' towards and interested in him after he speaks of Maria. Dâmaso, for his part, is delighted by Carlos's interest in him, henceforth using Maria as bait with which to attach himself to his idol. Indeed, his '*romance divino*' (p. 199) with her turns out to be 'fictício',[87] a fabrication designed to provoke Carlos's jealousy and dependency upon him. Dâmaso demonstrates a primary interest in Carlos, whereas the latter only expresses interest in Dâmaso insofar as he dangles the real carrot of Maria Eduarda. The asymmetry in their relationship is similar to that of Pedro da Maia and Tancredo, although Carlos now commands the advantage once held by the Neapolitan. A period of triumph follows for him; he appears, at least, to have corrected his father's 'mistake'.

Dâmaso, however, will not be defeated so easily, beginning his revenge by sullying Carlos's name around Lisbon. Ega summarises his story:

> É a velha história; diz que te apresentou, que te meteste de dentro, e como para essa senhora é uma questão de dinheiro, e tu és o mais rico, ela lhe passou o pé... Vês daí a infamiazinha. (p. 394)

> [It's the same old story; he says he introduced you to her, that you got involved, and that since money is all that matters to the woman, and you are richer than he is, she gave him the slip... You can see the scandal in the making.]

Besides feeling used by Carlos, Dâmaso reduces the love story to a simple question of money in which the two friends are ranked according to their net value, pre-empting his devastating revenge at the end of the novel, when he indirectly forces this 'corruption' of love on his friend. He furthers his vengeance with a slanderous article in a newspaper, but his final blow in fact comes from his uncle, Guimarães, who, seemingly by chance, the night before his departure to Paris, reveals to Ega the incestuous nature of Carlos's affair with Maria Eduarda. Ega, horrified, is quick to blame Guimarães for the revelation and wishes he had never appeared:

> E esta confusão, esta ansiedade, ia-se resolvendo lentamente em ódio ao Sr. Guimarães. Para que falara aquele imbecil? Para que insistira em lhe confiar papéis alheios? Para que lho apresentava o Alencar? Ah! se não fosse a carta do Dâmaso... Tudo provinha do maldito Dâmaso! (p. 588)

> [And all his confusion and worry slowly morphed into hatred for Mr Guimarães. Why had that imbecile spoken? Why had he insisted on trusting him with the papers of others? Why did Alencar introduce him? Ah! if it hadn't been for Dâmaso's letter... Everything stemmed from that damned Dâmaso!]

*Tudo provinha do maldito Dâmaso.* In the end, Guimarães only meets Carlos and Ega because of his disapproval of his nephew's humiliation in the Lisbon press. The secret of Carlos and Maria's consanguinity is only ever 'outed' because of Dâmaso's wrath at Carlos's valuation of him as a means to an end. Carlos, even when in the seemingly advantageous position in the love triangle, is nonetheless brought down by his (mis)use of Dâmaso's attachment. Carlos cannot redeem his father's sins because he too falls victim, despite his initial appearance as 'um ser de excepção', to a culture of exchange value that endows desire with the functional, instrumentalist purpose of (re)production. Carlos spurns Dâmaso's love — 'chegou a odiá-lo' [he grew to hate him] (p. 178) — and ultimately his sister's, unless it can serve, at some level at least, the advancement of his kin.

Carlos, therefore, cannot correct his father's 'mistake' (or indeed Dom Sebastião's): despite his 'perfect' English education, his virility and his lively interest in women, his life choices will leave him bereft of a satisfying future, just as he leaves his homeland bereft of him. By treating love and friendship as an investment, a feat that his father could not quite manage, he is brought down by what he has excluded to do so. Indeed, *Os Maias* concludes after the letter confirming Carlos and Maria's consanguinity literally arrives at its destination, to use a Lacanian turn of phrase,[88] and thus when all the repressed elements that allow their relationship to develop and function as an ostensibly perfect love affair over the course of the novel return with a vengeance.[89] Implicating the dominant culture of exchange in the problematic operation of desire, Eça tentatively offers non-normative desire — as in the case of Jorge and Sebastião in *Basílio* — as that which resists assimilation into patriarchal-capitalist structures of power, and which, in the case of *Os Maias*, returns to undo these. Phillip Rothwell ultimately arrives at a similar conclusion when he argues that it is Afonso da Maia's hypocritical endorsement of capitalism as the antidote to the nation's ills, after his initial revolutionary spirit, that leads to his family's demise: 'as is invariably the case when the antidoting system is one based on capitalism, the antidote itself transforms into a symptom'.[90] It is Afonso, indeed, who instils capitalist values in his grandson with his liberal, English education, disapproving of Maria Eduarda because of her father's links to the slave trade, whilst seemingly blind to the continued British and Portuguese trade with the remaining slave economies. Again, the failure of Portugal (and indeed its envied northern neighbours) to diminish its dependence upon ancient exploitative practices comes to the fore here. Carlos's transformation into a symptom of the system that he at first seems to have the power to change, reproducing a market culture that corrupts his relations with others, thus calls for a thorough reassessment of the social-sexual code and its structural role in the Western imperial history, echoing the Sebastianic allegory of *Basílio*.

The need for an upheaval in the logic of being and desiring is therefore the implication of a series of relationships that end in tragedy or simply lead to dead ends and disappointment, a theme that chimes with the author's gradual trend towards *vencidismo* [defeatism]. Desire can only find an acceptable expression when it promotes the perpetuation of patriarchal power and property: ownership of women, sons and capital. To violate the sexual code is to lose the power of exchange, and yet, in Eça, the normative route ultimately proves equally fruitless and probably more painful. Despite what are occasionally offered as ideal relationships — Carlos and Maria, Sebastião and Jorge — the interference of economics proves too strong to resist. Such a conclusion strengthens Lisboa's claim that the *desilusão* in *Os Maias* stems not so much from the revelation of kinship trouble as it does the reassertion of normative kinship. As Valério, Pires de Lima, and other critics have suggested,

*Os Maias* represents the spirit of *vencidismo* in its most complete form, an inability to put into practice the great plans of youth,[91] a sentiment that Eça, despairing its careless appropriation by the Portuguese press, defined in the following terms:

> para um homem, o ser vencido ou derrotado na vida depende, não da realidade aparente a que chegou — mas do ideal íntimo a que aspirava.[92]

> [for a man, being defeated or vanquished in life depends not on the apparent reality that he has reached, but on the intimate ideal to which he once aspired.]

The individual's most intimate, valued beliefs, in other words, are unable to be reconciled with the demands of social life. In this context, it seems fitting that an unacknowledged, non-normative desire — incestuous or otherwise queer, unable to be assimilated into the social and linguistic order — emerges as an escape from the pressures of capitalist economics only for it, too, to be quashed.

However, as we have seen, the transformation from *Geração de '70* to *vencidos da vida* was also motivated, in Eça's case in particular, by a loss of confidence in the epistemological and reformist potential of the Naturalist movement. Eça was flummoxed and frustrated by the silence in the immediate aftermath of the publication of his first major novel, *O crime do Padre Amaro*,[93] for example, and with the publication of *Os Maias* in 1888, his early revolutionary fervour is reduced to satire in the naive João da Ega.[94] Already in *Basílio*, the return to the Greek classics begins to frame and shape the narrative, a trend taken further in *Os Maias*, where the logic of social determinism is replaced with that of pre-determination, precipitated by an apparently chance moment of anagnorisis — a half-forgotten old box of cigars — that pointedly refutes grandiose Naturalist claims to absolute truth.[95] Fate comes to trump, in the end, the illuminative efforts of science. To the troublesome discourse of tragedy might be added Greek notions of beauty and friendship, or allegories of nationhood heralding the return of Dom Sebastião, all of which challenge bourgeois understandings of life and love and alter the register in which the Naturalist writer supposedly articulates his social commentary. The interruption of the narrative with older modes of representing being and desiring, undoing the lofty epistemological claims of the age in *vencidista* spirit, thus also returns us to questions of the Naturalist movement, cultural marginality and the canon. Jobst Welge contends that *Os Maias* is a 'genealogical fiction' whose concern with family breakdown reflects a society on the periphery of the dominant culture.[96] It is surely inviting to think of Portugal's marginal position as having contributed to the author's exploration of kinship to critique imported notions of literary-scientific 'truth' and free-market economics. This is the question I would now like to address, tying together my claims in this chapter with a reading of Eça's later novels, and most especially *A relíquia*, where the author definitively breaks with nineteenth-century narrative customs.

*Penso eu e pensa meu cunhado Crispim* [In the opinion of myself and my brother-in-law Crispim]: The Limits of Love, Literature and Truth in *A relíquia* and the Later Works

Published in 1887, written in Portugal during the same period as *Os Maias* and causing the author notorious difficulties and frustration,[97] *A relíquia* is in many ways the most puzzling of Eça's novels, adhering little to any particular literary style, while blending realism, fantasy and unreliable first-person narration. Oliveira Martins's praise for the novel — the only one the author submitted, unsuccessfully, for a prize[98] — goes some way towards illustrating its eclectic texture:

> *A relíquia* é o pandemónio mais incongruente, mais extravagante, mais inconcebível que se pode imaginar. Desde a farsa até à epopeia; desde a gargalhada, pelo sorriso, até ao patético mais puro; desde a aventura picaresca até aos episódios sublimes; desde a anedota do bacharel em viagem até ao quadro nobremente sereno da vida antiga; desde a troça desenfreada, até à história severa; desde a *pochade* grotesca, até à paisagem larga e monumental; desde a blasfémia, até ao hino — há de tudo neste livro, que é a obra acabada de um fantasista de raça. Literariamente, *A relíquia* é uma obra prima.[99]

> [*A relíquia* is the most incongruent, extravagant, inconceivable pandemonium imaginable. From farce to epic poetry; from smiles and laughter to pure pathos; from picaresque adventure to sublime encounters, from the anecdotes of a travelling bachelor to the nobly serene portrait of ancient life; from unbridled jokes to stern history; from grotesque *pochade* to broad, monumental landscapes; from blasphemy to the hymn sheet — everything finds its way into this book, which is the finished work of a distinguished fantasist. Literarily speaking, *A relíquia* is a masterpiece.]

*Há de tudo neste livro.*[100] The epigraph of the novel has become one of Eça's most famous lines — '[s]obre a nudez forte da verdade, o manto diáfano da fantasia' [covering the forceful nudity of truth, the diaphanous cloak of fantasy] — inscribed onto his statue on the Rua das Flores in Lisbon, and signalling the novel's interweaving of realism and fantasy. However, there is a significant dimension of *A relíquia* that, to my knowledge, has not been critically explored, and yet surfaces in the first line of the prologue: *meu cunhado Crispim* [my brother-in-law Crispim]. The narrator's relationship with Crispim, who begins the novel as his schoolboy lover and ends it as his brother-in-law, has not been read as significantly relevant to the novel's structure, inferred instead to be an illuminating reflection of the author's life. Coleman, for example, who describes Crispim simply as 'an old schoolmate',[101] draws on Coimbra Martins to argue that Teodorico's marriage to Crispim's sister at the end has 'glaring and instructive parallels' with the author's marriage to Emília de Resende.[102] Whilst I do not mean to refute or confirm these speculations surrounding Eça's personal life, I do wish to queer the narrator's relationship with Crispim and restore, like with Jorge and Sebastião in *Basílio*, its deceptively peripheral position to the centre of the novel's ideological concerns. As we shall see, the renunciation of illicit love in favour of patriarchal marriage echoes the *vencidista* trajectory of characters such as Jorge and Carlos, but in *A relíquia*, the use of first-person narration allows non-normative desire to haunt the act of writing the story, rather like in the later *A cidade e as serras*, but more pointedly bound up with epistemological questions and the refutation of Positivist claims to truth. Indeed, as I shall argue, Teodorico's eventual acceptance of the homosocial pact is the manifestation par excellence of his convictions surrounding the arbitrary nature of truth and signification. By questioning God, the Father's Name and the act of representation itself, *A relíquia* seems to position itself as far as possible from the principles of Naturalism, anticipating, as Frank de Sousa has argued,[103] the spirit of modernism (or even post-modernism), and troubling kinship and 'truth' in the same move.

A *relíquia* is the story of Teodorico Raposo, an *alentejano* orphaned at a young age and sent to live with his rich and draconian aunt, Titi Patrocínio das Neves. Titi is staunchly religious, believing nature to be 'quase obscena por ter criado dois sexos' [almost obscene for having created two sexes] (p. 34) and forbidding any activity that might be construed as 'andar atrás de saias' [chasing after skirts] (p. 34). Teodorico, coveting her vast fortune, leads a double life, touring churches to appear devout on the one hand, and seeking passions and carnal pleasures on the other. To complete his education, Titi sends him on a voyage to the Holy Land on her behalf, asking him to return with a sacred relic. Teodorico proves an indulgent, ignorant and irreverent traveller, falling in love with a British girl named Mary in Alexandria, who leaves him her unwashed petticoats as a titillating memento. Continuing onto Jerusalem with his companion, the German historian Topsius, Teodorico 'wakes up' to find himself at the time of Jesus, where he witnesses the latter's trial and crucifixion under Pontius Pilate, though almost missing both in order to smoke a cigarette and 'ir lá baixo às mulherinhas' [go downstairs to see the ladies] (p. 174). On his journey home, he finds a thorny branch which he resolves to present to Titi as having sprouted from the same tree as the crown of thorns worn at the crucifixion. Finally, returning to Lisbon, he reveals the relic to Titi, but unforgivably mixes up his parcels, unwrapping, instead, Mary's incriminating petticoats. Disowned and disinherited, Teodorico must abandon his plans for aristocratic ascendency, opting instead to sell sham relics to devout *lisboetas* before joining his friend Crispim's firm and marrying his sister, affording him a life of respectable bourgeois comforts.

In his closing lines, Teodorico finally offers readers his (and importantly, as we shall see, Crispim's) 'lição lúcida e forte' [strong and lucid lesson] (p. 5) that he promises at the beginning of his monograph: the need for a 'descarado heroísmo de afirmar' [shameless courage to affirm] (p. 256). Learning the (exchange) value of 'relics' — more still, the false foundations of Christianity, since the dream chapter implies that the crucifixion was staged to allow for the 'resurrection' — Teodorico claims that his greatest error was, in the end, not to have alleged to Titi that the fateful lingerie was no less than a gift from Mary Magdalene in the desert. This courage to affirm, or indeed lie, is, according to Teodorico, what creates the 'universal ilusão' sustaining 'ciências e ilusões' [sciences and illusions] (p. 256). Critics have long argued that this 'lição' represents the culmination of Eça's disillusionment with Naturalist thought. Mónica argues that the morality of *A relíquia* could not be more cynical;[104] for Coleman, the novel is a 'strategic ideological retreat' from the author's earlier, more pointedly Naturalist works.[105] Lisboa reads the novel as an undoing of religious and cultural history, a 'pseudo-cruzada supostamente santa' [supposedly holy pseudo-crusade],[106] working to strip the nation of its mythologised, grandiose past to leave little more than 'roupagens mais cómodas, mais caseiras' [more comfortable, homely garments], the 'bom burguês, feliz de regresso à sua lareira após jornadas tormentosas por mares já dantes navegados' [good bourgeois, happy to be back home after tempestuous journeys through seas already explored], strategically misquoting Camões.[107] She compares this sentiment to that expressed in Fukuyama's overzealous proclamation of the 'end of history' and 'victory' of Western values after the fall of the Soviet Union.[108] Such comparisons with more recent times seem especially apt for a work that appears to deny any coherent reason to the relationship between signifier and signified, so much so that a severed branch can lay claim to being the crown of thorns, or a stained petticoat an image of chastity and devotion. In a sense, the true relic of *A relíquia* — that which remains from the rubbish heap of history — is the empty signifier itself, now ripe for conversion to exchange value in a burgeoning capitalist order. It was not until the twentieth century that Saussure argued that the formation of the sign was arbitrary,[109] an insight more easily squared with writers such as Saramago than with the great novels of the nineteenth century, though Machado de Assis's *Dom Casmurro* tackles similar epistemological questions from the other side of the Atlantic.[110] The effect is a profound sense of despondency and resignation to accept, without enthusiasm, the disintegration of all cultural values save the power of exchange.

It is in this context of undoing the principles of Realist writing at their core, by questioning the bond between signifier and signified, indeed the viability of literary mimesis, that I would like to turn to the relationship that runs parallel to the narrator's trajectory from heir apparent to successful, if conventional and unremarkable, bourgeois patriarch. Like Luísa, Leopoldina, Jorge and Sebastião, Teodorico first meets Crispim at school; he is the son of the owners of a textile factory, and thus clearly marked as a member of the ascendent mercantile classes:

> Logo nas primeiras semanas liguei-me ternamente com um rapaz Crispim, mais crescido que eu, filho da firma Teles, Crispim & C.ª, donos da fábrica de fiação à Pampulha. O Crispim ajudava à missa aos domingos; e, de joelhos, com os seus cabelos compridos e louros, lembrava a suavidade de um anjo. Às vezes agarrava-me no corredor e marcava-me a face, que eu tinha feminina e macia, com beijos devoradores; à noite, na sala de estudo, à mesa onde folheávamos os sonolentos dicionários, passava-me bilhetinhos a lápis, chamando-me seu idolatrado e prometendo-me caixinhas de penas de aço... (p. 16).

> [During my first few weeks there, I bonded tenderly with a boy called Crispim, older than I was, the son of the firm Teles, Crispim & Co., owners of a textile mill in Pampulha. Crispim helped at mass on Sundays, and when he knelt down, with his long, blond hair, he recalled the gentleness of an angel. Sometimes he would take hold of me in the corridor and cover my face, which was soft and feminine, with devouring kisses. At night, in the study, across the table where

we leafed through the sleepy dictionaries, he passed me notes written in pencil, calling me his idol and promising me boxes of fountain pens...]

The instant attraction ('logo nas primeiras semanas') leads to a tender relationship that endures for several years. Despite seeming to find him angelically attractive, it is difficult to ascertain how much Teodorico reciprocates Crispim's behaviour: although he claims to be kissed rather than kiss, and receive notes rather than write them, he is rather laconic, ending here on an ellipsis, and writing as an older man and father. Interestingly, at school, another classmate calls Teodorico 'lambisgóia' (p. 19), a remarkably feminising insult probably related to *lamber* [to lick].[111] His reaction is to assault him in the toilets, bloodying his face 'com um murro bestial' [with a bestial punch], an act which Teodorico claims to leave him 'temido' [feared] thereafter (p. 19), and which seems at odds with his otherwise placid temperament. He wishes to cultivate an image of masculinity, perhaps, but his feminine features and older friend's advances complicate the task. It is not known whether the insult is related to Teodorico's relations with Crispim, but his phobic aversion to them is at least as apparent as his attraction towards them, foreshadowing his trajectory as an adult.

Crispim then disappears from the narrative until the very end, although in the Holy Land, despite granting his affair with Mary the greatest importance, Teodorico continues to display attraction to men, often referring casually to their beauty. This occurs particularly — and significantly — in the dream chapter, dreams being, for Freud, the 'blessed fulfillers of our wishes' revealing otherwise 'latent thoughts'.[112] Consider, for example, Teodorico's sighting of 'um homem formoso' [a handsome man] (p. 132), to whom he refers thereafter as 'o formoso Manassés' (p. 143). Later, in a similar manner, he notices 'um formoso moço' [a handsome boy] next to him in the crowd (p. 183). On arriving in Palestine, too, he remarks upon the Arab muleteer, 'tão airoso e lindo que eu' [as slender and handsome as I was] (p. 82); 'o nosso lindo arrieiro' [our handsome muleteer] (p. 105). Even his descriptions of the encyclopaedic Topsius sometimes distantly eroticise his figure in the dream sequence, with his 'lábios que pareciam clássicos e de mármore' [classical and marble lips] suggesting an 'irresistível intelectualidade' (p. 113). Teodorico watches him 'submissamente, como perante um mandamento celeste' [submissively, as though following a heavenly commandment], left to 'enfiar em silêncio as grossas botas de montar' [lace in silence his thick riding boots]. Fascinated with what he perceives to be his companion's irresistible intellectuality, when in fact Topsius is closer to a charlatan, Teodorico, as observed elsewhere in Eça, likens him to a classical figure with lips of marble, a godlike, celestial being inducing silent submission. As we shall see, Teodorico will later seek out this superficial bookishness in his wife. Despite such relationships in his youth, however, it is Mary who is most consciously recalled, being for Teodorico, 'talvez, em toda a vasta terra, o único coração em que o meu poderia repousar' [perhaps in all the vastness of the world, the only heart on which mine might rest] (p. 216).

In apparently privileging, like Jorge in *Basílio*, normative desire at the level of consciousness, Teodorico sets the stage for his entry into the homosocial pact at the end of the novel. Shortly after his return to Lisbon, he has a chance encounter with Crispim in the gardens of São Pedro de Alcântara, who upon hearing his friend's travails offers him a job at his firm. Times have changed, however: Crispim remarks that Teodorico is 'muitíssimo feio' [extremely ugly] (p. 250), and the latter, from hereon in, remarkably refers to his friend as 'Crispim & C.ª', or even 'a firma' [the firm] (pp. 251–52), a decidedly colder reincarnation of the *Sociedade Sebastião e Jorge*. With this nominal shift, in accordance with the novel's repeated emptying of signifiers, Crispim undergoes a conversion from a dear schoolfriend to a name on the stock exchange and provider of 'o queijo' [the cheese] (p. 250). Finally, to complete the transaction and partnership, he offers Teodorico his sister in marriage and a stake in the firm. Dona Jesuína is perhaps the least appetising woman he encounters in the novel: 'chamava-se D. Jesuína, tinha trinta e dois anos e era zarolha, [de] pele cor de maçã madura' (p. 252) [she was called Dona Jesuína, was thirty-two years old, and was cross-eyed, with skin like a ripe apple]. However, besides being Crispim's sister, other, seemingly bizarre attributes appear to interest Teodorico. Firstly, he admires her 'peito sólido e suculento' [solid and succulent chest], *suculento* being used to describe Mary's cheeks when the pair first meet (p. 68). He also perceives her to be well educated: 'sabia geografia e todos os rios da China, sabia história e todos os reis da França' [she knew geography and all the rivers of China, she knew history and all the kings of France] — rather like the historian Topsius, his idolised, if mediocre, model of intellectuality. Lastly, he admires her cookery skills and ability to consolidate his sense of masculinity: 'fazia um prato de ovos queimados: e o seu olho vesgo pousava, com incessante agrado, na minha face potente e barbuda de Raposão' [she made a dessert with burnt eggs, and her lazy eye rested, with unending pleasure, on the powerful, bearded face of the great Raposo]. The egg desserts no doubt remind him of those that he brings to Adélia, his first lover (p. 36). Jesuína is perceived and represented, in other words, as little more than a mélange of earlier characters' peculiarities that variously heighten Teodorico's sense of virility. Significantly, Teodorico's mother dies giving birth to him (p. 10), leaving him with no image to influence his future (Oedipal) object choice. It is therefore precisely Jesuína's ambiguous presentation that enables Teodorico to accept her as a bride, despite admitting that his inclinations towards her are loveless (p. 253). As a sufficiently empty signifier in her own right, Jesuína can stand in for Crispim, Topsius, Adélia and Mary, all former lovers in their own way, conjoined in a passably feminine body. Thus her gender is subtly clouded with ambiguity in speech: 'acho-a um belo mulherão; gosto-lhe muito do dote; e havia de ser um bom marido' ['I think she is a fine woman; I admire her dowry; and will be a good husband]. The use of the augmentative masculinises her, while the absence of a pronoun in the final clause allows her, in theory at least, to take the syntactic position of the 'bom marido'. The marriage is then sealed with a warm handshake between Teodorico and 'a firma', completing the homosocial pact. Crispim and Jesuína, then, are both ultimately related to in terms of their exchange value, the former as quite literally a brand, the creator of capital, and the latter as the means to that end, the *moeda corrente*, a body empty and unremarkable enough to figure as anything at all, if one has but the *descarado heroísmo de afirmar*.

The kind of love that Teodorico accepts at the end of *A relíquia* is thus the perfect expression of both the culture of exchange value and the loss of meaning in the wake of the death of God.

> Aren't we straying as through an infinite nothing? Isn't empty space breathing at us? Hasn't it got colder? Isn't night and more night coming again and again?[113]

In a world of such eroded values as that of *A relíquia*, where love and the individual are vanquished by the emptying power of exchange, it is difficult to imagine how more 'authentic' values might ever be recovered. Nietzsche's words, indeed, recall the closing image of *Os Maias*, the rising moonlight above Lisbon signalling an eternal night lit only dimly amid events that have 'unchained this earth from its sun'.[114] Have we arrived once more at the end of history or, perhaps, the end of the love story? Jesuína's gift of the 'última rosa do verão' [the last rose of summer] (p. 252) seems significant in this respect. It is the last expression of love that will ever bloom for man; 'love' will forever flower in this spurious form.

The need to accept this form of love, the last rose of summer, which is also to understand the invincible meaninglessness of capitalist society, is the crux of Teodorico's disquieting 'lição', a lesson shared, of course, by Crispim, as confirmed in the opening sentence of the text:

> Decidi compor, nos vagares deste verão, na minha quinta do Mosteiro (antigo solar dos condes de Lindoso), as memórias da minha vida — que neste século, tão consumido pelas incertezas da inteligência e tão angustiado pelos tormentos do dinheiro, encerra, *penso eu e pensa meu cunhado Crispim*, uma lição lúcida e forte. (p. 5, emphasis added)

> [I have decided to compose, during the summer holidays on my estate in Mosteiro (the ancient seat of the Counts of Lindoso), the memories of my life — which in this century, so consumed by the uncertainties of intelligence and anguished by the torments of money, teach us, *in the opinion of myself and my brother-in-law Crispim*, a lucid and forceful lesson.] (emphasis added)

Teodorico clearly locates his pessimistic 'lição' within the confines of the nineteenth century and its tempestuous obsession with both capital and post-Enlightenment claims to truth, now troubled by growing 'incertezas' in the *fin de siècle*. However, in claiming that his 'lição' is not just his but Crispim's, Teodorico makes *A relíquia* the literary child of their homosocial pact, a surrender to meaninglessness born of an exclusion, in adult life, of all values and sentiments resistant to the power of exchange. The very act of writing forges a homosocial bond, confirming the hegemony of heterosexuality and (re)productivity. Famously asking whether the pen is a 'metaphorical penis', Gilbert and Gubar contend that patriarchal ideology renders artistic creativity a predominantly masculine quality that, in its turn, works to cement the patriarchal order.[115] *A relíquia*, with its first-person narrator who ultimately accepts this order, assimilating his first lover to the position of brother-in-law and co-author, links the consolidation of normative sexuality and patriarchy to the revelation of 'truth' by man, once assured by an omniscient God, but now devoid of meaning — in the bourgeois, Western world at least — after His death, in spite of attempts by Eça and his generation to resurrect it as young men. If the pen is indeed a metaphorical penis, *A relíquia* details how that pen, perhaps in place of the penis, reaches the man's hand over the course and at the end of history, darkening his vision. Thus all that Teodorico receives from his Aunt's testament are her tinted spectacles, 'para ver o resto de longe' [to see the rest from afar] (p. 244), to look askance at what he has lost.

If the work of Eça de Queirós in general, and *Os Maias* in particular, troubles the foundations of the kinship system to reveal an excess that is denied and yet exploited for personal gain, *A relíquia* implicates this excess in the act of writing itself, a theme that surfaces frequently in the author's subsequent work. Teodorico's story and 'lição' rest on a homosocial pact that b(l)inds him to the restrictions of the patriarchal kinship system, his identification as a patriarch resting on a chain of empty signifiers. The novel explores the great ideological blind spots of Eça's 'scientific' age, a crisis of representation calling for unreliable first-person narration and the dreamlike 'manto diáfano da fantasia', shrouding the 'lição lúcida e forte' with alternative epistemologies that echo the return to the Greek classics in the author's earlier work. Interestingly, and as further evidence that *A relíquia* marks a pivotal moment in his career, Eça would return to similar ideas in his last novel, *A cidade e as serras* (1900),[116] which again features a first-person narrator, Zé Fernandes, haunted by his love for his 'belo príncipe', Jacinto.[117] Seemingly resolved once more through a homosocial pact with the narrator — Jacinto's marriage to Zé's closest relative, his cousin Joana — the novel is defined by the same unravelling of kinship and truth that characterises *A relíquia*. Indeed, despite the ostensibly more upbeat ending of *A cidade e as serras*, as Rothwell notes, few questions are left answered at the end. Failing to bury his ancestors' bones properly, despite fathering a child, Jacinto does not live up to his own expectations as the family's remaining patriarch, a turn of events that Rothwell reads as an inability to resolve (like Jorge in *Basílio*) the Oedipus complex. Zé Fernandes, meanwhile, resumes referring to Jacinto as his 'belo príncipe' at the end, devoting his story to his friend but never finding true love himself. 'O meu Príncipe, atrigueirado nas soalheiras e nos ventos da serra, a minha prima Joaninha [...] e eu, [...] trilhando um solo eterno, e de eterna solidez' [my Prince and I, bronzed by the sun and the winds of the hills, my cousin Joaninha [...] and I, [...] treading an eternal earth, of eternal solidarity] (p. 218), concludes the narrator, with a tinge of physical admiration for his newly countrified brother-in-law, whose marriage he oddly appears to complete, eternally, *até que a morte os separe* [unto death]. If there is any hope to be found in these stories of troubled bachelors and empty patriarchs, it is surely in these moments of longing for alternative forms of perfect union and harmony, first dreamed, perhaps, by Jorge and Sebastião, consummated but then spurned by Carlos and Maria Eduarda, and never quite acknowledged in the novels that follow.[118] Even in the formally more conventional *A ilustre casa de Ramires* (1900), penned in the third person, the protagonist can only dream of becoming a patriarch, glorifying his forefathers in literary endeavour, while never himself becoming a father, despite his phallic reconstruction of his family's ancestral tower.[119]

The complex epistemological and sociological critique developed by Eça in his later years is well exemplified by his short story 'José Matias' which, I believe, takes the philosophical blindspots of the *fin de siècle* as its chief focus. Published in 1897, after both *O Barão de Lavos* and *Bom Crioulo*, 'José Matias', again written in the first person, is a philosopher's tale of his incomprehension at the story's eponymous subject, narrated to an acquaintance at his funeral. In the spirit of courtly love,[120] José spends his life in silent adoration for the 'divina Elisa', a beautiful married woman who twice spurns him for other admirers, leading to José's premature death from spiralling alcoholism and financial ruin — rather like the Baron of Lavos, to whom I will return shortly. The narrator is baffled by José's capacity for self-destruction, calling him an 'espírito curioso' [curious spirit][121] who leaves him with more questions than answers; at the end, he defines him as 'talvez muito mais que um homem — ou talvez ainda menos que um homem' [perhaps much more than a man — or perhaps still less than a man] (p. 416). Quite what constitutes the great 'mystery' of José's character is not named or revealed, despite, as Cleonice Berardinelli notes, consistent attempts by critics to identify 'it' amid more than twenty 'expressões de dúvida' [expressions of doubt] and seventy-five ellipses.[122] More recently, Ana Paula Ferreira has proposed that Matias is a feminised figure, given to sentimentality and aesthetic beauty and thus coded as sexually non-normative, whom the narrator in vain 'wills to know' with his Positivist philosophy, echoing the 'homosexual panic' of the *fin de siècle*.[123] Sexuality in the story, in other words, is bound up with epistemological questions and the revelation (or complication) of truth. However, in the light of my reading of *A relíquia*, I would like to shift the focus of queerness away from José and onto the narrator himself who, like Teodorico at the end of his story, acknowledges only normative desire, but appears to harbour an interest in José himself, allowing for a more sinister reading of his character that again implicates writing and truth in the operation of patriarchy.

'[U]m rapaz airoso, louro como uma espiga, com um bigode crespo de paladino sobre uma boca indecisa de contemplativo, destro cavaleiro, duma elegância sóbria e fina' (p. 395) [A slender boy, blond as an ear of wheat, with the curly beard of a paladin knight beneath an indecisive, contemplative mouth, an agile gentleman of fine and sober elegance]. The narrator's initial description of his subject, 'um moço interessante' [an interesting boy], 'um suave camarada' [a sweet comrade], '[um] moço tão macio, tão louro e tão ligeiro' [a boy so soft, so blond and so gentle], is, importantly, physically flattering and curious, but not clearly erotic, echoing many other moments across Eça's work that allow for the possibility of physical attraction — the narrator also describes Elisa's new lover as a 'belo moço, rígido' [a strong, handsome boy] (p. 412) — without any move towards confirmation. However, some minor but structurally important details suggest that the narrator is in a much greater position of power than he prefers to admit. To begin with, he seems implicated in José's decision to retreat to Porto, out of respect for Elisa when her husband dies, which thwarts the first of two opportunities for José to declare his love legitimately:

> O José Matias abalava nessa noite para o Porto. [...] Num momento em que ele entrara na alcova, murmurei ao Nicolau, por cima do grogue: — 'O Matias

faz perfeitamente em ir para o Porto...' Nicolau encolheu os ombros: — 'Sim, pensou que era mais delicado... Eu aprovei. Mas só durante os meses de luto pesado...' (p. 403)

> [José Matias was leaving for Porto that night. [...] When he went to his room, I murmured to Nicolau, peering over my glass:
> 'Matias is right to go to Porto...' Nicolau shrugged his shoulders. 'Yes, he thought it was the tactful thing to do... I approved. But only during the months of deepest mourning.']

Why does the narrator mutter his advice to his friend when José leaves the room? We might surmise that he wishes to keep his designs for José a secret. It is curious that José misses two golden opportunities to propose to the widowed Elisa because of his prolonged absence in Porto, apparently encouraged by the narrator, and despite his (public) profession to see José married to Elisa. Secondly, the narrator's panic to analyse and explain is sometimes inflected with the language of sexual dominance, audible in his early reference to José's soft, bland appearance. The following passage relates his consternation on learning of Elisa's second marriage to the wealthy Torres Nogueira, apparently because of José's refusal to see her when in Porto:

> Ambos nos olhámos, e depois ambos nos separámos, encolhendo os ombros, com aquele assombro resignado que convém a espíritos prudentes perante o Incognoscível. Mas eu, Filósofo, e portanto espírito imprudente, toda essa noite esfuraquei o ato do José Matias com a ponta duma Psicologia que expressamente aguçara: — e já de madrugada, estafado, concluí, como se conclui sempre em Filosofia, que me encontrava diante duma Causa Primária, portanto impenetrável, onde se quebraria, sem vantagem para ele, para mim, ou para o Mundo, a ponta do meu Instrumento! (p. 405)

> [We both looked at each other and then we parted ways, shrugging our shoulders, with that resigned shock that comes to the aid of prudent spirits when contemplating the unthinkable. But I, a philosopher, and thus an imprudent spirit, spent the whole night drilling through the act of José Matias with the point of a psychology that I had expressly sharpened, and as morning broke, exhausted, I concluded — as one always concludes in philosophy — that I found myself before a primary, and therefore impenetrable, cause that would shatter, with no use to me, him or the world, the point of my instrument!]

Thus the narrator passes the night penetrating the mystery of José Matias with the point of his psychological instrument. The metaphor likening the will to know to an act of penetration — strikingly similar to that used in Zola's surgically inspired preface to *Thérèse Raquin* that became something of a Naturalist manifesto[124] — is well developed and might be said to prefigure Gilbert and Gubar's characterisation of the pen as a metaphorical penis. 'José Matias' is, in one sense, the story of how such a pen leads to the ink running dry — or, more formally speaking, an epistemological crisis, in which the narrator tries to enunciate his subject's 'secrets' without, apparently, apprehending the hidden, authoritative ideology of the supposedly clarifying enunciative act. Here, the sense that Eça has turned against Zola's literary methods is especially palpable.

## Concluding Remarks

Beginning with his early work and ending with the untrustworthy narrators of *A relíquia* and 'José Matias', this chapter demonstrates how Eça's well-charted journey towards disillusionment with Naturalism accompanies and entails a detailed exploration of family and sexual politics, kinship, desire and love. The seeds of his development of a narrative style perhaps more at home in the twentieth century, reminiscent of the later works of Machado de Assis, are arguably sown as a young author; already in *O crime* and especially in *Basílio*, his critique of nineteenth-century social codes involves a series of departures from contemporary approaches to love, friendship and literary praxis. The 1880s, however, would prove a decisive turning point for the author. If *Os Maias* marks the end of the road for Naturalism and its supposedly objective approach to society and literature, *A relíquia* and the later works blow apart the principles of Realist narration entirely, diegetically assimilating the limits of language and kinship in resignation to the absence of truth and meaning in modern society. The consistency of *A relíquia* and *A cidade e as serras* in this respect, the protagonists of which both marry their best friend's closest relation in an apparent attempt to reconcile intimate desires with social constraints, is quite remarkable, and these later novels may indeed be less optimistic than they at first seem, at least as far as revolutionary change is concerned. Either way, it is difficult to dissociate Eça's characteristically critical engagement with Naturalism from his detailed deconstruction of the patriarchal family and the multiple meanings and values it (re)produces across time, from the original colonial experiment to the bourgeois family. Given the struggles in the following century for recognition and acceptance of other ways to love and desire, as well as for the end of colonialism the world over, the emptiness of Teodorico's Oriental adventures and subsequent marriage, or the convivial, stay-at-home life dreamed by Jorge and Sebastião as young men, may be considered remarkably radical and farsighted, even if they entail a return to older epistemologies and philosophies.

We will never quite know, of course, why Eça de Queirós was so concerned with questions of kinship and forbidden desire. Some will point to the author's own life and his uncle's refusal to consent to his marrying his cousin, with whom he had amorous relations in his youth,[125] though this explanation, of course, collapses meaning back into the author, that other, little god. Others will pursue more ideological explanations rooted in the author's anarchistic political convictions. However, if, as I have argued, the problematisation of kinship in his work questions the foundations of patriarchal capitalism, it is surely apt that such a critique should emerge from a country that was declining in influence within this socio-economic system in its increasingly accelerated and globalised form, made especially visible during the various crises of the nineteenth century. Just as important as the country's growing marginality in this respect, indeed, is surely its former centrality and ongoing imperial project,[126] which in Eça is reimagined as a historic error mobilised by a flawed logic of desire and conquest. Eça thus works in the other direction to Botelho: whilst both authors implicate kinship, and even Dom Sebastião, in the country's ills, for Botelho, it is its normative manifestation that spells a return to prosperity, whereas for Eça, this is in fact a *parentesco postiço* [feigned kinship] offering only the last rose of summer, heralding the dissolution of love and values forever more. The physical degeneration of José Matias (and indeed of Eça's 'sociedade podre') is therefore not, as with the Baron of Lavos, the inevitable culmination of decadence and pernicious heredity, but rather bound up with his adherence to an archaic model of true love with no place[127] in a modern Portugal governed by exchange value, repressing (violently perhaps, in the case of 'José Matias') non-normative love in pursuit of its own truth. Only a thorough replacement of the foundations of society can provide an answer to the mistakes of the nation's past.

Eça's novels as a whole, therefore, can be theorised as a gradual process of dismantling the parameters of love and 'science' in a world of products, plantations, productivity and reproduction. Rather than attempting to reaffirm, tirelessly as in *Lavos*, the language of science, Eça dwells on its ambiguities and internal confusion, surrounding what is accepted and perceived — exchanged? — with indeterminacy and incomprehension. Harold Bloom, who describes intra-poetic relationships as 'parallels of family romance',[128] identifies the 'weak' modern poet as akin to Adam, reproducing the father's law, and the 'strong' poet as Satan, who rejects the incarnation of God's son.[129] To continue the analogy, Eça's writing verges on the Satanic, rejecting Naturalist claims to truth but also, in the end, acknowledging the banishment of defeat to preserve what remains of the *ideal íntimo a que se aspirava*. Thus the short story 'O Senhor Diabo' expresses awe and respect for the fallen angel, 'a figura mais dramática da História da Alma' [the most dramatic figure in the history of the soul]:

> em certos momentos da história, o Diabo é o representante imenso do direito humano. Quer a liberdade, a fecundidade, a força, a lei. É então uma espécie de Pã sinistro, onde rugem as fundas rebeliões da Natureza.[130]
>
> [At certain moments in history, the Devil is the immense representative of man's rights. Be it freedom, fecundity, force or law. Then he becomes a kind of sinister Pan, in which the deepest rebellions of nature growl.]

To see the world as Satan is to reject the father's law in search of the most ardent desires of human nature. Eça takes up Satan's mantle to find far more dimensions to man's desiring than the various gods throughout history have generally allowed, whether these be religious, literary, monarchical or republican. In so doing, he exposes the *parentesco postiço* of a country whose sons and daughters, in counter-Hegelian fashion, cannot escape the problematic relations of the past, awaiting the return of a king who cannot live up to his father's muddled name. Clearly, Eça's socio-historical critique is many times more nuanced than that of Abel Botelho, who largely upholds an imported pathological discourse even if he gestures towards its own weaknesses. For the latter, the historic logic of desire and conquest is something to be recovered and reinstated by 'science', whereas for Eça, science cannot escape its grip and at its worst, offers only the same mistakes. If Eça sees with the eyes of Satan, Botelho acts at the most as an anxious Adam, peering into the fires of Hell, perhaps, but wearing the blackened spectacles bequeathed to Teodorico. Such a characterisation is doubtless reflected in the different canonical positioning of the two authors. But they do have something striking in common: both explore their nation's changing position within the structures of Western power by disrupting the logic of patriarchal kinship, and both concede victory to the bourgeoisie as the old order visibly disintegrates. Moreover, be it through allegory, metaphor, dreams and fantasy, or the return to Greek modes of being and desiring, both authors, at some level, pit Naturalism against itself, modifying its discourse to contemplate an empire represented, in an almost 'natural' fashion at the *fin de siècle*, as decadent and peripheral. These are defining contours of the movement in Portugal that, as we shall see, would prove no less important and influential in Brazil.

## Notes to Chapter 2

1. Eça de Queirós, O primo Basílio, in Obras completas de Eça de Queirós (Lisbon: Círculo de Leitores, 1980), vol. I, p. 252. All page references are to this edition.
2. This reading is also set out in David J. Bailey, 'Com o odioso guarda-chuva entre os joelhos: Queer Male Desire, Weak Paternity, and Kinship Trouble in the Novels of Eça de Queirós', The Modern Language Review, III (2016), 413–33 (p. 414).
3. Machado de Assis in his critique of O primo Basílio. See <http://www.literaturabrasileira.ufsc. br/documentos/?action=download&id=8274> [accessed 31 March 2016].
4. See e.g. João Gaspar Simões, Vida e obra de Eça de Queirós (Lisbon: Livraria Bertrand, 1973), p. 498, and Carlos Reis, História da literatura portuguesa: o realismo e o naturalismo (Lisbon: Publicações Alfa, 2001), p. 157. The work of other critics in this respect will be considered in this chapter.
5. See Alexander Coleman, Eça de Queirós and European Realism (New York: New York University Press, 1980), p. 49.
6. Rafael Bordalo Pinheiro, O funeral..., in A Paródia, I (1900), pp. 292–93, Biblioteca Nacional de Portugal.
7. Cited by Carlos Reis in História crítica da literatura portuguesa (Lisbon: Editorial Verbo, 1994), p. 94.
8. Eça de Queirós, Correspondência (Lisbon: Caminho, 2008), p. 135.
9. Ibid, p. 235.
10. Simões, p. 561.
11. Eça de Queirós, A relíquia, in Obras completas, vol. V, p. 143.
12. António José Saraiva, As ideias de Eça de Queirós (Lisbon: Gradiva, 2000), p. 115.
13. Coleman, pp. 247–85.
14. Carlos Reis, Estatuto e perspectivas do narrador na ficção de Eça de Queirós (Coimbra: Livraria Almedina, 1984), p. 235.
15. Correspondência, p. 135.
16. See Carmo Salazar Ponte, Oliveira Martins: a história como tragédia (Lisbon: Imprensa Nacional–Casa da Moeda, 1999), p. 31.
17. See Eça de Queirós, 'O francesismo', in Obras de Eça de Queirós, (Porto: Lello e Irmão, 1948), vol. XI, pp. 333–57 (p. 333).
18. Hélder Macedo, for example, describes the central incestuous relationship in Os Maias as symptomatic of the 'situação estagnada de Portugal' [Portugal's stagnated situation]. See introduction to The Maias, trans. by Patricia McGowan Pinheiro and Ann Stevens (London: Everyman, 1986), p. vii. António Coimbra Martins makes a similar argument in Ensaios Queirosianos (Lisbon: Publicações Europa-América, 1967), pp. 268–87. Isabel Pires de Lima, meanwhile, describes the implied homosexual relations of Charlie Gouvarinho in Os Maias as reflecting the 'atmosfera dolente de Lisboa' [pitiful atmosphere of Lisbon]. See Isabel Pires de Lima, As máscaras do desengano (Lisbon: Editorial Caminho, 1987), p. 178.
19. See Maria Manuel Lisboa, Teu amor fez de mim um lago triste: ensaios sobre 'Os Maias' (Porto: Campo das Letras, 2000).

20. Ana Paula Ferreira, 'Amores vicários: "José Matias" e o pânico homo/heterossexual', in *Congresso de Estudos Queirosianos: IV Encontro Internacional de Queirosianos* (Coimbra: Livraria Almedina, 2000), vol. I, pp. 327–37.

21. Ibid., note to p. 328.

22. José Carlos Barcellos, *Literatura e homoerotismo em questão* (2006), p. 203, available at <http://www.dialogarts.uerj.br/admin/arquivos_emquestao/%5B1%5Dlit_e_homo.pdf> [accessed 15 January 2015].

23. Anna Klobucka, 'Libaninho', in *Reading Literature in Portuguese*, ed. by Cláudia Pazos-Alonso and Stephen Parkinson (Oxford: Legenda, 2013), pp. 136–40.

24. Phillip Rothwell, *A Canon of Empty Fathers* (Lewisburg, PA: Bucknell University Press, 2007), p. 79.

25. Literally the 'burnt patriarchal church' owing to the edifice that once stood there, and now known as Príncipe Real, an area celebrated for its splendid mansions. It was once the rubbish dump of the Bairro Alto, regenerated in the nineteenth century, and thus epitomises the ascent of the bourgeoisie. See <http://lisboaverde.cm-lisboa.pt/index.php?id=4304> [accessed 29 March 2016].

26. The authoritative narrative tone is audible in, for example, the description of Leopoldina's fado singing: 'falava-se nas "raivas do ciúme, nas rochas de Cascais, nas noites de luar, nos suspiros da saudade", *todo o palavreado mórbido do sentimentalismo lisboeta*' [she sang of 'outbursts of jealousy, of the rocks of Cascais, of moonlit nights, of pangs of yearning', *all the morbid twaddle of Lisbon sentimentality*] (p. 160, emphasis added).

27. Silviano Santiago, 'Eça, Autor de *Madame Bovary*', in *Uma literatura nos trópicos: ensaios sobre a dependência cultural* (Rio de Janeiro: Rocco, 2000), pp. 47–65.

28. Incidentally, 'camarada' — English 'comrade' — ultimately derives from Latin *camera* ('bedroom, chamber'), which was modified in Spanish to mean 'one with whom one shares one's bedroom', thus originating in notions of physical proximity. See <http://www.etymonline.com/index.php?term=comrade> [accessed 9 April 2014].

29. Queirós, 'Carta a Teófilo Braga', in *Correspondência*, p. 51.

30. See Plato, *Symposium*, trans. by Benjamin Jowett (Rockville, MD: Serenity Publishers, 2009), p. 52.

31. Michel Montaigne, 'On Affectionate Relationships', in *The Complete Essays*, translated from the French by M. A. Screech (London: Penguin, 2004), pp. 205–19 (p. 211).

32. Lisboa, p. 352.

33. Ibid, p. 361.

34. This is the overarching argument laid out in Lisboa, *Teu amor fez de mim um lago triste...*

35. See e.g. Sigmund Freud, 'On Narcissism: an Introduction', in *The Standard Edition of the Complete Psychological Works of Sigmund Freud*, trans. and ed. by James Strachey and Anna Freud (London: Hogarth, 1957), vol. XIV, pp. 67–102.

36. For a discussion of the influence of opera on Eça's work, see Maria de Carvalho, 'Eça de Queirós e a ópera no século XIX em Portugal', *Revista Colóquio/Letras*, 91 (May 1986), 27–37.

37. Friedrich Engels, *The Origin of the Family, Private Property and the State* (London: Penguin, 1986).

38. Michael Warner, 'Homo-Narcissism; or, Heterosexuality', in *Engendering Men: The Question of Male Feminist Criticism*, ed. by Joseph A. Boone and Michael Cadden (London: Routledge, 1990), pp. 190–206 (pp. 190–01).

39. Freud, 'Three Essays on the Theory of Sexuality', in *Standard Edition*, vol. XVII, pp. 125–248 (p. 145).

40. See, for example, Freud, 'On Narcissism...', p. 91.

41. E. M. Forster, *Maurice* (London: Penguin, 1972), p. 18.

42. For Lisboa, Eça's recourse to Greek tragedy is evident even in his first novel, *O crime do Padre Amaro*, where it interrupts the discourse of social determinism. See Lisboa, pp. 333–93.

43. 'Se D. Sebastião não fosse absoluto, não teria ido *enterrar em Alcácer Quibir a nação portuguesa, as últimas esperanças da pátria*.' (Emphasis added). See Quental, 'Causas da Decadência...'.

44. 'Fazei, Senhor, que nunca os admirados | Alemães, Galos, Ítalos e Ingleses, | Possam dizer que são pera mandados, | Mais que pera mandar, os Portugueses' (to paraphrase in English:

my King, ensure that the wondering Germans, Gauls, Italians and English can never say that the Portuguese take orders, but rather give them). Luís de Camões, *Os Lusíadas* (Porto: Porto Editora, 2006), p. 284 (Canto x, estrofe 152).

45. As we shall see, *A relíquia* also allegorises the futility of Portuguese imperialism in Teodorico's irreverent travels in the Middle East.

46. Edward Said, for example, writes of the 'feminine penetrability' and 'supine malleability' of the Orient as conceived by the West. See *Orientalism: Western Conceptions of the Orient* (London: Vintage Books, 1979), p. 206.

47. In *Os Lusíadas* (see note 44), Venus rewards the explorers for their valour with a paradisiacal island, abundant with ripe fruit and populated by naked nymphs for their enjoyment.

48. Lisboa, p. 61.

49. 'Ó vã cobiça | Desta vaidade, a quem chamamos Fama!' [O vain pursuit | Of this vanity we call fame!]. Camões, p. 120 (Canto iv, estrofe 95).

50. Eça de Queirós, *A ilustre casa de Ramires*, in *Obras completas*, vol. ix.

51. Eça de Queirós, *Uma campanha alegre*, in *Obras completas*, vol. xiv, p. 102.

52. In Vicente's famous play of 1509, which predates *Os Lusíadas* by some decades, the success of the voyages of discovery is undermined by adultery and domestic turmoil during the oblivious husband's absence. See Gil Vicente, *Auto da Índia* (Porto: Porto Editora, 2018).

53. See Lisboa, pp. 333–93.

54. Eça de Queirós, *Os Maias*, in *Obras completas*, vol. vi. All page references are to this edition.

55. I discussed this text in the Introduction; see Judith Butler, *Antigone's Claim: Kinship Between Life and Death* (New York: Columbia University Press, 2000).

56. Rothwell discusses the homoerotic implications of Jacinto's characterisation as a 'belo príncipe' by his friend and narrator, Zé Fernandes. See Rothwell, p. 79.

57. Lisboa, p. 255.

58. Barcellos, p. 186.

59. Kaja Silverman, *Male Subjectivity at the Margins* (New York: Routledge, 1992), p. 194.

60. Ibid., p. 200.

61. Eça de Queirós, *O crime do Padre Amaro*, in *Obras completas*, vol. iv, p. 224.

62. Eça de Queirós, *A correspondência de Fradique Mendes*, in *Obras completas*, pp. 30–36.

63. Montaigne, p. 211.

64. Lisboa, p. 181.

65. Pires de Lima, *As máscaras do desengano*, p. 240.

66. Lisboa, p. 255.

67. In *Os Maias*, the word 'irmão' is used to describe several male friendships. Alencar describes Carlos as like a brother to him, and Cohen uses the word interchangeably with 'amigo': 'um amigo, um irmão' (p. 169).

68. Lisboa refers to Ega as Carlos's 'amigo-irmão' (p. 239).

69. Montaigne, p. 211.

70. Klobucka, p. 139.

71. See Gayle Rubin, 'The Traffic in Women: Notes on the Political Economy of Sex', in *Towards an Anthropology of Women*, ed. by Rayna Reiter (New York: Monthly Review Press, 1975), pp. 157–210 (p. 180).

72. Macedo, p. vii.

73. Lisboa, p. 81.

74. Ibid., p. 108.

75. Ibid., p. 102.

76. Lima, p. 25.

77. Ibid., p. 42.

78. Lisboa, pp. 227–38.

79. Irigaray, p. 181.

80. Christopher Castiglia, 'Rebel Without a Closet' in *Engendering Men: The Question of Male Feminist Criticism*, ed. by Joseph A. Boone and Michael Cadden (London: Routledge, 1990), pp. 207–24 (p. 207).

81. Fernando Curopos, *L'Emergence de l'homosexualité dans la littérature portugaise (1875–1915)* (Paris: L'Harmattan, 2016), p. 36.

82. Lisboa, p. 234.

83. Lima, p. 65.

84. Ibid., p. 67.

85. Incidentally, there are several similarities between character and king. Both Carlos and Dom Sebastião lost their fathers at a very young age (in the monarch's case, eighteen days before he was born) and were abandoned by their mothers: Carlos, when Monforte elopes with Tancredo, and Sebastião when his mother Joanna of Austria, shortly after his birth, was called to Madrid to become queen regent of Spain. Both Carlos and Sebastião, furthermore, were raised by grandparents. See <http://www.arqnet.pt/dicionario/sebastiao1rei.html> [accessed 1 April 2016].

86. Lisboa, p. 217.

87. Ibid., p. 211.

88. Lacan uses the metaphor of the purloined letter in Poe's eponymous short story to illustrate the 'debt' that must be paid when the Imaginary and the Symbolic do not correspond. See Jacques Lacan, 'Seminar on the Purloined Letter,' in *Écrits*, trans. by Bruce Frink (London: W. W. Norton and Co., 2007), pp. 6–48.

89. See Lisboa, pp. 117–31, for a reading of Maria Eduarda as the return of the repressed mother.

90. Rothwell, p. 74.

91. Elisa Valério, *Para uma leitura de 'Os Maias'* (Lisbon: Presença, 1997), p. 15.

92. Cited by Joaquim Gomes Monteiro in *Vencidos da vida: relance literário e política da segunda metade do século XIX* (Lisbon: Edição Romano Tôrres, 1944), p. 13.

93. See Clodomir Moog, *Eça de Queirós e o século XIX* (São Paulo: Delta, 1966), p. 219.

94. Ega's similarity to the author (orthographically, a mere pen-stroke) has long been suggested by critics. See e.g. Antero Vieira de Lemos, *Eça de Queiroz, o seu drama e a sua obra* (Porto: Edição do Autor, 1945), p. 202. See also Valério, p. 30.

95. Lisboa, pp. 382–93.

96. Jobst Welge, *Genealogical Fictions: Cultural Periphery and Historical Change in the Modern Novel* (Baltimore, MD: Johns Hopkins University Press, 2014), pp. 120–41.

97. Interestingly, Maria Filomena Mónica points out that Eça never managed to write well in Portugal, and spent weeks travelling around the country with Ramalho Ortigão looking for 'um sítio limpo de maçadores, de moscas e de cozinheiros, para acabar de escrever *A relíquia*' [a place free of cretins, flies and cooks, in order to finish writing *A relíquia*]. The very process of writing in his peripheral country (as opposed to France and Britain, where he wrote most of his work) figures as an impediment to careful Naturalist study. See *Eça de Queirós* (Braga: Quetzal, 2001), p. 202.

98. See Mónica, pp. 206–09.

99. Oliveira Martins cited by Alfredo Campos Matos in *Eça de Queirós: uma biografia* (Lisbon: Edições Afrontamento, 2009), p. 472.

100. See also Ernesto Guerra da Cal, *A relíquia, romance picaresco e cervantesco* (Lourenço Marques: Sociedade de Estudos de Moçambique, 1972) for an exploration of the eclectic nature of *A relíquia*.

101. Coleman, p. 176.

102. Ibid., p. 181.

103. Frank de Sousa, '*A relíquia*: do Realismo/Naturalismo a uma estética da imperfeição,' in *Suplemento ao Dicionário de Eça de Queirós*, ed. by Alfredo Campos Matos (Lisbon: Editorial Caminho, 2000), p. 569.

104. Mónica, p. 206.

105. Coleman, p. 167.

106. Maria Manuel Lisboa, *Uma mãe desconhecida: amor e perdição em Eça de Queirós* (Lisbon: Imprensa Nacional–Casa da Moeda, 2008), p. 148.

107. Ibid., p. 163.

108. Ibid., pp. 188–200. See Francis Fukuyama, 'The End of History?', *The National Interest* (Summer 1989), <http://www.wesjones.com/eoh.htm> [accessed 5 May 2016].

109. Ferdinand de Saussure, *Course in General Linguistics* [1916], trans. by Roy Harris (London: Bloomsbury, 2013), p. 78.

110. See Joaquim Machado de Assis, *Dom Casmurro* (Lisbon: Guerra e Paz, 2016), where a definitive answer to the question of Capitu's faithfulness to the narrator is withheld throughout. As I have indicated elsewhere, of all the authors not considered in this book, Machado is perhaps the most conspicuous candidate for further research in this line of enquiry.

111. See <http://www.dicionarioweb.com.br/lambisgóia/> [accessed 15 March 2016].

112. Freud, *The Interpretation of Dreams*, trans. by James Strachey (Harmondsworth: Penguin, 1976), pp. 212–15.

113. Friedrich Nietzsche, *The Gay Science*, trans. by Josefine Nauckhoff (Cambridge: Cambridge University Press, 2001), p. 120.

114. Ibid.

115. Sandra M. Gilbert and Susan Gubar, *The Madwoman in the Attic: The Woman Writer and the Nineteenth-Century Literary Imagination* (New Haven, CT: Yale University Press, 2000).

116. Eça de Queirós, *A cidade e as serras*, in *Obras completas*, vol. VIII.

117. See Rothwell, p. 79.

118. Although Rothwell asserts that in *A cidade*, the love of Jacinto and Zé Fernandes is at one point 'reduced to a coarse sexual act' (p. 41), he does not provide a citation and this reader at least can find no evidence of such a consummative incident. The narrator's references to 'Sodoma' and 'Lesbos' (p. 74) to which Rothwell may here be referring are used to describe the supposedly decadent people of Paris, and not ostensibly the pair themselves, who are viewing the city from a physical and critical distance. We could of course read this as Zé's oblique warning to Jacinto and thus something of an unintended admission of guilt, but again the ambiguity is insoluble.

119. David Frier also questions the extent to which the later novels *A cidade* and *A ilustre casa* end successfully with regards to paternity and future security. See 'Transcender o passado ou perder-se no passado? À procura de comunidades imaginadas n'*A ilustre casa de Ramires* e n'*A cidade e as serras*', *Queirosiana*, 21–22 (2010–11), 57–73.7

120. See Alanda El Fahl, 'José Matias: Um amor fora de lugar', in *Fólio — Revista de Letras*, 6.2 (2014), 11–23.

121. Eça de Queirós, 'José Matias' in *Contos*, in *Obras completas*, vol. IX, pp. 395–416 (p. 395). All page references are to this edition.

122. Cleonice Berardinelli, 'José Matias', *Convergência Lusíada*, 13 (1996), p. 44.

123. Ferreira, pp. 327–37.

124. See Émile Zola, Preface to the 1st edn of *Thérèse Raquin*, trans. by Andrew Rothwell (Oxford: Oxford University Press, 1992), p. 2.

125. See Edmundo Moniz, *As mulheres proibidas: o incesto em Eça de Queirós* (São Paulo: José Olympio, 1993), p. 27.

126. As discussed in the Introduction, Boaventura de Sousa Santos characterises Portugal's identity in the nineteenth century as both centre of its own world and at the margins of British and French imperialism.

127. I am drawing here on El Fahl's concept of the *amor fora de lugar*.

128. Bloom, p. 8.

129. Ibid., p. 20.

130. Eça de Queirós, 'O Senhor Diabo' in *Contos*, in *Obras completas*, vol. IX, pp. 33–47 (p. 35).

# CHAPTER 3

# Aluísio Azevedo

### Introduction: um Naturalismo nos Trópicos

The publication of Cruz e Sousa's *Missal* (1893) offers critics one of those felicitous moments in which an apparently minor detail neatly captures the intellectual zeitgeist. The collection of poetry, written by a black poet from Florianópolis and published in Rio de Janeiro, is followed by the subtitle 'Brasil — Sul' [Brazil — South].[1] The geographical marker seems ingenuous enough, but when we pose the question of its purpose — as did Adolfo Caminha, with a tone of great frustration, after its publication[2] — it is clear that the publisher was pulling a particular set of ideological strings relating to race, climate, environment and intellectual life. As we have seen earlier in this study, the supposedly pernicious effects of a hot climate were readily used, in intellectual circles, to cement the perceived cultural superiority of centres of dominance in temperate Northern Europe, contrasted against the presumed licentiousness and slovenliness of the 'Sotadic Zone' beginning at the Pyrenees.[3] Considerations of climate, meanwhile, slipped into questions of race and sexual practices. What is interesting in this case, however, is how the logic is reproduced, in near-perfect symmetry, to the south of the equator. In Brazil, of course, the most temperate regions are found in the south of the country, and the publisher of *Missal* once more relates a cooler climate to a more refined intellectual capacity, contrasted in this instance, presumably, with the fiercely hot *Nordeste*. The contrast was perceived to be all the more pronounced by the fact that the south of Brazil was also, and remains today, racially whiter and economically more advantaged than the north of the country, being specifically chosen by the government to attract European immigrants at the end of the nineteenth century.[4] The words 'Brasil — Sul' thus fracture Brazilian cultural output against putative criteria of climate and degeneracy imported from Europe. As usual, *fin-de-siècle* thought has a remarkable ability to proliferate analytical categories in its insatiable thirst for purity, homogeneity, clarity and binary formulations. The inconspicuous subtitle, however, exposes something of the particular trouble with such ideas in Brazil: whilst they had popular currency and could apparently mobilise the identifications of an overwhelmingly white readership culturally aligned with Europe (in this case, no doubt, luring them to the work of one of Brazil's first black poets), they often operated so as to pit the country against itself.

As a case in point, Caminha's extensive criticism of the words 'Brasil — Sul', which is characteristically pointed and insistent, ties itself in the same theoretical knot. Like most of the Brazilian Naturalist writers, including Aluísio Azevedo, whose work I will consider in this chapter, Caminha was from the 'underdeveloped' Northeast and thus well positioned to critique the supposed cultural superiority of the South. He mentions at the end of the piece, for example, that a key reason for the differences in cultural output between the north and south of the country is their differing proximity to the metropolis.[5] However, despite this gesture towards a social-constructivist argument, most of the text is in fact devoted to replacing one theory of climate with another, including drawing on Montesquieu to argue that the heat of the tropics heightens, rather than depresses, intellectual sensibilities: '[o] calor, *acelerando as forças vivas* da natureza humana, empresta ao homem *certa energia moral...* ao contrário do gelo, do frio e das brumas, que produzem *uma enervação doentia* e grande abatimento d'alma' [hot weather, accelerating the living forces of human nature, lends man a certain moral energy... unlike frost, cold and mist, which produce a sickly state of nervousness and disturbances to the soul].[6] The north–south logic is reversed, but the underlying discourse of pathology remains essentially unchanged. Similarly, if not without some contradiction, Caminha goes on to argue that the Northeast is in fact the most temperate region of Brazil, if 'temperate' is taken to mean constancy and stability.[7] The intellectual dilemma is clear: an essentialising 'science' is deployed to convey authority, but that same science works to degrade large swathes of the country. And of course, what are flattened here as geographical regions in fact disguise different demographics, and ultimately if not exclusively, differing distributions of races within Brazil.

This intellectual dilemma is one of the most salient characteristics of Naturalist literature from Brazil: adopting hierarchical theories of race, heredity and climate — where authority increasingly rested — entailed an acceptance of Brazil as, at best, struggling to float above the bottom of that hierarchy. It is a double bind that bears some similarities the Portuguese experience, since, as we have seen, works such as *O Barão de Lavos* also draw their authority from theories of degeneracy in ways that denigrate the nation and its past. However, whilst degeneration theory may have marginalised Portugal in relation to its northern neighbours, in Brazil, the racial makeup of the population was such that hierarchies of degeneracy could cast a wider net, identifying large swathes of the population that were thought to pose a problem for the nation's future, and thus lending the theory a redoubled sense of perceived relevancy and urgency that greatly influenced national politics. Adopted and disseminated by the *Escola do Recife* in the 1870s and 1880s, of which many of the Naturalist writers were admirers,[8] Positivist ideas quickly brought racial theories into the mainstream and, as we have seen, Brazil pursued a policy of *branqueamento* in the latter part of the nineteenth century with the explicit aim of producing a whiter, 'viable' future population.[9] Meanwhile, the proponents of racial theory trod an impossibly fine line between staying faithful to the theories they admired and maintaining some hope for the nation's future, often giving rise to contradictory formulations broadly analogous to Caminha's critique in 'Norte e Sul'. Sílvio Romero, for example, the most prominent figure of early racial theory in Brazil and member of the *Escola do Recife*, did so first by stressing the potential benefits of miscegenation, paving the way for the 'whitening' solution, and later of educating the general populace in a more social-constructivist turn,[10] though always with the fraught aim of *overcoming* the supposedly *inherent* inferiority of the Brazilian 'stock'. I will explore some of Romero's ideas in more detail over the course of this chapter, but suffice it here to say that the Naturalist movement in Brazil was underpinned by an energetic intellectual debate surrounding heredity and environment, and that in this debate each was put forward as a form of resistance to the marginalising implications of 'scientific' thought. The importance of heredity was underlined in Darwinian theories of evolution, which explained evolution by the survival and reproduction of those best adapted to the environment,[11] whilst in theories based on those of Jean-Baptiste Lamarck, which remained popular in late nineteenth-century Brazil,[12] the supposedly altering effects of the environment were taken to be the chief drivers of evolutionary change. In the Brazilian texts especially, heredity and environment are important, if problematic, concepts for analysis, explored systematically in the works of Azevedo and Caminha, and with the emphasis often shifting from one to the other to problematise the conclusions of European theorists.

Drawing as it does on this precarious theoretical framework, Naturalist literature in Brazil has not, generally speaking, attracted broad critical acclaim. Whilst Eça de Queirós probably rescued the movement from near oblivion in Portugal, its reception in Brazil varies between cautious praise, scandal and ridicule. Earlier criticism tends to focus on a perceived weakness of style and crude preoccupation with sex, typically compared against Zola's model. As Josué Montello writes, 'as quatro figuras representativas do Naturalismo brasileiro, inclinaram-se pela cópia da realidade, com um ou outro traço de tinta violenta e crua' [the four representative figures of Brazilian Naturalism tended towards copying reality, leaving the odd streak of violent and crude paint].[13] Dorothy Loos writes that style, for the Brazilian Naturalists and in contrast to Zola, was 'unimportant', and that they 'came to concentrate more and more upon what was evil, to stress the sensational, the crude and the lascivious'.[14] Indeed, some critics suggest that lascivious bedroom scenes work as a convenient excuse to avoid contemplation of pressing social issues, most obviously the continuation of slavery.[15] More recent criticism has focused on the role of racial prejudice in the Brazilian Naturalist novel. David Brookshaw identifies Naturalism as notably 'responsible' for the continuing animalisation of black people and circulation of racial stereotypes, and asserts that writers such as Caminha and Azevedo, even if pro-Abolition, were not so 'for any love of the negro', being instead 'products of an expanding urban bourgeoisie, who were committed to the ideals of technology and free skilled labour as instruments of economic development',[16] sentiments enshrined in the Brazilian flag as *ordem e progresso* [order and progress]. For Murray MacNicoll, meanwhile, Azevedo's *O mulato* is too reliant on racial prejudice to work as anything other than 'an exposé of provincial pettiness',[17] as he criticises the author for 'finding it difficult to attain an atmosphere of scientific objectivity in dealing with his native province',[18] again suggesting that departure from Zola's model constitutes a literary weakness. Of all

Brazilian Naturalist works, only Azevedo's *O mulato* and *O cortiço*, Caminha's *Bom Crioulo*, and perhaps Inglês de Sousa's *O missionário*[19] have reached anything close to canonical status. Even then, it is rather symbolic of the lacklustre appreciation of Brazilian Naturalism that the handsome, *azulejo*-tiled house of Azevedo, the star of the movement in Brazil, stands in ruins on the Rua do Sol in São Luís do Maranhão, now earmarked for redevelopment into a car park.[20] There is perhaps a certain irony in this instance of disregard for the cultural heritage of a movement that took heritage itself as one of its central concerns. After Caminha and Azevedo, the names become increasingly obscure, with Júlio Ribeiro's *A carne*, as I mentioned elsewhere, repeatedly described as the worst book in the history of Brazilian literature.[21]

There have, nonetheless, been attempts by critics to rescue Caminha and Azevedo from scholarly disregard, and I will consider these in this chapter as I turn, once more, to the representation of kinship to arrive at a different, less straight(forward) understanding of these texts. Most notably, Antônio Cândido's now classic essay, 'De Cortiço a Cortiço' [From Slum to Slum], praises Azevedo's adaptation of Zola's model to represent Brazilian social realities, which, he argues, results in a greater reliance on allegory to reflect a society in which social classes were still in the process of being spatially segregated.[22] As with the Portuguese authors, I will be paying close attention to the Brazilian Naturalists' use of allegory, by no means limited to *O cortiço*, as well as to the process of adaptation and 'copying' of an imported model, looking not at how 'successfully' these authors follow Zola's model, but at how they deal with the problems of its inadequacy in Brazil. This inadequacy was, after all, widely discussed at the time: Araripe Júnior went as far as to assert that Naturalism could not succeed in Brazil because of the country's detrimental ('entorpecente') climate that supposedly impeded careful study,[23] reminiscent of Eça's complaints about the heat and ever-circling flies while writing *A relíquia* in Portugal.[24]

For those familiar with conceptual problems in Brazilian culture, the anecdote of 'Brasil — Sul', and indeed the paradoxical adoption of degeneration theory in a supposedly 'degenerate' Brazil, will appear as symptomatic of a wider phenomenon in which European ideas of questionable relevancy are copied and imported, a process that Roberto Schwarz identifies compellingly as 'misplaced ideas', or *ideias fora de lugar*.[25] For Schwarz, there is an inescapable 'caráter imitativo' [imitative character] to Brazilian cultural life, a 'contradição entre a realidade nacional e o prestígio ideológico dos países que nos servem de modelo' [contradiction between the national reality and the ideological prestige of the countries that serve as our model].[26] Thus in the nineteenth century, Liberalism circulated amongst an elite whose wealth, literacy and social position nevertheless derived primarily from slavery and, after its abolition in 1888, a continuing culture of 'favour' and dependency, leading to an inescapable antagonism at the level of ideas.[27] In this sense, Brazilian Naturalism, drawing as it does heavily on theories of degeneracy that marginalised Brazil itself, rehearses the dilemma of misplaced ideas particularly keenly.

However, arguably the most surprising aspects of these texts, as Cândido's article demonstrates, come into view when focusing precisely on the problematic process of cultural 'importation'. As Schwarz, Cândido's pupil, goes on to argue, if cultural 'borrowing' in Brazil is taken to be antithetical to 'authentic' national cultural production, it can be overcome neither by 'subtracting' the imported element from the whole nor by conducting a facile philosophical deconstruction of the concept of copy.[28] Instead, any 'originality' in Brazilian cultural production is to be found in the potentially transgressive, supplementary space that opens up in the process of reiteration. This idea is also developed by Silviano Santiago who, as we have seen, reads Eça's *O primo Basílio* not just as a 'copy' of *Madame Bovary*, of which it was accused at the time, but as a reflection on the prior work and transgression of the model, working to complement Flaubert's novel.[29] For Santiago, this corruption of the model is no less than the organising principle of Lusophone literatures of the time:

> Talvez pudéssemos aqui generalizar e propor como ponto de partida para o nosso raciocínio a conclusão a que esperamos chegar. Tanto em Portugal, quanto no Brasil, no século XIX, a riqueza e o interesse da literatura não vem tanto de uma originalidade do modelo, do arcabouço abstrato ou dramático do romance ou do poema, mas da transgressão que se cria a partir de um novo uso do modelo pedido de empréstimo à cultura dominante. Assim, a obra de arte se organiza a partir de uma meditação silenciosa e traiçoeira por parte do artista que surpreende o original nas suas limitações.[30]

> [Perhaps we could generalise here and propose, as a departure point for our train of thought, the conclusion that we hope to reach. In Portugal, as in Brazil in the nineteenth century, the richness and interest of literature does not owe itself to any kind of original model, any abstract or dramatic sketch of a novel or poem, but to the transgression that arises from the new use of a model borrowed from the dominant culture. As such, the work of art organises itself as a silent and treacherous meditation by the artist, who surprises the original in its limitations.]

In this view, reading Brazilian texts vis-à-vis their European models becomes necessary to their understanding, unveiling the space in which the writer's meditation is compelled to reside. If, in other words, ideas are generally misplaced in Brazil, there is yet scope for these ideas to be altered and made one's own, consciously or otherwise.

Naturalism, therefore, which presents the Brazilian writer with a particularly unpalatable set of misplaced ideas, emerges as a conspicuous candidate for a reading of what Santiago terms the 'entre-lugar' [space in between] of Latin American discourse.[31] Indeed, its cultural loans were not restricted to European theories of race, sex and criminality: the Brazilian Naturalists drew extensively on fictional texts by their most admired writers, in particular Zola, Flaubert and Eça de Queirós. The latter especially was vexed that his works were adapted to stage without his permission in Brazil,[32] and many of his novels were plagiarised, retold and adapted, even though, as I will argue, he himself drew on the work of Azevedo. As Vieira asserts, '[o]s brasileiros achavam que tudo o que fosse escrito em português podia ser reproduzido por eles' [the Brazilians thought that they could reproduce everything written in Portuguese]; the problem of plagiarism was deemed so grave that a legal agreement was eventually signed between Portugal and Brazil, protecting literary and artistic production from each country, in September 1889.[33] Its impact is debatable: both *O mulato* (1881) and Caminha's *A normalista* (1893) are, to a similar extent, 'copies' of *O crime do Padre Amaro*, suggesting a continuum here between appropriation and plagiarism, a process acquiring legal and financial implications, and reflecting the lucrative state of the Lusophone Naturalist literary market. Moreover, and importantly for this study, the engagement — often strategic, as we shall see — with Portuguese texts, and the degree of influence that Brazilian authors themselves had on their Portuguese counterparts, suggests a dialogical, transatlantic exchange of ideas that Eurocentric allegations of plagiarism and 'copying' airbrush and oversimplify. This exchange is visible not only in the obvious similarities in plot between novels such as *Lavos* and *Bom Crioulo*, but in the deployment of similar techniques, such as allegory and Greek tragedy, to supplement and problematise the 'scientific' method. *A normalista* in particular warrants further discussion here, as it neatly exemplifies the Brazilian Naturalists' productive engagement with Portuguese texts, often surprising the reader with what might be termed, to misquote Silviano Santiago, *um naturalismo nos trópicos*.

*A normalista*, Caminha's first novel, broadly follows the plot structure of *O crime do Padre Amaro*, Eça's tale of abuse in the Catholic Church, in which Amélia is seduced, impregnated and finally abandoned by her priest and confessor, Amaro, who then separates her from her baby, precipitating her death. In Caminha's 'version', Maria do Carmo is a vulnerable, orphaned schoolgirl brought up in the care of her godfather, João da Mata, in Fortaleza, Ceará. Taking advantage of his patriarchal position in a manner similar to Amaro, he seduces his goddaughter, who becomes pregnant and is sent into hiding in the house of an old cashew-fruit seller, the *velha dos cajus*. Despite her reputation for growing sweet, ripe fruit, she is a careless midwife and allows the baby to fall to the floor at birth. The heartless João da Mata is relieved at the baby's death, while Maria do Carmo's initial distress appears to give way to indifference as she is found, years later, happily married to a police sergeant, imagining before her 'um futuro largo, imensamente luminoso, como um grande mar tranquilo e dormente' [a long and bright future, like a calm, sleeping sea].[34] As we shall see, this final plot development is significant insofar as it constitutes a departure from *O crime*. The influence of Eça, in fact, readily becomes a dialogue analogous to that which Eça himself performs with *Madame Bovary* in *O primo Basílio*. Thus one remarkable passage has Maria do Carmo read a copy of *Basílio* that she borrows from her friend Lídia Campelo:

> — Acabei *O primo Basílio*!
> — Que tal?
> — Magnífico, sublime! Olha, vem cá... E dando o braço à outra dirigiu-se para o banheiro [...].
>  Uma vez ali, sentadas ambas num caixote que fora de sabão, única mobília do banheiro, Maria sacou fora *O primo Basílio*, cuidadosamente embrulhado numa folha da Província. Queria que a Lídia explicasse uma passagem muito difusa, quase impenetrável à sua inteligência.
> — É isto, menina, que eu não pude compreender bem. E, abrindo o livro,

leu: ...e ele (Basílio) quis-lhe ensinar então a verdadeira maneira de beber champanha. Talvez ela não soubesse! — Como é? perguntou Luísa tomando o copo. — Não é com o copo! Horror! Ninguém que se preza bebe champanha por um copo. O copo é bom para o Colares... Tomou um gole de champanha e num beijo passou-o para a boca dela, Luísa riu..., etc., etc...

— Como explicas tu isso?

— Tola! fez a Campelinho. Uma coisa tão simples... Toma-se um gole de champanha ou de outro qualquer líquido, junta-se boca a boca assim... E juntou a ação às palavras.

— ...e pronto! bebe-se pela boca um do outro. Tão simples...

— E que prazer há nisso?

— Sei lá, menina! tornou a outra com um gesto de nojo, cuspindo. Pode lá haver gosto... Depois, as duas curvadas sobre o livro, unidas, coxa a coxa, braço a braço, passaram à sensação nova. Lídia apressou-se em dizer que as mulheres do mundo é que sabem essas coisas... Quanto a ela não conhecia outras sensações além dos beijos na boca, às escondidas, fora os abracinhos fortes e demorados, peito a peito, isto mesmo com pessoa do coração... Contou então que o seu primeiro namorado, um estudante do Liceu, um fedelho, tentara certa vez... Concluiu baixinho ao ouvido de Maria, com receio de que alguém as estivesse observando.

— E consentiste?

— Qual! Dei-lhe com um não na cara, e o tolo nunca mais me fez festa.[35]

['I finished *Cousin Basílio!*'

'How was it?'

'Magnificent, sublime! Look, come here...' And offering her arm to her friend, she took her to the bathroom.

Once there, sitting on an old soap box, the only piece of furniture in the room, Maria took out her copy of *Cousin Basílio*, carefully wrapped in a sheet from *The Province*. She wanted Lídia to explain to her a very diffuse paragraph, difficult for her mind to grasp.

'This is the part I couldn't understand properly.' And, opening the book, she read out: '... and he (Basílio) wanted to teach her the proper way to drink champagne. Perhaps she didn't know! "What's it like?" asked Luísa, holding her glass. "You don't use a glass! How dreadful! No one with any self-respect drinks champagne from a glass. A glass is for the likes of Colares..." He took a sip of champagne and, kissing her, passed it from his mouth to hers, Luísa laughed, etc., etc...'

'How do you explain that?'

'You silly girl!' said Campelinho. 'Such a simple thing... You take a sip of champagne or any other drink, put your mouths together like this...' and she gave a demonstration.

'And that's it! You drink from the other's mouth. So easy...'

'And what pleasure is there in that?'

'What should I know!' replied the other with a gesture of disgust, spitting out the drink. 'It can't be very pleasant...' Then the two of them, leaning over the book together, their hips and arms touching, moved on to the 'new sensation'. Lídia was quick to say that the women of the world know all about those things... As for her, she hadn't heard of anything other than kisses on the mouth, given in secret, and of course long and tight embraces, chests held

together, with someone you love... Then she spoke about her first sweetheart,
a cheeky boy from school who had once wanted to try.
'And did you let him?'
'What? I said no to his face, and the silly boy never touched me again.']

Caminha recreates, in this passage, the titillating relationship between Luísa and
Leopoldina in *Basílio* that we saw in the previous chapter. The language describing
their interaction is familiarly Queirosian in its flirtatious use of repetition, leading
to suggestive phrases such as 'coxa a coxa, braço a braço'. Their acting-out of the
champagne kiss, taught to Luísa by her cousin during an amorous afternoon at their
love nest, and here abandoned by the narrator in ellipses and etceteras, underscores
the didactic and mimetic potential of *Basílio* and suggests that the much-commented
'sensação nova' will soon follow in the girls' education.[36] The atmosphere is made
to appear correspondingly clandestine; the two friends sit hunched in a cramped
bathroom and confidences are uttered discreetly.

Regina Zilberman, having identified this passage as a moment of dialogue with
Eça, finds in it little significance other than its prominence as 'o depoimento mais
sincero da rendição dos intelectuais brasileiros ao charme do ficcionista nascido em
Portugal' [the sincerest declaration of Brazilian intellectuals' rendition to the charm
of the Portuguese novelist].[37] For Carlos Bezerra, meanwhile, the passage exposes
an ambivalence, on the part of the author, towards Eça's novels, 'entre censura
e admiração' [between reproach and admiration].[38] However, if we observe the
textual interaction with Eça's work closely, *A normalista* emerges as a commentary
on Naturalism and its reception in Brazil. Whilst Luísa, in *Basílio*, acts out the
Romantic novels she reads, most notably those of Walter Scott in a thinly veiled
criticism of the vacuous ideals of Romanticism, Maria do Carmo takes precisely *O
primo Basílio* as her formative model, the very work that presents itself as an antidote
to 'delusional' Romantic thought.[39] We might interpret this not as an attack on
*Basílio* per se, or indeed as praise, but as an illustration of the way in which, in
Brazil at least and perhaps in Portugal, the transformative potential of Naturalism
misfires, doing no more than Romanticism, in the end, to effect social change.
Hence, in *A normalista*, we see the alteration of the tragic ending of *O crime*, such
that Maria do Carmo is married, apparently happily but evidently for convenience,
and with the chilling metaphor of the future as a stupefying 'mar dormente' — an
ending more easily aligned with the final moonrise and *vencidismo* of *Os Maias*
than the more dramatic, revolutionary spirit of Eça's early novels. Whilst Amélia
in *O crime* dies after forced separation from her baby, and Luísa in *Basílio* suffers
a gruesome death, Maria do Carmo recovers and ultimately forgets the abuse to
which she is subject throughout the novel, just as Ceará forgets her supposedly
scandalous pregnancy, much-publicised in the local press. Caminha transposes the
intransigence and hypocrisy of the Catholic Church in *O crime* to bourgeois *cearense*
society. At the same time, he carefully exposes the paradox of misplaced ideas with
his apparent mistrust of the cultural relevance of the movement within which he
himself writes. Thus one of the novel's most comic lines is uttered in earnest by
the municipal judge who, hoping that the president of Ceará will recover from

a bout of yellow fever, asserts, '[a] ciência faz milagres' [science works miracles]. The 'scientific' method that Eça uses to attack the Church in *O crime* becomes, in Caminha's novel, oxymoronically miraculous, assimilated into the same provincial religiosity that it was designed to counteract. By reading *A normalista* in light of its dialogue with cultural loans, then, rather than merely its dependency on them, we can determine that its author was highly creative in his 'copy' of *O crime do Padre Amaro*, addressing cultural problems relevant, if not necessarily unique to Brazil, and complementing the 'original' work — itself widely accused of being a 'copy'[40] — from the margins of Western culture. In the readings that follow, I will be paying close attention to intertextuality and the often 'corrupting', transgressive potential of cultural dependency with which the authors rework notions of kinship in Brazil, writing against nature and collaborating, sometimes treacherously, with the Portuguese Naturalists in the process.

The discussion of *O primo Basílio* in Caminha's *A normalista* also goes some way towards illustrating the immense popularity of Naturalist literature in Brazil at the time, despite its relative obscurity today. Aderbal de Carvalho wrote in 1894 that *Basílio* arrived in Brazil 'como uma verdadeira bomba de dinamite' [like a bombshell].[41] Meanwhile, *O mulato*, often regarded as the first Brazilian Naturalist novel,[42] was an unprecedented success, selling two thousand copies in São Luís alone within a few days of its publication,[43] an exceptional number for a relatively small city with a low literacy rate. In 1919, Domingos Barbosa wrote that no other book had been so successful in Brazil, and still in 1941, Álvaro Lins wrote that the success of *O mulato* had 'rarely been repeated in Brazilian letters'.[44] As usual, the relationship between popularity and canonicity is a complex one, and the financial success of many Brazilian Naturalist novels did little to assure their immortality; indeed, often the opposite was true, and critical work consistently reproduces a characterisation of Azevedo's work into two strands, his 'serious' novels, including *O cortiço*, *Casa de pensão*, *O coruja* and *O mulato*, and what Loos describes as his 'pulp productions', which he allegedly wrote hurriedly for money, including *Filomena Borges* and *O homem* (both of which I will nevertheless be referring to in this chapter).[45] Lúcia Miguel Pereira went as far to describe these 'lesser' novels by Azevedo as 'unreadable'.[46] Meanwhile, strong book sales did not necessarily indicate straightforward popular approval. When Maria do Carmo reads *Basílio* in *A normalista*, despite being fixated by it, she criticises it for being 'escabroso demais' [too scabrous]. Contemporaneous critics widely condemned Naturalism for its supposed 'immorality' and readiness to depict sex scenes.[47] As Loos puts it, 'the purported obscenity of a work was an assurance of its success with the public'.[48] Thus the frenzied reception of Naturalism in Brazil, encompassing wonderment, excitement, scandal and offence, reflects a movement that fulfilled the desires of readers as much as it did shock them, that attracted and repelled them with the characteristic contradictions of *fin-de-siècle* thought. As we negotiate questions of popularity and canonicity, then, Naturalism in Brazil emerges as a movement that at once captured, reproduced and challenged the status quo, in line with Marx and Engels's formulation of the *principle of contradiction* that I referred to in the

Introduction,[49] laid bare too in the narrative movements of *O Barão de Lavos*. These contradictory but inseparable forces will continue to inform my analysis in these two chapters.

The theme of kinship has not, to my knowledge, been explored in any depth in the work of Aluísio Azevedo, to which I now turn in this chapter.[50] However, I believe it is a particularly productive one, not least since his novels often revolve around questions of incest and, to a lesser extent, queer desire. Whilst the latter, if not the former, has attracted attention from critics, particularly surrounding the exoticised lesbian sex scene in *O cortiço*, it has not been brought far beyond the bounds of degeneration theory: as we saw in the Introduction, Cândido describes this and other such episodes across Lusophone literature as an 'ato desnatural' [unnatural act] and thus a 'degradação do enfoque "natural" de Zola' [degradation of Zola's 'natural' focus].[51] Building on my previous readings, I would like to problematise the notion of the 'natural' in these works, relating kinship trouble to the author's distortion of Naturalism through allegory, tragedy and myth. In so doing, I aim to show how Azevedo's *naturalismo nos trópicos* engages closely with the analytical categories that buttressed the bourgeois identity of the *fin de siècle*, adapting its discourse to reimagine notions of family, race and degeneracy in Brazil.

I will begin with *O mulato*, a novel that has received little critical attention in recent decades, perhaps best known as a literary endorsement of abolition, miscegenation and *branqueamento*.[52] A remarkable aspect of this novel has not been adequately explored: the incestuous nature of the central, interracial relationship and its function within an Oedipal story strikingly similar to that of *Os Maias*, published some eight years later.[53] Indeed, considering the latter novel, *O mulato* arguably initiates a transatlantic dialogue that exemplifies the Lusophone Naturalists' willingness to exchange literary ideas, often surrounding the legacy of colonialism. A comparison of the two novels will thus prove productive, I hope, in eliciting their cultural specificities and formal similarities. Both *O mulato* and *Os Maias* deploy the story of Oedipus to rethink the foundations of society, but in revealingly different ways. I then move through Azevedo's work chronologically to *Casa de pensão*, arguing that the author becomes increasingly interested in the transformative power of the environment over heritage, which corresponds, on the plane of kinship, to a replacement of blood ties with bonds of economic convenience, allegorising the family in the fashion of Eça and Botelho, and implicating similar social concerns. If, as Cândido argues, *O cortiço* functions as an allegory of a diverse but divided Brazil, kinship will be seen to dissolve into the picture, with the terminology of relationality assimilated into a fast-changing social order, characterised by free-market capitalism and the patriarchal hangover of slavery and colonialism.

## Oedipus in Brazil: Aluísio Azevedo's *O mulato*

Azevedo's second novel was published in 1881 when the author had yet to turn twenty-five, and was soon recognised as marking the beginning of the Naturalist movement in Brazil.[54] *O mulato* resonates clearly with the dilemma contained in the words 'Brasil — Sul', taking as its focus the steamy northern province of Maranhão, Azevedo's birthplace, and portraying it in a characteristically unflattering, at times disdainful Naturalist light. The opening chapter, as a case in point, depicts the stifling climate of São Luís, 'entorpecida pelo calor' [deadened by the heat] and host to an 'ar fúnubre' [funereal air], where 'só os pretos' [only the blacks] appear able to resist the hostile environment,[55] a portrait coloured with the lens of Darwinism. Several critics suggest the novel's 'extremely combative spirit'[56] in part reflects the author's personal grudge against his native Maranhão, evidenced by characters modelled 'with little doubt' on contemporary figures of *Maranhense* high society.[57] As a 'copy' of *O crime do Padre Amaro*, *O mulato* transports the pettiness of Leiria to the streets of São Luís do Maranhão. The similarities in plot to *O crime* are significant, seen primarily in the pivotal role played by a corrupt Catholic Church, but they are insufficient in themselves as an explanation for the novel's structure.[58] Ana Rosa, daughter of the businessman Manuel Pescada, is an innocent local beauty who falls in love with her long-lost cousin, the highly educated mulatto, Raimundo. Disapproving of miscegenation and hoping to secure and expand his business interests, Manuel wishes for his daughter to marry his sly Portuguese employee, Dias, refusing Raimundo's request for his cousin's hand in marriage. The two plan to elope but, manipulated by the villainous Cônego Diogo [Canon Diogo], Ana Rosa confesses that she is carrying Raimundo's child, whilst Dias and the canon, calculating the strength of their relationship, conspire to foil their plot to escape. Raimundo is shot in the street by Dias, while Ana Rosa miscarries upon seeing his dead body paraded through the city. Years later, however, she is found apparently happily married to Dias in a clear victory for the old, racist institutions represented by Manuel and Cônego Diogo. Maranhão, '[g]eographically isolated' and historically 'the periphery of colonial Brazil',[59] remains, at the end of the novel, and like Leiria in *O crime*, stubbornly immune to the social changes embodied in the voice of the Naturalist narrator.

However, as I have already indicated, *O mulato* bears as many similarities to Eça's *Os Maias* (1888) as it does to *O crime*, although this comparison has not, to my knowledge, been explored by critics. It is of course impossible that Azevedo drew on *Os Maias*, written and published several years later, although it is quite possible, if perhaps less orthodox, to suggest that Eça drew on *O mulato*, given, as we have seen, that he followed Brazilian literary production closely, including where writers 'plagiarised' his work. The novel begins with Raimundo's arrival in São Luís, reminiscent of Carlos's arrival in Lisbon in the opening chapters of *Os Maias*. Raimundo, like Carlos, is educated in Coimbra, where he learns modern ideas, graduating in law. He is well-travelled and cosmopolitan, in stark contrast to his religious and often superstitious compatriots. Azevedo's characterisation of Raimundo, Manuel and Cônego Diogo is archetypal, throwing their ideological differences into relief:

> Por esse tempo aqueles três surgiam na rua, formando cada qual mais vivo contraste com os outros: Manuel no seu tipo pesado e chato de negociante, calças de brim e paletó de alpaca; o cônego imponente na sua batina lustrosa, aristocrata, mostrando as meias de seda escarlate e o pé mimoso, apertadinho no sapato de polimento; Raimundo, todo europeu, elegante, com uma roupa de casimira leve, adequada ao clima do Maranhão, escandalizando o bairro comercial com o seu chapéu-de-sol coberto de linho claro e forrado de verde pela parte de dentro. Formavam, dizia este último, chasqueando, sem tirar o charuto da boca, uma respeitável trindade filosófica, na qual, ali, o Sr. Cônego representava a teologia, o Sr. Manuel a metafísica, e ele, Raimundo, a filosofia positiva, o que, aplicado à política, traduzia-se na prodigiosa aliança dos três governos o do papado, o monárquico e o republicano! (p. 109)

> [Around then the three of them appeared in the street, each one striking a contrast with the others: Manuel, like the stiff businessman he was, wore cotton trousers and an alpaca jacket; Canon Diogo, imposing in his cassock, lustrous and aristocratic, revealing his scarlet silk stockings and delicate feet, which fitted snugly into his polished leather shoes; Raimundo, as European as they came, elegant in his light cashmere shirt, well suited to the climate of Maranhão, scandalised the neighbourhood with his bright linen sunhat lined in green. They formed, joked the latter with a cigar in his mouth, a respectable philosophical trinity, in which Canon Diogo represented theology, Manuel metaphysics, and he, Raimundo, Positivist philosophy which, applied to politics, amounted to the prodigious alliance of the three bodies of governance, the papal, the monarchical and the republican!]

Raimundo, then, like Carlos, is educated with ideas greatly at odds with his new environment — *fora do lugar*, perhaps? — and the stage is set for a clash of ideologies as well as personalities. There is already a hint of mockery in the narrator's description of Raimundo as 'todo europeu', and the position of the narrator will prove critical as Raimuindo attempts to reconcile his European ideas with his family history in Maranhão. Raimundo, consciously at least, comes to the province to sell his ancestral properties with hopes of establishing himself later in Rio de Janeiro. In an extended 'flashback' chapter detailing his family history, however, again similar to the second chapter of *Os Maias*, we then learn that he is the son of José da Silva — Manuel Pescada's brother — and, unbeknown to him and Ana Rosa, his slave and lover, Domingas. José da Silva, whose wealth derives from the illegal slave trade, is married to the cruel Dona Quitéria, who achieves infamy for lashing her slaves in brutal attacks of sadism. She despises her husband's affection for Raimundo, conceived before their marriage, leading her to burn Domingas in an act of genital mutilation. The young Raimundo watches his mother's torture and subsequent descent into madness before being despatched from the family *quinta* of São Brás to live with Manuel Pescada in São Luís. Ana Rosa is born and the two are briefly brought up as siblings, Raimundo being treated as a son by Manuel's wife Mariana, who deeply regrets not marrying for love. Meanwhile, José da Silva discovers that the young Cônego Diogo is having an affair with his wife, Dona Quitéria, whom he strangles to death. Diogo then fatally shoots José in revenge, using his influential position to orchestrate a cover-up. Raimundo is sent to be educated in Lisbon and Coimbra, unaware of his origins and afterwards, like Carlos da Maia, travels Europe saturated with Positivist ideas. When he returns to his ancestral home in São Luís, past turmoils apparently forgotten, he and his cousin who, like Carlos and Maria Eduarda, once shared a cradle in infancy, fall passionately in love with each other as Raimundo compulsively tries to discover his heritage. Finally learning of his maternal ancestry through Manuel Pescada after being refused Ana Rosa's hand in marriage, Raimundo comes close to fathoming Cônego Diogo's dark secrets, offering the reader a fleeting promise of a just resolution to events. However, the canon skilfully dispels Raimundo's doubts about his father's death and history is set to repeat itself: Diogo has Raimundo murdered like his father before him, securing the public interpretation of the death as a suicide, and the social order, briefly perturbed by Raimundo's reappearance in São Luís, returns to its former state.

The similarities with *Os Maias* are compelling, seen principally in the authors' deployment of an Oedipal framework disrupted in the youngest generation such that the identity of the mother is repressed, her name erased from the family past.[60] The repressed mother then returns problematically in the form of a long-lost sister — biologically so in *Os Maias*, and functionally so in *O mulato*. Thus Ana Rosa and Raimundo are described as 'companheiros de berço, criados juntos, *que nem irmãos*' [cradle companions, brought up *closer than brother and sister*] (p. 101, emphasis added), and soon after meeting each other as adults, Ana Rosa comments to Raimundo that she laments not having a brother. To Raimundo, meanwhile, Ana Rosa figures as 'uma irmã, de quem ele estivera ausente desde a infância' [a sister from whom he had been separated since childhood] (p. 105). Both sets of 'siblings' in *O mulato* and *Os Maias* share a cradle in infancy and begin sexual relations in adulthood, a common detail too remarkable to miss, anticipating the Freudian schema in which sexual desires in adulthood are modelled on experiences of intimacy as a child, the mother's image typically becoming the unconscious object of desire for a grown boy.

It is in this sense that Ana Rosa's passive temperament can be read in a more productive light than one which reduces it to evidence of misogyny on the part of the author. This is the conclusion of Elizabeth Marchant, who argues that whilst Azevedo seeks to represent race as a social construction in *O mulato*, he naturalises gender such that Ana Rosa's character is 'more in keeping with nineteenth-century scientific ideas about femaleness' than Raimundo's is with contemporary ideas about race.[61] Whilst I do not mean to dispute such accusations of misogyny, I do propose that Ana Rosa's passivity has broader structural repercussions within the novel, endowing her with a servile attitude that aligns her closely with Raimundo's slave-mother Domingas, and thus approximating her to Raimundo's unconscious image of the mother. The alignment is hardly subtle: when Ana Rosa realises she is in love with Raimundo, she wishes to 'tornar-se passiva, servi-lo como uma escrava amorosa, dócil, fraca' [become passive, serve him like a slave, loving, docile and weak] (p. 124). Even before meeting him, she imagines herself marrying a man 'a quem ela pudesse amar abertamente como amante e obedecer em segredo como escrava' [whom she might love openly as a lover and obey in secret as a slave] (p. 26).

In a crisis of passion, she exclaims to her cousin, 'É uma escrava que chora a teus pés!' [A slave weeps at your feet!] (p. 265). Losing her mother at a young age, 'justamente quando mais precisava do amparo maternal' [just when she most needed maternal support] (p. 21), Ana Rosa is greatly influenced by her wet nurse or *mãe-pretinha*, Mônica, such that she herself has a slave as a model for identification — a slave who, having bought her own freedom, continues to serve the family regardless. Raimundo, meanwhile, is clearly titillated by his cousin's submissive and servile tendencies. Imagining their happy marriage together, he concludes a lengthy interior monologue with the words, '[a]lém de que, com um filho nas entranhas, ela lhe obedeceria como escrava!...' [besides, with a child in her belly, she would obey him like a slave!] (p. 312). Therefore, whilst Azevedo may make use of misogynistic tropes, these are used productively to rework the (European) Oedipal matrix for the Brazilian context, where Raimundo is fatefully attracted to his banished slave-mother, functionally reincarnated in the figure of his cousin-sister. In *Os Maias*, Carlos seeks to return to the repressed mother who is rejected for her ancestral links to the slave trade; in *O mulato*, the slave herself is banished from the family home (principally by Quitéria), and it is the image of slavery that is then unwittingly sought by her son. Thus although in *O mulato*, the question of slavery is more central, both novelists cast it early on as a historic mistake that continues to have repercussions in the present, deploying a (tragic) Oedipal motif to explore its effects. This compulsive return to the relations and economics of the past, by a self-described Positivist mulatto who is both victim of racism and beneficiary of the spoils of the illegal slave trade, will be of central importance in my subsequent understanding of the text.

Azevedo develops the Oedipal framework in *O mulato* particularly clearly, including, like the Portuguese Naturalists, references to classical texts. Cônego Diogo, who regularly utters obscure Latin phrases as a means to convey authority, is the figure who consistently works to bury kinship trouble in the past, offering Ana Rosa a 'remédio' [treatment] for the abortion of her mulatto baby, advising Manuel against recognising Raimundo as his nephew, suppressing knowledge of José da Silva's murder of his adulterous wife, and plotting the assassination of Raimundo to avoid any probing into that of his father. He succeeds in all these attempts whilst maintaining the image of a saintly and humble servant, terms in which his fellow *maranhenses* often describe him. 'É um santo homem!' [He's a saintly man!]; 'Um santo! Um verdadeiro santo!' [A saint! A true saint!] (p. 60). On two occasions, to dodge a response when asked a difficult question, Diogo remarks, '*Davus sum non Aedipus!*' (pp. 182, 292). This line is taken from Terence's *Andria*,[62] uttered by Davus in an attempt to dodge an uncomfortable question. In the classical play, Davus is the slave trickster whose private schemes, like those of Diogo, remain unheeded by the other characters. He references Oedipus's encounter with the Sphinx to define his opposite rhetorical role: if Oedipus is the solver of riddles and, ultimately if tragically, unearths kinship trouble from the past, Davus works in the other direction, obscuring this past from view. These words, in *O mulato*, become Diogo's mantra, *raison d'être* and structural function within the novel as he strives to prevent the social order from confronting the contradictions that Oedipus, or Raimundo, both contains and threatens to reveal.

Raimundo, indeed, is drawn inexorably towards the void in his knowledge of the past that Cônego Diogo artfully constructs over the decades. First and foremost, it is of great structural importance in *O mulato* that Raimundo is not consistently recognised as mixed race, meaning he can remain unaware of his ancestral past. Marchant argues that '[h]is relative whiteness may be read as a means to garner the sympathy of a white reading audience' and as an affirmation of the supposed virtues of *branqueamento*.[63] Again, whilst I do not mean to dispute this, it is surely more significant for its role in sustaining a missing page in Raimundo's memory of the past, a page he seeks to recover over the course of the novel. Raimundo therefore asks himself who his mother is at five different points, and uncertainties surrounding his heritage haunt him from the moment in the narration that he develops free indirect discourse; namely when, as a child in Lisbon, he receives a letter from Mariana, Manuel's wife:

> as suas reminiscências não iam além da casa do tio; no entanto, queria parecer-lhe que a sua verdadeira mãe não era aquela senhora, aquela vinha a ser sua tia, porque era a mulher de seu tio Manuel; e até, se lhe não falhava a memória, por mais de uma vez ouvira dela própria falar na outra, na sua verdadeira mãe... Mas quem seria a outra? Como se chamava?... Nunca lho disseram!... (p. 69)

> [his memories did not extend beyond his uncle's house; however, he was inclined to think that woman was not his real mother, she was his aunt, because she was Uncle Manuel's wife; and he even thought, if his memory served him correctly, that he'd heard her talking more than once about the other woman, his real mother... But who might she be? What was her name?... They had never told him!]

The lengthy sentence, with its incomplete clauses suggesting erratic thought, followed by repeated ellipses and questions, gestures towards the lacuna in Raimundo's self-knowledge that propels, on some level, his future journey of discovery in Maranhão. Thus although he repeatedly affirms that his sole desire there is to 'liquidar os meus negócios e pôr-me ao fresco!' [liquidate my capital and be on my way!] (p. 52), his travels are marked from the beginning by a desire to (re)discover his heritage. His 'maior empenho' [greatest endeavour] when travelling to inspect his properties with Manuel is to visit the most worthless financially, his ruined birthplace of São Brás, in the hope of learning something of his ancestry; when Manuel refuses to go there first, he agrees, but 'praguejando entre dentes contrariado e cheio de tédio: Que grandíssima estopada! O diabo da tal fazenda do inferno parecia fugir diante deles!...' [cursing between his teeth, cross and irritated: what a dreadful bore! The damned plantation seemed to vanish before their eyes!] (p. 193). This mirage-like figuration of São Brás metaphorises that same void in Raimundo's consciousness that spurs his voyage through his ancestral past, a journey that he refuses to acknowledge as important with corresponding insistency. Travelling to Maranhão, in another passage of free indirect discourse, he will only admit to economic concerns as the motive for his travels:

Raimundo perdia-se em conjeturas e, malgrado o seu desprendimento pelo passado, sentia alguma coisa atraí-lo irresistivelmente para a pátria. Quem sabia se aí não descobriria a ponta do enigma?... Ele, que sempre vivera órfão de afeições legítimas e duradouras, como então seria feliz!... Ah, se chegasse a saber quem era sua mãe, perdoar-lhe-ia tudo, tudo!

O quinhão de ternura, que a ela pertencia, estava intacto no coração do filho. Era preciso entregá-lo a alguém! Era preciso desvendar as circunstâncias que determinaram o seu nascimento!

Mas, no fim de contas, refletia Raimundo, em um retrocesso natural de impressões, que diabo tinha ele com tudo isso, se até aí, na ignorância desses fatos, vivera estimado e feliz!... Não foi decerto para semelhante coisa que viera à província! Por conseguinte, era liquidar os seus negócios, vender os seus bens e por aqui é o caminho! O Rio de Janeiro lá estava a sua espera!

Abriria, ao chegar lá, o seu escritório, trabalharia, e, ao lado da mulher com quem casasse e dos filhos que viesse a ter, nem sequer havia de lembrar-se do passado!

Sim, que mais poderia desejar melhor?... Concluíra os estudos, viajara muito, tinha saúde, possuía alguns bens de fortuna. Era caminhar pra frente e deixar em paz o tal passado! O passado, passado! Ora adeus! (pp. 51–52)

[Raimundo lost himself in conjecture, and despite his detachment from the past, he felt something luring him irresistibly towards his homeland. Who was to say whether he wouldn't reach the crux of the enigma there?... He, who had always been an orphan when it came to lasting and legitimate affection — how happy he would be!... Ah, if only he knew who his mother was, he would forgive her everything, everything!

The portion of tenderness owed to her was intact in her son's heart. He had to give it to someone! He had to find out the circumstances leading to his birth!

And yet, in the end, reflected Raimundo in a natural reversal of thought, what the devil did he have to do with it all if he had lived happily, until now, in ignorance of the facts!... It certainly wasn't why he had come back to the province! It was a case of liquidating his capital, selling his possessions and he'd be on his way! Rio de Janeiro was there, waiting for him!

When he got there he would open his office, work, with his future wife and two children at his side, he wouldn't even remember his past!

Yes, what more could he want?... He had finished his studies, travelled widely, was in good health, had a small fortune... He had to keep moving forward and leave the past in peace! The past, the past! Goodbye to it!]

The promising future that Raimundo sees for himself is similar to that envisaged for Carlos da Maia by his friends and family. However, as with Carlos, there are already ominous signs for what lies ahead. The past is a continuing source of fascination and mystery, shrouded in vagueness: 'sentia alguma coisa atraí-lo irresistivelmente para a pátria' is a conspicuously superstitious sentiment for a man who laughs derisively at the concept of superstition just weeks later, when Maria Bárbara, Ana Rosa's uncompromisingly racist grandmother, claims her granddaughter is victim of a curse (p. 104). (I will return later to the significance in *O mulato* of superstition and myth, which work as a disruptive counterpoint to Raimundo's Positivist thought.) Mystery and conjecture then produce excitement and resolve; '[e]ra preciso entregá-lo a algúem! Era preciso desvendar [...]!' However, despite Raimundo's keen interest in his past, he vehemently denies any such interest, again repeating his mantra that 'era liquidar os seus negócios [...] e por aqui é o caminho!'. This dubious denial then becomes arrogance and flippancy: 'o tal passado! O passado, passado! Ora adeus!', these words signalling precisely the imminent return of the repressed. Two contradictory forces thus govern Raimundo's journey: the compulsion to return to his ancestral past, and his denial of any interest in doing so. When he says 'Ora adeus!' to the past, we can almost hear the words of the naive Oedipus dismissing the prophet Tiresias — 'Once gone, you will not trouble me again'.[64]

## Race, Incest and *Bumba-meu-boi*: Rethinking the Oedipal Model

Having explored Azevedo's development of an Oedipal story in O *mulato*, anticipating with his return to classical texts, like Eça, problems that would be explored in greater depth by Freud, I would now like to turn more specifically to how he adapts the model for the social milieu of nineteenth-century São Luís. Some such adaptations have already arisen in the analysis: Ana Rosa's passive temperament, for example, acquires a new significance in the context of an ancestral history of slavery represented by the mad slave mother, Domingas. As we shall see, these modifications to Sophocles' model seek to articulate modes of kinship peculiar to Brazil, fashioned by colonialism and slavery, but they also point, at the level of narrative, to Azevedo's tendency to write against the Naturalist movement as conceived in Europe.

Perhaps the most conspicuous modification to the Oedipal framework in O *mulato* is the loosening of the degree of consanguinity in the central incestuous relationship, both in relation to *Oedipus Rex* and, retrospectively of course, *Os Maias*. Indeed, although I have suggested that Raimundo and Ana Rosa are *functionally* siblings, as is stressed repeatedly in the text, they are nevertheless biologically cousins. We should read this not as an attempt to render their relationship more palatable to a prudish readership, but as a means to shift the focus of the European texts onto questions of race. It is, of course, only by removing consanguinity by one degree that Raimundo, in contrast to his cousin-sister, can carry the blood of black slaves,[65] such that Ana Rosa becomes, according to Maria Bárbara, 'a primeira que na família sujava o sangue!' [the first in the family to tarnish the blood!] (p. 237). At the same time, restoring sibling relations in functional form preserves the intimacy of infancy, having lain dormant for decades, that precipitates a compulsive return to the lost 'mother' in adulthood. It is a clever literary trick, tinkering with the European model to move the goalposts of social commentary onto a Brazilian playing field. There is also, perhaps, something of Zola's 'experimental' approach here, proposed as the watermark of Naturalism in the preface to *Thérèse Raquin*, in Azevedo's calculated adjustments to the variables of race and kinship.

By introducing the blood of slaves into the Oedipal family, Azevedo is able to develop a constructivist critique of racial thought. Being Ana Rosa's cousin, carrying her father's name and fortune, and yet deemed wholly unfit to marry her precisely because of his ancestry, Raimundo sits at the point in which the *maranhense* attitude towards race is seen at its most contradictory. Loosening a degree of consanguinity should lift the constraints of the incest taboo, but their marriage is nevertheless refused because of a conviction that their blood should not, like those of siblings, be mixed. In the terse words of Maria Bárbara, 'Preto é preto! branco é branco! Nada de confusões!' [Black is black! White is white! Don't confuse things!] (p. 243). However, it is just these 'confusões' that Raimundo's Oedipal discovery gradually threatens to expose. The fact that his appearance is racially ambiguous, aside from recreating the 'blindness' that Tiresias attributes to Oedipus in relation to his identity, situates the problem of race within language.[66] If, according to Butler and as we saw in the introduction, Antigone's struggle is one of recognition within the kinship system that reveals shortcomings in the latter's terminology, a problem explored in detail by Eça, Raimundo's struggle is against the language and categories of race into which he is not 'adequately' assimilated since, distanced from his family, his self-image does not correspond to his place in the symbolic order of Maranhão. Thus when he finally learns of his ancestry, he studies himself in the mirror in an unquenchable search for 'truth':

> Em um destes passeios, parou defronte do espelho e mirou-se com muita atenção, procurando descobrir no seu rosto descorado alguma coisa, algum sinal, que denunciasse a raça negra. Observou-se bem, afastando o cabelo das fontes; esticando a pele das faces, examinando as ventas e revistando os dentes; acabou por atirar com o espelho sobre a cômoda, possuído de um tédio imenso e sem fundo. (p. 228).

> [On one such occasion, he stopped in front of the mirror and looked at himself very carefully, trying to discover on his discoloured face anything, any sign that would denounce the black race. He observed himself well, separating his hair at the roots, stretching the skin on his cheeks, examining his nostrils and teeth; finally he flung the mirror onto the dresser, consumed by an immense and fathomless dissatisfaction.]

This passage echoes some of the darker reaches of fin-de-siècle thought, relating the moment in which Raimundo's own ideas turn chillingly against himself; as he stretches his skin and examines his nostrils, he reproduces the contemporaneous fascination with medical-observational practices, enthusiastically applied to the study of race. Unsurprisingly, then, the more he observes himself, the less he is satisfied, until he throws the mirror onto the chest of drawers, his frustration 'sem fundo' reflecting the perennial insufficiency of 'scientific' racial discourse itself. Raimundo's problem is not that he is mixed race, in any case far from obvious, but that he is coded as such by his kinsmen. Accordingly, his Oedipal discovery is the moment when, to use a Lacanian trope, the Imaginary is reconciled with the Symbolic or, in this case, when his self-image is belatedly assimilated into the racist order of his homeland. Or, in more literal terms, when he ceases to be addressed as the respected 'doutor', as at the beginning, when he is greeted by 'grandes apertos de mão' [warm handshakes]; and becomes 'Um cabra! [...]. É um filho da negra Domingas! alforriado à pia! É um bode! É um mulato!' [A mule! [...] The child of the negress Domingas! Freed at the baptismal font! A half-caste! A mulatto!] (p.

304) — as Maria Bárbara addresses him at the end. Indeed, one could go as far as to suggest that Raimundo's most significant discovery in *O mulato* is not of who *he* is, but of who others see him as. This is why Diogo has him assassinated, as he threatens to expose race as the social construction on which the white elite of São Luís precariously depend.[67]

One key way in which Azevedo modifies the Oedipal model, then, is to displace incest with race as the central concern, Antigone's claim becoming Raimundo's struggle against a symbolic order that cannot accommodate him. At this point I would like to introduce another current in *O mulato* that performs a similar renegotiation of family and narrative: Azevedo's engagement with the now-famous *maranhense* myth, *Bumba-meu-boi*, here juxtaposed with the myth of Oedipus. The festival of *Bumba-meu-boi* is a vigorous display of cultural hybridity, developed amongst slaves in colonial Brazil,[68] and incorporating aspects of African, Indian and Christian traditions.[69] There are many variations to the story and the festival is celebrated widely around Brazil, but it is most closely associated with Maranhão where, between 1861 and 1868 — Azevedo's childhood — it was prohibited,[70] dismissed by contemporaries as 'the stupid immoral merrymaking of slaves'.[71] Today, vast processions fill the streets of São Luís in the months of June and July to celebrate the festival. The general storyline is as follows: the slave Pai Francisco lives with his pregnant wife, Mãe Catarina, on a *fazenda* owned by a Portuguese immigrant, usually known simply as Amo [Master]. Mãe Catarina develops cravings for *língua de boi* [ox tongue], and will only be satisfied by eating the tongue of the finest bull on the *fazenda*. Worried for his wife and the unborn child, Pai Francisco leads Amo's favourite ox into the woods, kills it and gives the tongue to his wife, who cooks and eats it, while the rest of the animal is divided amongst the slaves. The master, noticing the missing bull the next day, sends for his slaves and *caboclos*, one of whom, having missed out on the bounty of meat, tells Amo that he sighted Pai Francisco leading the bull away into the forest. The ox's carcass is found, provoking the wrath of Amo, who orders Pai Francisco to resuscitate the bull or face death himself. A Portuguese doctor tries to resuscitate the animal to no avail. Finally, an Amerindian healer arrives and successfully restores the bull's life; all are forgiven, and the miracle is celebrated through the night.[72] In another, somewhat queerer version of the story, Francisco and Catarina flee in terror, returning regretfully only years later after learning of their master's continuing grief. Their son blows into the anus of the bull and his life is restored.[73]

The myth of *Bumba-meu-boi* thus draws on a range of traditions, but perhaps the most salient structurally is Christian mythology, transported to the environment of the Brazilian *fazenda*, with the *língua de boi* analogous to the forbidden fruit with which Eve tempts Adam to break the Father's Law. The resurrection of the bull leads to the forgiveness of the lovers' sins and they can once more serve their 'father' faithfully. But just as *O mulato* twists the Oedipal story to problematise race, so does the myth of *Bumba-meu-boi* adjust the structure of Christian mythology to account for a different configuration of the patriarchal family, shaped by the economics of slavery. If, as Eugene Genovese argues in relation to the Southern United States, the nineteenth-century slave-owning household functions as a one whole 'family, white and black',[74] with slaves and young children both subject to the corrective measures of their 'parents', a dynamic outlined similarly in Gilberto Freyre's *Casa-Grande e senzala*,[75] it is not difficult to view *Bumba-meu-boi*, with its origins as a form of resistance amongst slaves 'to denounce and ridicule colonial slave owners',[76] as a refocusing of the Christian patriarchal tradition to bring into view the specific patriarchal abuses of the *fazenda*. As such, it becomes ripe for juxtaposition with the Oedipal story developed in *O mulato*, itself adjusted to account for the dynamics of slavery and its aftermath. The parallel is drawn both structurally and in textual references, the most significant of these being the words of a travelling *sertanejo* [musician from the *Sertán*] during the local *festas juninas* [June festivals] who, after directing his verses at specific characters at a dinner party as he collects his tips, withdraws mysteriously:

> E virou de costas e retirou-se, a dançar, cantando uma passagem do Bumba-meu-boi:
>
> > *Isto não, isto não pode sê.*
> > *Isto não, isto não pode sê*
> > *A filha de meu amo casar com você!...*
> > *O caboclo me prendeu,*
> >
> > *Meu amor!*
> > *Foi tão certa da razão,*
> > *Coração!*
> > *Que o cabo...*
>
> E perdeu-se nas fundas sombras do mangueiral a voz do sertanejo e o som da viola. (p. 149)

> [And he turned around and went away, dancing, singing a passage from the *Bumba-meu-boi*:
>
> > *This cannot be.*
> > *This cannot be.*
> > *My master's daughter marrying thee!*
> > *The Indian arrested me,*
> >
> > *My love!*
> > *You were so sure,*
> > *Sweetheart!*
> > *That the Ind...*
>
> And the voice of the *sertanejo* and the sound of his guitar were lost in the shadows of the mangroves.]

The two verses, which appear to be Azevedo's own, perhaps transcriptions or interpretations of words the author himself heard, explicitly draw on the myth of *Bumba-meu-boi* and clearly echo the relationship of Raimundo and Ana Rosa, the 'filha do amo' [master's daughter] whose love for her cousin leads fatefully to his assassination. Importantly, this period of festivity in São Luís, which includes *Bumba-meu-boi*, celebrated by the lower classes at the time and thus heard later by Raimundo only as 'um sussurro longínquo de Bumba-meu-boi' [a faraway whisper of the *Bumba-meu-boi*] (p. 174), is also of pivotal structural importance in the novel, being the moment when he resolves to ask Manuel for his cousin's hand in marriage and, at the same time, when Diogo and Maria Bárbara discover from his belongings that he is not a Christian, leading them to conclude that '[é] preciso pôr esse homem fora de cá!' [we need to kick this man out!] (p. 184). The festival of forbidden passions, *Bumba-meu-boi*, marks the moment in the novel that Raimundo goes against his uncle's wishes and assumes his love for Ana Rosa, securing his fate within the family.

I mentioned above that there is an air of mystery to the *sertanejo*'s musical withdrawal, which we can see in the ellipsis of the final syllable of the word *caboclo*, lost in the 'fundas sombras do mangueiral'. This not only adds a certain semantic weight, or sense of intrigue, to the episode, but is part of a wider narrative current in *O mulato* whereby the Naturalist outlook — epitomised in the opening chapter with the description of the afternoon heat in São Luís — is undercut by a fascination with myth and mystery, indeed the metaphysical, an epistemological system that the Positivist agenda of Naturalism and Realism resoundingly dismissed, or claimed to dismiss. Just as the incorporation of *Bumba-meu-boi* seeks to articulate kinship trouble in *O mulato* in peculiarly Brazilian terms, echoing, perhaps, the nationalist efforts of contemporaneous figures such as Sílvio Romero, who collated songs and stories of Brazilian folklore,[77] so does it stand, alongside other myths in the novel, in opposition to the 'scientific' method.

There are many instances in *O mulato* in which the metaphysical counteracts the supposedly enlightening Naturalist perspective, particularly where the abandoned *fazenda* of São Brás is concerned, the geographical point upon which the secrets of the past converge. When Diogo attributes Dona Quitéria's death to an 'espírito maligno que se lhe havia metido no corpo' [a malign spirit that had entered her body], covering up José da Silva's murder, São Brás becomes shrouded in superstition: 'criou a sua lenda e foi aos poucos ganhando a fama de amaldiçoada' [it spawned a legend and slowly rose to fame as a cursed place] (pp. 56–57). Domingas, the slave mother who turns mad after her mutilation, becomes phantasmagoric: '[a]nos depois, contavam que nas ruínas de São Brás vivia uma preta feiticeira, que, por alta noite, saía pelos campos a imitar o canto da mãe-da-lua' [years later, it was said that the ruins of São Brás were home to a black witch who roamed the fields at the dead of night, imitating the call of the poor-me-one] (p. 68). The *mãe-da-lua* (potoo or poor-me-one), is a nocturnal bird with a frightful appearance native to the hottest regions of Central and South America. According to legend, the bird's haunting call is the voice of an Indian tribeswoman mourning her lover, killed by her father in an act of jealousy. In the Peruvian Amazon, meanwhile, the poor-me-one's song is said to be that of a baby abandoned by a tribe so as not to die from an impending plague, forever crying for its mother.[78] Both stories resonate in *O mulato*, the tale of Raimundo's quest for his lost mother and subsequent murder at the hands of the townsfolk to prevent his marriage to Ana Rosa. The *mãe-da-lua*, already incorporated into the mythology of São Brás by the people of Maranhão, appears in the novel on the night that Raimundo sees (without recognising) his mother for the first time, the eve of his visit to his ancestral *fazenda*:

> O silêncio era completo; de repente, porém, a uma nota harmoniosa de contralto sucederam-se outras, prolongadas e tristes, terminando em gemidos.
> O rapaz impressionou-se; o canto parecia vir de uma árvore fronteira à casa. Dir-se-ia uma voz de mulher e tinha uma melodia esquisita e monótona.
> Era o canto da mãe-da-lua. O pássaro levantou vôo, e Raimundo o viu então perfeitamente, de asas brancas abertas, a distancar seus gorjeios pelo espaço. Considerou de si para si que os sertanejos tinham toda a razão nos seus medos legendários e nas suas crenças fabulosas. Ele, se ouvisse aquilo em São Brás lembrar-se-ia logo, com certeza, do tal pássaro que canta a finados. Segundo a indicação do guia, continuava a pensar, a tapera amaldiçoada ficava justamente para o lado que tomara a mãe-da-lua. Devia ser naquelas baixas, que dali se viam. Não podia ser muito longe, e ele seria capaz de ir lá sozinho... Veio distraí-lo destas considerações um frouxo vozear misterioso, que lhe chegava aos ouvidos de um modo mal balbuciado e quase indistinguível. Prestou toda a atenção e convenceu-se de que alguém conversava ou monologava em voz baixa por ali perto. Quedou-se imóvel a escutar. Não havia dúvida! Desta vez ouvira distintamente! Chegara a apanhar uma ou outra palavra! Mas, onde diabo seria aquilo?... (pp. 206–07)

> [All was quiet. Suddenly, however, the dulcet tones of a contralto could be heard, sad and prolonged, ending in wails.
> This made quite an impression on the young man; the song seemed to come from a tree at the front of the house. It sounded like a woman's voice and had a simple, eerie melody.
> It was the call of the poor-me-one. The bird took flight and Raimundo saw it perfectly, its white wings spread wide, warbling through the night. He thought to himself that the people of the *Sertão* were quite right to believe in their mythical fears and legends. No doubt if he were to hear the bird in São Brás, he would think it was singing for the dead. Then he remembered that according to the guide, the cursed ruin was in the same direction that the poor-me-one had taken, down there in the hollow. It wasn't very far off, and he could make his own way there... These thoughts were interrupted by a faint, mysterious murmur that reached his ears in broken and muffled tones. He listened carefully and was convinced that someone was muttering close by, either with someone or alone. He stood still and listened again. There was no doubt about it! This time he had heard it clearly! He had caught a word or two! But where the devil was it coming from?]

I have quoted this passage at length because it demonstrates neatly the opposing forces of myth and reason in *O mulato*. On the one hand, the strange bird becomes, within the novel, a narrative realisation of the local myths surrounding São Brás, its call heard ominously on the eve of his great discovery. The narrator thus indulges in the air of mystery: words such as 'esquisita', or 'frouxo vozear misterioso', stand clearly in contrast to the supposedly demystifying language of Naturalism, a motif that we observed, albeit briefly, in the cave-like living conditions of the ageing Baron of Lavos. Meanwhile, the use of the verb 'parecer' in 'o canto parecia vir de uma árvore fronteira à casa', and the conditional 'dir-se-ia', establish limits in the narrator's perspective, darkening the reader's vision. However, Raimundo seems relatively unfazed by the incident, quickly reasserting his perceived superiority of reason. 'Considerou *de si para si*' suggests an exclusive epistemological standpoint in his contemplation of the incident, contrasted clearly with that of the *maranhenses*, who develop 'medos legendários' and 'crenças fabulosas'. When he concludes that they have 'toda a razão' in their beliefs, it is not to concede that they are in any way true, but to assert the supremacy of his 'enlightened' perspective, without which the myths could not be 'properly' understood. Raimundo's position is thus similar to that of the young Eça, determined to show society its 'falsas interpretações e falsas realizações' [false interpretations and false realisations].[79] Two epistemological currents run through the novel: the power of myth and the metaphysical, working to hide the traumas of the past, and that of Positivist ideas, represented by Raimundo, working to uncover them. Note, however, that the narrator makes use of both, often slipping into the language of secrecy and legend, and structuring the story in line with local myths, 'numa curiosa mistura' [in a curious blend], as Cândido identifies with the use of allegory in O *cortiço*, 'de lucidez e obnubilação' [of clarity and obfuscation].[80]

## Conclusions on O *mulato*: Narrative Dialectics and the Triumph of Maranhão

Azevedo's curious integration of myth into the Naturalist method entails a narrative structure that is perhaps the key to positioning O *mulato* within the contemporaneous literary space. I wish to part here with a claim that runs consistently through criticism of the novel: that Raimundo is an idealised character, transcending the dictates of degeneration theory, affirming the strategy of *branqueamento* and designed to elicit the sympathy of readers.[81] The deployment of myth and legend in O *mulato* is, crucially, narratologically uneven, shared by the narrator in his enthusiastic appropriation of *Bumba-meu-boi* and the *mãe-da-lua*, and broadly by the superstitious residents of Maranhão, but *not* by Raimundo, who reacts to myth with a mixture of amusement, derision, boredom and indifference. As we have seen, he mocks Maria Bárbara's claim that Ana Rosa is victim of a curse. Later, too, he displays mortal tedium when listening to Freitas, a family friend, describe the local *festas juninas* that incorporate those of *Bumba-meu-boi*. At the first sign of a conversation in this direction, which ends up lasting several pages (pp. 89–95), Raimundo lies about having read a magazine on the subject to avoid elaboration. When this fails, he complains of being too hot, which backfires as Freitas leads him away onto the balcony. His subsequent behaviour exudes impatience: 'Raimundo ria-se por delicadeza, e espreguiçava-se na cadeira, bocejando' [Raimundo laughed politely and sat back in the chair, yawning]. 'Raimundo soltou um suspiro profundo e mudou de posição' [Raimundo sighed heavily and changed position]. 'Raimundo quis levantar-se; o outro obrigou-o a ficar sentado, pondo-lhe as mãos nos ombros' [Raimundo tried to stand up, but the other man made him stay seated, putting his arm around him]. ' — Ah! gemeu Raimundo' ['Ah!' groaned Raimundo]. He shows no interest in the local traditions, his behaviour proving aloof and arrogant. Similarly, when Manuel asks him, on the journey to São Brás, whether he prays, 'Raimundo não pôde conter uma risada' [Raimundo couldn't stifle a laugh]. The true conflict of ideas in *O mulato* is not, perhaps, between the narrator and the people of Maranhão, as suggested by criticism that claims the novel's 'extremely combative spirit'[82] reflects the author's disdain for his native province,[83] but between an 'enlightened' Raimundo and his conservative compatriots, with the narrator adopting an ambivalent position, in which a fascination with local history and myth undercuts the recognisably Naturalist style, challenging the supposedly superior epistemological perspective of the Positivist protagonist.[84]

The novel's questioning of Naturalist principles is further evident in the above passage detailing the appearance of the *mãe-da-lua*, where, despite Raimundo's recourse to and faith in his reason, the myth ultimately gets the better of him as he is compelled to follow the nightbird's call, interrupted only by the murmur of hushed voices in the night. 'Ele seria capaz de ir lá sozinho...' Indeed, whatever Raimundo's efforts, in nineteenth-century Brazil, myth is the form of interpretation that ultimately wins out against science.[85] When Raimundo is murdered like his father, history repeats itself — contrary to Hegel's proclamations, of course — and by the following morning the circumstances of his death are being wildly distorted: '[c]ontava-se o fato de mil modos; inventavam-se lendas, improvisavam-se romances' [the events were told in a thousand different ways; legends were invented, novels were drafted]. For Casusa, a family friend, 'aquilo fora, nada mais, nada menos, do que um suicídio, e [...] Raimundo viera até à porta da rua nas agonias da morte' [it had all been nothing more, and nothing less, than a suicide, and [...] Raimundo had gone to the door in his death throes] (p. 319). For all his Positivist education, Raimundo is powerless in his fight against the tide of myth and legend that smothers his past and into which he himself is ultimately assimilated. Thus when he is on the cusp of discovering the truth surrounding his father's murder and confronts Cônego Diogo, demanding '[v]á dizer-me quem matou meu pai!' [you will tell me who killed my father!], he cowers before his appearance of sanctity:

> Raimundo, com efeito, estava imóvel. Ter-se-ia enganado?... À vista do aspecto sereno do cônego chegara a duvidar das conclusões dos seus raciocínios. Seria crível que aquele velho, tão brando, que só respirava religião e coisas santas, fosse o autor de um crime abominável?... E, sem saber o que decidir, atirou-se a uma cadeira, fechando a cabeça nas mãos. (p. 233)

> Raimundo, indeed, was motionless. Had he got it wrong?... At the sight of the serene appearance of the Canon he had begun to doubt the conclusions of his reasoning. Was it really possible that that gentle old man, who lived and breathed religion and holiness, was the author of such an abominable crime? And without knowing what to think, he flung himself into a chair, holding his head in his hands.]

His education and apparently broader world view are still no match for Diogo's ability to breathe and manipulate much older, epistemological systems — the cultural weight of Christianity, in this case, but also the power of myth and superstition in others. Even if Raimundo has morality on his side, and Cônego Diogo is the unambiguous villain of the story, the author does not, apparently, display great faith in the efficacy, in Maranhão at least, of his protagonist's philosophy.

The reasons for such mistrust on the part of the author, reflected in the dialectical movement of the narration, are best considered by returning to the problems of the economic system that shaped the contemporaneous culture of misplaced ideas. As I signalled earlier, Raimundo embodies the dilemma of *ideias fora do lugar* not just because of his European ways of dressing and thinking in the sleepy province of Maranhão, but because every facet of his education since leaving Brazil as a child, including his refined fashion sense, depend nevertheless on the spoils of slavery. Inheritor of his father's wealth, amassed from the continued trafficking of African slaves, Raimundo's disdain for the 'mesquinhos escrúpulos' [petty scruples] (p. 222) of his compatriots seems culturally precarious, hypocritical even, made all the more so by his failure to contemplate the origins of his privilege. Indeed, Raimundo expresses disinterest, on a conscious level, in all aspects of his heritage, from the traditions of his homeland to his mysterious family history of slavery and the slave trade, which, as we have seen, he disavows with his insistence that his sole purpose is to liquidate his ill-gotten capital and leave Maranhão forever. Perhaps, allegorically speaking, Raimundo represents not the new Brazilian but the disdainful European, quick to criticise the 'backwardness' of the postcolonial world, but quietly forgetting his dependency upon it. In this respect, and as more evidence of the influence the novel would have on Eça, Raimundo is conspicuously similar to Afonso da Maia, who disavows Maria Monforte for her father's links to the slave trade, only to embrace British mercantilism, quietly forgetting its complicity with the ongoing practice of slavery in the Americas. Indeed, Raimundo is no greater bearer of meaningful change than the Portuguese characters in the novel,[86] including Dias and Manuel Pescada, who are motivated almost entirely by profit, distinguished only thinly from the mass of unfavourably portrayed Portuguese capitalists in São Luís, seen dragging their 'grandes barrigas' [portly bellies] around the city warehouses.[87] Either way, Raimundo's lack of patience for local customs and avowed devotion to new ideas, despite his wealth deriving from slavery, aligns him more easily with the coloniser than the colonised. This twist of characterisation explains the curiously ambivalent position of the narrator in *O mulato*: familiar with new ideas, perhaps even admirer of them, but fascinated too with local custom and wary of the exploitative European, the narrator is constructed as a (white) Brazilian vis-à-vis his Europeanised protagonist. In the process, the Naturalist vision is coloured with the lens of local myth — shunned by the Positivist Raimundo — whilst European cultural loans, including that of Oedipus (itself anti-Naturalist as a tragedy, of course), are adapted to articulate the specificities of the more peripheral experience of Brazil, still shackled to its dark colonial past. Naturalism, in other words, is reconfigured to construct a Brazilian voice whose authority stems as much from the deployment of 'science' as it does from folklore and the rejection of the supremacy of European ideas.[88] This is Azevedo's *naturalismo nos trópicos* that appropriates and complements the inherited model.

In her reading of *O mulato*, drawing on MacNicoll and Patai, Marchant asks whether Maranhão, with its fierce climate that destroys European complexions,[89] creating an atmosphere of stifling immobility, might not be 'the true protagonist of the novel'.[90] Indeed, one wonders whether Maranhão is not just the protagonist but the ultimate victor in *O mulato*, both within the novel's storyline, and at the structural and narratological level, the Naturalist style becoming infused with local colour that tentatively mocks the movement as conceived in Europe and represented by Raimundo. I mentioned earlier that theories of race and degeneracy, in Brazil especially, engaged closely with questions of heredity and environment, pitted against each other in the course of the individual's destiny. In *O mulato*, despite an intense preoccupation with ancestry and heredity, perhaps unrivalled in any Brazilian work from the period, it is the environment, arguably, that wins out in the end — not just because the social order of Maranhão is restored in the final chapter, but because the narrator, metaphorically speaking, is seduced by the haunting call of the *mãe-da-lua*.

If Azevedo's Naturalism is an inherited one, the author counters the power of his heritage by emphasising the cultural power of his homeland. Thus *O mulato*, in contrast to its *fora-do-lugar* protagonist, adapts the ideas to the place. To disentangle the ties of kinship in *O mulato* is to journey through the natural and cultural history of Maranhão. To approach this journey as Raimundo, returning to reclaim his slave money with the eyes of a modern, cosmopolitan liberal, is to repeat the mistakes of the past, including those of his father who, in a chilling parallelism, flees the then-state of Grão-Pará in 1831 to avoid execution by his slaves in the *Setembrada* revolts against slavery and absolutism. He settles 'incólume' [unharmed] in Maranhão with his booty — 'conseguia sempre salvar algum ouro' [he managed to save some of the gold] — and past evils are buried. His son, in turn, sets out to leave Maranhão with the same fortune a generation later. Here we are surely reminded of the words of Freud from 1914: 'the patient does not *remember* anything of what he has forgotten and repressed, but *acts* it out. He reproduces it not as a memory but as an action; he *repeats* it, without, of course, knowing that he is repeating it'.[91] Thus when Raimundo is surprised by his mother in São Brás, not knowing who she is, and perturbed by her intimate behaviour, he instinctively raises his whip like the *fazendeiros* of old.[92] Thus too does he seek his forgotten mother in his servile cousin-sister. If, in *O mulato*, Raimundo is tragically compelled to repeat the mistakes of his father, the novel works, above all else, to expose the contradiction that sustains the cycle of repetition: namely, the European's disavowed dependency upon the exploitative brutalities of the (post-)colonial world, that marginal cultural space over which he ceaselessly asserts his superiority. The finest historical example of this hypocrisy in colonial times, besides John Locke's private investments in the slave trade,[93] is that of the British objection to slavery when they brazenly spun cotton grown by slaves in Brazil and elsewhere.[94] The greatest strength of *O mulato*, perhaps, is its development of a Brazilian voice sensitive to these cultural blind spots of the 'enlightened' European.

One need only contrast *O mulato* with the book it seems to have inspired, that novelistic centrepiece of the Lusophone canon, *Os Maias*, for its distinctly Brazilian articulation of the problems of patriarchy, race and colonialism to come into relief. Nevertheless, both authors question the supposedly egalitarian principles of liberal capitalism that divided the nineteenth-century world, and both cast Portuguese colonialism as a still-unheeded mistake. Remarkably, they deploy Greek tragedy to develop their critique: in each case the mother, her identity repressed owing to her associations with slavery, resurfaces from the past, against the logic of Positivism, to thwart the promising attempts of the 'liberal' new generation to 'modernise' their homeland, calling into question their ideas in a world that still, until 1888 at least, depended on the exploitation of slaves. The similarities between *O mulato* and *Os Maias*, encompassing crucial details of child development and broader structural and philosophical influences, exemplify well the transatlantic literary techniques developed to examine and problematise the Lusophone (post-)colonial world, challenging too the dominant view of how ideas circulated within it. And whilst in *O mulato*, slavery and racism are surely more central concerns, it is still through an exploration of kinship, the matrix that organises and reproduces economic relations within the family and society, that Azevedo deconstructs the power structures of the period, with the troublesome arrival of Oedipus in Brazil.

## The Dis-solution of the Family: Kinship and Allegory in *Casa de pensão*

*O mulato* is unique amongst Azevedo's novels for the centrality it gives to ancestry and heritage, but already environment is presented as a significant counterweight to its influence. When we move forward chronologically through his work, the balance shifts still further and environment takes centre stage, made manifest by the titles of his subsequent most 'significant' novels,[95] *Casa de pensão* [The Guesthouse] (1884) and *O cortiço* [The Slum] (1890), which displace *O mulato*'s overt concern with ancestry with a pointed focus on space and place. If Azevedo disengages somewhat with questions of biological ancestry, however, he does not move away from questions of kinship, but rather undoes their apparent foundations in blood ties, constructing allegorical 'families' whose fragile cohesion owes more to bonds of shared environment and economic convenience than consanguinity.[96] There are aspects of *O mulato* that anticipate this trajectory. As we have seen, Azevedo splinters the kinship function from biological ties when he seeks to represent Raimundo as effectively his cousin's brother. Ana Rosa, too, finds a functional mother in her *mãe-pretinha*, Mônica, whilst Mariana, her biological mother who dies when she is still a child, figures as a functional mother for Raimundo. Mothers, fathers, sisters, cousins and aunts, in short, need not be biological to serve their societal functions, an insight shared later by Lacan, who abstracted Freudian notions of father and mother to position them as structuring forces in the subject's psyche.[97] This insight will underscore my subsequent analysis of *Casa de pensão*, where I examine how Azevedo allegorises a profitable Rio guesthouse as an unhappy family and indeed Brazil itself, stretching — queering? — the kinship system over the contours of economic and international relations to expose their complicities. Once more, the mystifying force of allegory, adducing a further layer of signification, pressures the representation of the family as 'natural'. Thus whilst I take several cues from

Cândido's work on the use of allegory in *O cortiço*, which he identifies as Azevedo's most salient adaptation to Zola's model, I wish to focus more specifically on *Casa de pensão* where, as in *O mulato*, a disruption to the normative structure of the family is reflected in something 'queer' at the level of the text. In this sense, the novel chimes with other Lusophone Naturalist works that project national and colonial allegories onto what are ostensibly stories of families and urban life.

Azevedo's second major work, again received with great popularity at the time, has nevertheless attracted far less critical attention than *O mulato* and *O cortiço*. Indeed, there is very little structural analysis of *Casa de pensão* at all, with the fortunate exception of an article by Angela Fanini,[98] to which I will return shortly. The novel tells the story of Amâncio, a young, wealthy *maranhense* representing the older slave-owning classes, who settles in Rio de Janeiro to study medicine.[99] He is quickly marked as an excessively Romantic type, 'um sonhador, um louco' [a dreamer, a madman] (p. 22), provoked by the harsh, authoritarian rule of his Portuguese father and the peaceful refuge he finds in his indulgent mother. Living initially in the house of Campos and his wife Hortênsia, old family friends, he quickly longs for greater freedom and establishes himself in the guesthouse of João Coqueiro and his older, French wife, Madame Brizard, whom he meets early in his studies. Whilst they claim to have their 'friend's' best interests at heart, in secret they covet his money and in particular his hand in marriage to Coqueiro's sister, Amélia, a match that would lift the trio from relative poverty and recover their past riches. Despite a promising start, the plot fails as Amâncio appears more interested in Hortênsia and the guest Lúcia, both married women, leaving Coqueiro and Madame Brizard increasingly exasperated in their matchmaking efforts. Coqueiro sues Amâncio in court, accusing him of seducing his sister and then refusing to marry her. The case, which clearly echoes that of the *Questão Capistrano* of 1876,[100] is ruled in Amâncio's favour, but in a characteristically dramatic finale, Coqueiro murders him, the final scene depicting Amâncio's distraught mother finding her son's bloodied corpse on a visit from Maranhão.

Fanini's reading of the text identifies a 'movimento pendular' between Romantic and Naturalist ideas in *Casa de pensão*,[101] a tension beginning with the opposing attitudes of Amâncio's mother and father, traceable through his passionate love affairs that conflict with Coqueiro's calculating, rationalist approach to their 'friendship', and resolved tragically in murder at the end. Compellingly, Fanini demonstrates this pendular movement within the narrative, the narrator at once idealising maternal love and representing paternal authority with the lens of supposed objectivity.[102] She sets this dialectic in the context of the clash of economic models present in Brazil at the time, one based on slavery, which she associates with Romanticism, and the other on free-market capitalism, associated with Naturalism and the bourgeoisie. This latter model leads inexorably (as we saw in Eça's works) to a mercantilisation of social relations,[103] which sees Amâncio's provincial innocence consistently exploited for financial gain. With this backdrop of pendular narration between Naturalism and Romanticism (not dissimilar to the use of myth in *O mulato*), I would like to turn to the allegorisation of kinship. Allegory, after all, is itself characteristic of Romanticism, not least in Brazil, where Alencar's *Iracema* presents the romance between the Portuguese Martim and the Indian *virgem dos lábios de mel* [honey-lipped virgin] as the foundational moment of the Brazilian nation.[104] However, again taking allegory to be a two-way street between signifiers and signifieds, rather than reproducing what Paul de Man identifies as 'the asserted superiority of the symbol over allegory',[105] I hope to show how, as in *O Barão de Lavos*, the allegorical plane pressures the integrity of its own symbolic system — in this case, the normative family.

The title of the novel, *Casa de pensão*, introduces the dialectic that structures the subsequent allegory. On the one hand, 'casa' signals the comforts of the family home, of rest, shelter and community. On the other, 'pensão', derived from Latin *pensio*, meaning 'rent',[106] signals exploitation, profit and social division. The central relationships in *Casa de pensão* contain this tension between the semblance of family and the reality of financial greed, beginning in earnest when Amâncio goes to live with Campos and his wife prior to meeting Coqueiro and Madame Brizard. On his arrival, Campos speaks to Hortênsia in private and tries to convince her of the need to 'oferecer-lhe a casa' [offer to let him stay at their house] (p. 19) due to his indebtedness to Vasconcelos, Amâncio's uncle:

> É uma questão de gratidão!... Devo muitos obséquios à família deste rapaz! Lembras-te daquele velho, de que te falei, aquele que foi que me deu a mão lá no Norte?... Pois este é o sobrinho, é filho do Vasconcelos. Não nos ficaria bem recebê-lo assim, sem mais nem menos! (p. 20)

> [It's a question of gratitude!... I owe a great many favours to that boy's family! Do you remember that old man I have spoken about before, the one who helped me out up north?... Well this is his nephew, Vasconcelos's son. It wouldn't be right for us to treat him as any old guest!]

Receiving Amâncio is not the selfless act it might appear, but instead figures as a repayment for past favours. When Campos rejoins the room where Amâncio is waiting, however, he offers him some lighter clothing, invites him to join him for dinner and, finally, utters the words, '[v]enha para cá; faça de conta que minha família é a sua!' [come and stay; you can count on my family as though it were your own!] (p. 21), pressing him to stay at his house. He then acts in a consistently paternal manner towards Amâncio:

> [O] Campos estava sempre a lhe moer o juízo com as matrículas, com a entrada na academia, com o inferno de obrigações a cumprir, cada qual mais pesada, mais antipática, mais insuportável!
> — Olhe, seu Amâncio, que o tempo não espicha — encolhe!... É bom ir cuidando disso!... Repetia-lhe o negociante, fazendo ar sério e comprometido.
> — Veja agora se vai perder o ano! Veja se quer arranjar por aí um par de botas!... (p. 39)

> [Campos was always getting on his nerves about the matriculations, his admission to the academy, about all the darned things he had to do, each one more grating, more unpleasant, more insufferable than the last!
> 'Look, Amâncio, time is of the essence — don't let it slip by!... You'd better see to it!...' repeated the businessman seriously, with an air of responsibility. 'Don't risk missing the year! Watch you don't get yourself into trouble!']

Campos, in other words, does not just repay his 'debt' to Vasconcelos by offering Amâncio board and lodging, but takes him into his 'family', declaring him a rightful member, and acting as a father towards him by reminding him repeatedly of his obligations, or the Law (of productivity), with an 'ar sério'. Amâncio's juvenile irritation with this Law, meanwhile, is audible in the repetition in the phrase 'mais pesada, mais antipática, mais insuportável!'. The pretence to a relationality of kinship, a day after meeting each other as strangers, is an exchange of services and not founded on authenticity, a dynamic not dissimilar to that of the 'brotherly' relationships we saw in *Os Maias* in the previous chapter. However, in this apparently seamless complicity of 'family' and economics, of *casa* and *pensão*, where the Father's Law exercises tight control, cracks will soon emerge as kinship acquires increasingly allegorical meanings that contort the system itself.

The allegorical shift takes place when Amâncio establishes himself in Madame Brizard's guesthouse. To begin with, the complicity of (pseudo-)kinship and economics continues with ease. Immediately, Amâncio is taken in as both a tenant and member of the 'family'. When he first meets Coqueiro at an extravagant lunch for which he foots the bill, the latter tries to persuade him to move to the *casa de pensão* which, he insists, 'não é um hotel, é uma — casa de família! Não temos hóspedes, temos amigos!' [it's not a hotel, it's a family home! We don't have guests, we have friends!] (p. 56), a claim that the novel's title evidently undermines. When Amâncio arrives at the guesthouse, Coqueiro demands, ' — [p]õe-te à vontade, filho! [...] *em ar quase de censura*' ['make yourself at home, son!' [...] *in an almost censorial tone*] (p. 93, emphasis added), positioning Amâncio as son in the 'family' both lexically and in his mode of expression. Similarly, shortly afterwards, he remarks:

> 'Tu, aqui, não quero que sejas um hóspede, mas um amigo, um colega, *um filho da família, uma espécie de meu irmão*, compreendes? São dessas coisas que se não explicam — questão de simpatia! Conhecemo-nos de ontem e é como se tivéssemos sido criados juntos; em mim podes contar com um amigo para a vida e para a morte! (p. 103, emphasis added)

> [When it comes to you, I don't want you to be a guest but a friend, a colleague, *a son of the family, a kind of brother to us*, do you understand? It's one of those things that can't be explained — a matter of kindness! We got to know each other yesterday and yet it's as though we grew up together; you can count on me as a friend for life and for death!]

Coqueiro explicitly invokes kinship to try to demonstrate the sincerity of his emotion which is, of course, only cold calculation. Several such tropes are invoked — filiality, brotherhood, a shared upbringing, and eternal commitment — as Coqueiro establishes himself as the 'father' of the house early on. 'Serás tratado como um filho... Agora, quanto a certas visitas... [...] isso, filho, tem paciência... Lá fora o que quiseres, mas daquela porta para dentro...' [you will be treated like a son... Now, as regards certain visits... [...] with that, son, you'll have to be patient... Do whatever you want out there, but within these walls...] (p. 104). As in the traditional bourgeois family home represented by Campos and his wife, Coqueiro's *casa de pensão* apparently has a strict sexual code enforced by the *dono de casa*; Amâncio is quickly positioned beneath the Law. Coqueiro's tactic which, as we shall see, will ultimately prove unsuccessful, is to treat Amâncio as his child, and indeed 'uma espécie de irmão' [a kind of brother] (a brother can be many things, of course), with the exclusive desire of controlling his wealth. As he says to his wife after first meeting him, '[é] um achado precioso! [...] é filho único e tem a herdar uma fortuna! [...] a coisa vai para além de quatrocentos contos!... [...] se o metermos em casa e se conduzirmos o negócio com um certo jeito, não lhe dou três meses de solteiro!' [he's a precious find! [...] an only child set to inherit a fortune! [...] we're talking more than four hundred *contos*!... [...] if we take him in and steer the matter with a little flair, I bet he won't last three months as a bachelor!] (p. 88).

The law of the house, however, proves to be weak in *Casa de pensão*, the appearance of a family order thinly disguising the lawlessness underneath. Thus Coqueiro, who prohibits amorous visits to the house 'para a boa moral' [for the sake of propriety], does not practise what he preaches, and is later spied by Amâncio leaving the house with 'uma mulher gorda' [a fat woman] (p. 153) at the dead of night. Amâncio, too, receives tiptoe visits from Lúcia, and alludes to Coqueiro's hypocrisy when the latter reproaches him — 'sei, tão bem como tu, que aqui nem todos são santos!...' [I know as well as you do that we're not all saints in this place!] (p. 204). There is a generalised sense in *Casa de pensão* that the house is not merely hypocritical, but a troubling, sometimes hideous distortion of the supposedly saintly bourgeois family. On the night that Amâncio catches his friend with his lover, the house descends into a hysterical argument about noise and indecency, provoked by the wakeful wife of the poor composer Mendes who, frustrated by her husband working into the small hours, demands that he turn out the light. 'Deixa isso! Anda! E apaga o diabo dessa luz! [...] Arre, com os diabos! Que nem se pode dormir!' [Stop it! Come on! And turn of that damned light! [...] Grrr, may the devil take you! I can't sleep a wink!] (p. 157), she cries, in a particularly expletive outburst. When he warns her calmly about the neighbours, she dismisses his words: ' — Os vizinhos que se fomentem! Berrou ela, embrulhando-se na colcha e fazendo tremer o soalho com seus passos de granadeiro. — Não como em casa deles, não preciso deles para nada!' ['To hell with the neighbours!' she shouted, wrapping herself in the duvet and making the floor shudder with her heavy steps. 'I don't eat in their house, I don't need them at all!']. Her response epitomises the underlying individualism in Coqueiro's supposed 'casa de família'. Within minutes, a loud argument breaks out at three o'clock in the morning:

> O moço do n.º 7 expectorou com mais força e pôs-se a gemer.
> — Ora, com um milhão de demônios! Gritou o guarda-livros, morava no n.º 6. — Não é possível sossegar neste inferno! Quando não é a tosse e o gemido da direita, é a rezinga e a briga da esquerda! Apre! Antes morar num hospital de doidos!
> [...]
> — Os incomodados são que os que mudam! — gritou ela.
> [...]
> Nesse momento, o Campela, o tal esquisitão do n.º 4, que até aí não dera sinal de si, levantou-se tranquilamente, tomou o seu clarinete, e começou por

acinte, a tirar do instrumento as notas mais estranhas e atormentadores que se podem imaginar. O guarda-livros respondeu-lhe batendo com a bengala nas paredes de tabique e berrando, como um doido, o *Zé Pereira*.

— Ai, meu Deus!, ai, meu Deus!, continuava a gemer arrastadamente o pobre sujeito do n.º 7.

Já pelas escadas, Amâncio ouviu as vozes do *gentleman*, do Melinho e de Lúcia, que acordaram espantados, e em gritos reclamavam contra semelhante abuso.

No andar de baixo, o Piloto, o Dr. Tavares, o Fontes, e a mulher, abriam as portas dos competentes quartos, para indagar que diabo queria aquilo dizer. [...]

Amâncio já estava entre os lençois, quando o Coqueiro percorreu toda a casa, de *robe-de-chambre* e castiçal na mão.

[...]

O guarda-livros, no dia seguinte pela manhã, declarou a Mme. Brizard que se retirava da casa de pensão.

— Oh! Disse. — Não estava disposto a suportar por mais tempo aquele zungu! Os seus vizinhos eram uma gente impossível! — Não se passava uma noite em que não houvesse chinfrinada! (pp. 158–60)

> [The young man in no. 7 coughed more heavily and started to moan.
> 'For all the fires of hell!' shouted the bookkeeper who lived in no. 6. 'You can't rest for a minute in this dreadful place! If it isn't the coughing and moaning to the right, it's the griping and fighting to the left! Damn it! I'd rather live in a mental asylum!'
> [...]
> 'If you don't like it, move out!' she shouted.
> [...]
> Then Campela, the oddball from no. 4, who until then hadn't shown any sign of life, rose calmly, took up his clarinet, and deliberately started to extract from it the strangest and most disturbing noises imaginable. The bookkeeper responded by rapping his cane on the wall and shouting, like a madman, the *Zé Pereira*.
> 'God help me! God help me!' moaned the poor boy in no. 7.
> Climbing the stairs, Amâncio could hear the voices of the gentleman, Melinha and Lúcia, who awoke in shock, shouting in protest at such impropriety.
> On the floor below, Piloto, Dr Tavares, Fontes and his wife opened the doors to their rooms, asking what on earth was going on. [...]
> Amâncio was already between the sheets when Coqueiro ran through the house in his *robe-de-chambre*, candlestick in hand.
> [...]
> The following morning, the bookkeeper announced to Mme. Brizard that he was leaving the guesthouse.
> 'Oh!' he said. 'He wouldn't put up with that rookery any longer! His neighbours were impossible! Not a single night went by without a pandemonium!']

In this passage, the weakness of the Father's Law that ought to govern the structure of the family is seen in the collapse of the division between public and private. As Foucault argues in relation to the great institutions of the eighteenth and nineteenth centuries, the creation and policing of sexuality during this period was realised in the configuration of space, with boys' dormitories, for example, designed with curtains and partitions to prevent sexual contact whilst implicitly acknowledging its potential to arise.[107] In the episode above, the divisions between rooms, and even floors, break down, eliciting a scandalised response from the more prudish guests. As the bookkeeper, who leaves soon afterwards, succinctly puts it, 'quando não é a tosse e o gemido da direita, é a rezinga e a briga da esquerda!'. That which ought to maintain the integrity of the public and private spheres fails on the night that Amâncio discovers that Coqueiro is committing adultery, and thus himself undermining the sexual-spatial code. Accordingly, Coqueiro paces hopelessly through the commotion in his dressing-gown, his phallic candlestick only a pretence to paternal authority. The narrator emphasises the increasing confusion of private and public space by identifying each character according to their room number, and using numerals, which adds to the sense in which the cacophony of voices and instruments cuts across the supposedly rationalised space. As Coqueiro's Law is gradually weakened, revealing itself as complicit in perpetuating a *parentesco postiço* that hides a chaotic sexuality and individualism underneath, there appears to be something rather queer, or devious perhaps, about the *casa de pensão.*

The narrator himself seems to suggest such a possibility when he describes the upbringing of Amélia, Coqueiro's sister, where again the 'family home' figures as a corrupting influence characterised by an excess of intimacy:

> Amélia, por conseguinte, cresceu em uma — casa de pensão. Cresceu no meio da egoística indiferença de vários hóspedes, vendo e ouvindo todos os dias novas caras e novas opiniões, absorvendo o que apanhava da conversa de caixeiros e estudantes irresponsáveis; afeita a comer em mesa-redonda, a sentir perto de si, ao seu lado, na intimidade doméstica, homens estranhos, que se não preocupavam com lhe aparecer em mangas de camisa, chinelas e peito nu. (p. 79)

> [Amélia, as a result, grew up in a guesthouse. She grew up amid the selfish indifference of the many guests, watching and listening to new faces and new opinions daily, absorbing what she grasped from the conversations of salesmen and irresponsible students, growing accustomed to eating at a round table, and feeling close to her, at her side, in the intimacy of her home, strange men, who took no exception to wearing short sleeves, sandals and unbuttoned shirts.]

Here, the tension identified earlier between *casa* and *pensão* comes to disturb the Father's Law that ought to hold them together. On the one hand, there is an 'egoística indiferença' on the part of the paying guests, who come and go with the times, having no qualms about appearing in public dressed in an informal attire that pushes the boundaries of the acceptable in front of a young lady — not scandalous, perhaps, but certainly suggestive, with chests, arms and feet on display. However, we find the same 'confusion' of space that characterises the episode of the argument, with the round table facilitating contact between strangers who, judging by their clothes at least, are not quite fit for the private sphere, or 'intimidade doméstica', as the narrator puts it. Their dissonance at her side is emphasised further with the almost tautological clauses 'a sentir perto de si, ao seu lado, homens estranhos', which also carry a sibilance suggestive of whisper and scandal. The complicity of *casa* and *pensão*, in other words, which Coqueiro uses consistently to attract guests, and which brings lodgers into the 'intimidade doméstica', results in a disturbance to the former in its services to the latter. Coqueiro's mercantile approach to the guesthouse brings about the corruption of precisely the bourgeois family that he invokes as his business model.

This distortion of the bourgeois family is confirmed in the sterility of the 'mother' and 'father' of the house who, despite their symbolic roles, do not have children of their own. Queerer still, this sterility is due to Madame Brizard's old age; at fifty, when she marries the much younger Coqueiro, a second-year student at the time, she is too old to have children. The great difference in age between husband and wife is viewed as distinctly odd by onlookers. Soon after meeting Coqueiro, 'Amâncio jurava corresponder àquela amizade, mas, no íntimo, ria-se do Coqueiro, que agora lhe parecia tolo, e cujo casamento com a francesa velhusca o tornava, a seus olhos, cada vez mais ridículo' [Amâncio swore to return the friendship, but deep down he laughed at Coqueiro, who now seemed silly to him, and whose marriage to the old Frenchwoman, in his eyes, made him more and more ridiculous] (p. 103), the pejorative suffix — *usca* indicating his disapproval of the intergenerational marriage. When Campos learns of Amâncio's court case, he immediately blames himself for not foreseeing the calamity:

> Mas, onde diabo tinha eu esta cabeça, para não ver logo que um homem, que se casa especulativamente com uma velha do feitio de Mme. Brizard; um homem que consente à irmã receber presentes e mais presentes de um estranho; um homem que especula com tudo e com todos, um maroto! (p. 304)

> [But where on earth was I not to realise immediately that this man, who speculatively marries an old crone like Mme. Brizard; a man who allows his sister to receive gifts from strangers; a man who speculates with everything and everyone, a trickster!]

It seems reasonable to suggest that Coqueiro's marriage is perceived as 'queer', identified immediately as a primary reason to distrust him, echoing Foucault's concept of the 'will to know', the odd difference in age taken as a privileged site for understanding Coqueiro's character. And yet despite its queerness in the eyes of the bourgeoisie, it is precisely bourgeois interests that govern his marriage to Madame Brizard who, being the widow of a Parisian hotelier, presents herself as the ideal partner to relaunch the guesthouse that closed with the death of Coqueiro's mother. 'Toda a sua vida, todos os seus recursos, seriam empregados para o mesmo fim: facultar ao marido os meios de estudar, os meios de crescer, desenvolver-se, luzir' [all her energies, all her resources would be geared towards the same goal: provide her husband with the means to study, grow, develop and shine] (p. 83). There is something motherlike in Madame Brizard's desire to provide for Coqueiro's 'upbringing'. Choosing a capitalist mother for a wife, Coqueiro places commercial interests first, but in so doing, his marriage becomes a disturbed reflection of the patriarchal, bourgeois family, his Law weakened irreparably, with no sons to transmit his name and bloodline. Thus Madame Brizard does not take Coqueiro's name at any point in the novel, but retains her nominal connection to the Parisian hotelier. As Coqueiro himself says, in earnest as much as in jest, '[s]ou casado [...]. Isso, porém, nada quer dizer' [I am married [...]. That, however, doesn't mean anything] (p. 54).

With this curious 'deformation' of the family, arising paradoxically from its complicities with the same capitalist order it ought to underpin, we perhaps glimpse the queer at the level of the text. There is without doubt a precedent within the Naturalist movement for 'typological' characters such as Coqueiro and Madame Brizard, who approach all social relations with the principles of exchange. Particularly noteworthy in this respect is Octave Mouret from Zola's *Les Rougon-Macquart* series who, in *Au Bonheur des Dames*, believes he will conquer the intransigent Denise with spiralling offers of money.[108] However, Madame Brizard's nationality, age and sterility invest the *casa de pensão*, with its comically diverse array of guests, with national-allegorical meaning. As I have indicated, the Brazilian Romantics often deployed allegory to create 'foundational' myths of the Brazilian nation. But if, as Fanini neatly demonstrates, *Casa de pensão* wavers between Romanticism and Naturalism, might this not be the point where the two reach a deadlocked synthesis, in which the allegories of the former, forging family, nation and future, meet the cold, 'rational' perspective of the latter which, in Brazil at least, was significantly associated with the new, mercantile classes, vehemently opposed to European influence?[109]

This distortion of the foundational family, which is also, in its recourse to allegory, a now-familiar technique of the Lusophone Naturalists, explored by Botelho in his intergenerational 'pathology', is perhaps best illustrated through a comparison with Alencar's much-celebrated *Iracema* (1865), which I cited earlier as typifying the Brazilian Romanticist 'foundational' tradition. The novel, a 'fantasy of American-European miscegenation',[110] tells the story of Martim, a Portuguese coloniser, his *pitiguara* friend, Poti, and Iracema, a *tabajara* girl with whom he falls in love, and who dies after giving birth to their child.[111] The child of Martim and Iracema thus carries both European and, according to Maria Manuel Lisboa:

> just enough Indian blood [...] to sustain the novel's status as foundation text, but not enough viably to secure the continuity of the line that died with his mother. Iracema, too, remains what she always was: sweet, fertile, destructible, and at the last dead.[112]

A comparison of the figures of Iracema and Madame Brizard reveals a symmetrical inversion of the (misogynistic) portrayal of women, typically dichotomised in Western culture as angels or whores. Iracema, representing the Indian line that was already all but decimated by the time of the novel's publication, is culturally sublimated, selfless, procreative, and ultimately dead. Madame Brizard, by contrast, represents the continuing European presence in Brazil, much maligned by the Naturalists and mercantile classes,[113] and already criticised by Azevedo in *O mulato*, a criticism he consolidates in the later *O cortiço*, in which the miserly Portuguese capitalist, João Romão, constructs an exploitative empire in the form of a tenement in Rio de Janeiro.[114] Madame Brizard thus epitomises the European's sense of superiority in relation to the New World — 'Ah! Ela, a francesa, sabia perfeitamente como tudo isso se arranjava no Brasil' [Ah! She, the Frenchwoman, knew just how it all worked in Brazil] (p. 84), she remarks to Coqueiro as she plots the much-coveted 'casamentão' [the big marriage]. And being European, the 'mother' of the story becomes everything that a mother 'ought' *not* to be: calculating, businesslike and imposing — she is obese[115] — and, finally, old and sterile. We will encounter a remarkably similar figure in Caminha's *Bom Crioulo* in the following chapter. If Madame Brizard is placed against Iracema, the foundational allegories of the Romantics are inverted and rendered barren by the Naturalists' close and 'demystifying' attention to the social environment, still conspicuously absent of slaves in the case of *Casa de pensão*, but saturated with the meddling influence of Europe.

If Madame Brizard is taken as the European (anti-)mother in *Casa de pensão*, the other characters in the novel complete the allegorical picture. Amâncio, as Fanini demonstrates, represents the older, slave-owning classes from the provinces, lost and adrift in the cosmopolitan milieu of Rio de Janeiro. Coqueiro, deprived of his aristocratic fortune at a young age by his frivolous father, represents the new, republican bourgeoisie, abandoning the economic models of the past in the hope of making a fortune in business and, crucially, seduced by the French Republican fugitive,[116] Madame Brizard. The great hope is that his sister Amélia will provide the child to secure the future viability of the family and its capital. However, despite her 'gestozinhos passarinheiros' [bird-like little gestures] and pretence to 'virtue', she amounts to little more than the carrot dangled by Coqueiro and Madame Brizard to attract the prize,[117] strictly instructed by the latter, prior to Amâncio's arrival, to avail herself of 'muita habilidade e alguma esperteza' [a great deal of skill and wit] with the aim of finding 'um marido rico' [a rich husband] (p. 89). With Amélia reduced structurally to an instrument of temptation in *Casa de pensão*, a sterile triad emerges, a loveless love triangle encompassing Amâncio (old Brazil, slavery), Madame Brizard (the exploitative European) and Coqueiro (the 'new' Brazilian nevertheless seduced — like Raimundo? — by the latter). Despite hopes that this triad will, with the impassive help of Amélia, become a happy family at the end, bringing together the conflicting classes and nationalities in *fin-de-siècle* Rio, the result is mutual destruction, with Amâncio murdered, Coqueiro arrested, and his guesthouse forever discredited. *Casa de pensão* thus participates in a sterilisation — through allegorisation — of families and love triangles that is prevalent across Naturalists works from Portugal and Brazil, echoing the childless Sebastians of *Basílio*, perhaps, and anticipating the violent trio of *O Barão de Lavos*.

There is an ideological deadlock, a pained stalemate of dominant classes and ideas, in Azevedo's (anti-)foundational allegory of Rio society, where there are certainly no winners, except, unsurprisingly if not convincingly, Madame Brizard, who appears to be absent at Amâncio's funeral, her name, in contrast to those of Amâncio and her husband, decidedly intact. The guesthouse is dissolved towards the end, with the (pseudo-)community of bookkeepers, bohemians, students, opportunistic lovers, foreigners and *provincianos* gradually moving elsewhere, either through choice or by force. But as the allegory develops in the meantime, two oppositional forces are set in motion that restore dynamism to the text. On the one hand, there is a movement from family to city and nation, from kinship to relations of class and nationality, adducing an allegorical plane in a pattern that we have observed repeatedly in previous chapters. On the other, there is a countermovement from the nation to the family, from (post)colonial and class relations to relations of kinship. And here the patriarchal family is pressured by its allegorical referent, recast as an anti-family, a sterile non-unit reflecting the excesses of market capitalism yoked to the stubborn presence of European power in Brazil. If the family of *Casa de pensão* is to be considered 'queer', it is equally bound up with something queer at the textual level, that is, the recourse to national allegory that Cândido identifies as a distinctive deviation from Naturalist principles in *O cortiço*. Azevedo thus inverts the mystifying allegories of the Romantics in his novel, shifting the focus onto the continuing abuses of the present day. In so doing, he exposes the internal contradiction of the patriarchal family, whereby its instrumental role in the accumulation and transmission of capital leads to the precise conditions for a foreclosure of patrilinear inheritance. At the beginning, perhaps, to cite a contemporaneous work that draws heavily on allegory,[118] the family shows the smiling face of the ageless Dorian Gray; at the end, we see its grotesque portrait after it has sold its soul. However, in *Casa de pensão*, it is not just moral decadence and an erosion of values, but continuing European influence that rears its ugly allegorical head. Azevedo thus sits somewhere between Eça and Botelho, using allegory to call for an end to colonialism, but still finding kinship trouble to be a ruinous, rather than redemptive, theatre of social upheaval.

That said, and perhaps to a greater degree than *Lavos*, Azevedo does allow other epistemologies to creep into his sterile representation of the family in *Casa de pensão*. These are most visible when contemplating the single character who remains outside the net of 'scientific' thought, Madame Brizard's hysterical second daughter, Nini, whose husband dies young, inducing madness and compelling her to live with her mother. Nini shows no concern for the bourgeois sexual code, at one point entering Amâncio's room and trying to smother him with kisses, much to his shock and dislike: 'sentiu cair sobre ele um corpo gordo e mole' [he felt a soft, fat body fall onto him] (p. 144). Azevedo's representation of the hysteric, however, differs from what one might expect from the period, with a consistent emphasis on the perversion of those who observe and analyse her. When she appears at the dinner table for the first time, '[u]m silêncio formou-se em torno de sua chegada; percebia-se que pensavam nela' [silence fell upon her arrival; they were evidently thinking about her] (p. 109). Shortly before her arrival, the guests discuss possible cures for her ailment, with Sr. Lambertosa predictably citing the 'fisiologistas' and proposing marriage as the miracle cure. She is repeatedly patronised as guests talk about her in the third person in her presence — '[p]ouco, Sr. Lambertosa, dê-lhe pouco!' [don't give her much, Mr Lambertosa, just a little!] (p. 113), orders Madame Brizard as he offers her the compote. 'Vítima inocente dos imprenetráveis caprichos de Deus' [an innocent victim of God's unfathomable caprices] (p. 143), affirms Dr. Tavares at a subsequent dinner. The focus of the narration shifts from the hysteric to those who observe her,[119] and as they attempt to circumscribe her experience, to locate her outside the symbolic order, a degree of autonomy is subtly restored. Nini's stare provokes intense disconcertion:

> Nini largou a colher no prato, sem dizer palavra, e pôs-se de novo a encarar para Amâncio, com um olhar tão dolorido e tão persistente, que o rapaz ficou impressionado.
> E não lhe tirou mais a vista de cima. O estudante remexia-se na cadeira, importunado por aqueles dois olhos grandes, rasos, de um azul duvidoso, que se fixavam sobre ele, imóveis e esquecidos.
> Disfarçava, procurava não dar por isso, nada, porém, conseguia. Os dois importunos lá estavam, sempre assentados sobre ele, a lhe queimar a paciência, como se fossem dois vidros de aumento colocados contra o sol.
> — Que embirrância! Dizia consigo o provinciano. (p. 109)

> [Nini set her spoon down on the plate without saying a word and again turned to face Amâncio, giving him such a pained and persistent stare that the young man was troubled.
> And she didn't take her eyes off him for the rest of the dinner. The student couldn't sit still in his chair, put off by those two flat, gaping eyes, with their odd blue colour, fixed on him, motionless and distant.
> He pretended not to be bothered, but nothing he did set him at ease. There they were, the two pests, settled on him, trying his patience, like two magnifying glasses held to the sun.]

Amâncio's frustration, demonstrated both in his thoughts and in his restlessness when facing her inscrutable gaze, suggests that Nini sees something in him that he does not wish to be seen, and which perhaps even he himself cannot see, given the blinding metaphor that is employed in relation to her penetrative eyes. Her stare is invariably focused on Amâncio in the novel; at one point, her eyes observe him 'sem pestanejar' [without blinking] (p. 115). The narrative thus creates two contrasting perspectives: the reductive, 'scientific' gaze of the guests, observing Nini, and the latter's uncanny, mysterious ability to transcend their circumscription. That she consistently observes Amâncio, introduced himself as 'um louco' by the narrator, instates an alternative epistemological axis that repudiates the bourgeois, 'scientific' gaze and gestures towards an arrangement of relationships stripped of economic concerns and restored instead with passion, which is the governing principle of both Amâncio and Nini.

However, in trying to exclude Nini from the order of the *casa de pensão*, and by extension the (allegorical) order of the 'new' city and nation, the guesthouse seals its fate, deafening itself to the chaotic clamour of human passion that ultimately engulfs it. Hence in a similar vein, Azevedo pinpoints the moment in Amâncio's youth when he represses his non-normative urges, a decisive moment in an upbringing that sees his wild behaviour as a young child 'domesticado', according to his schoolmaster, in a particularly lucid display of bourgeois ideology. When he is just twelve, he declares to his family that he wants to join the navy: '[a] farda seduzia-o. Nada conhecia "tão bonito" como um oficial de marinha' [he was taken by the uniform. He didn't know anything 'as pretty' as a navy officer] (p. 32). His embarrassment, provoked by his mother who looks 'em torno de si, chamando a atenção para o desembaraço do filho' [around her, drawing attention to her son's embarrassment], marks a turning point as he develops his veneer of conformity and impassiveness thinly hiding the 'louco' underneath, a madness that only Nini can see. In these moments of confrontation with queer bodies and desires, where the narration makes visible their repression and control in society, Azevedo's prose seems much more aligned with that of Eça, whose characters also flirt with non-normative desires in youth, than the moralising diagnoses of Botelho.

## Concluding Remarks

My discussion, in this chapter, of two of Azevedo's rather less studied novels, *O mulato* and *Casa de pensão*, and not the better-known *O cortiço*, is partly strategic since it serves to show, I hope, the wealth of work by this remarkable author that is ripe for readings of the kind that Cândido performs, attentive to 'deviant' writing practices, even when he himself describes the remainder of Azevedo's novels as 'geralmente medíocre'.[120] I do not mean to dispute *O cortiço*'s pre-eminence as his greatest novel, and it remains arguably the one that most convincingly problematises the diversity of Brazilian society, expanding the allegory of *Casa de pensão* to include a fuller range of classes and races. Perhaps, however, Azevedo's 'lesser' novels have too often been flattened in critical readings, read against Zola's precedents as a measure of 'success', as though the author had no mind or pen of his own, a literary automaton from an 'inauthentic' culture. Instead, we should surely take Cândido's cue and look for the points at which the 'copy' does not measure up to the model. In both *O mulato* and *Casa de pensão*, these are perhaps the moments of greatest literary interest, when the blind spots of contemporaneous European discourses are enthusiastically brought to light in a culture marginalised by, but nevertheless implicated in them. Hence the liberal, abolitionist Raimundo's disavowal of his dark family past; hence too the seductive, yet ultimately pernicious, influence of the European in *Casa de pensão*, disrupted by the terrifying stare of Nini. In a sense, the manifest limitation of Naturalist thought in Azevedo's work — the recourse to myth, allegory and the metaphysical — works to articulate the uneven pressures of a burgeoning global capitalism, a theme surely no less relevant today than it was in the late nineteenth century. Azevedo's less celebrated works remain strikingly insightful in this respect.

The Naturalist movement in Brazil, however, sowed the seeds for its relative unpopularity in the twentieth century with its penchant for racist, misogynist and xenophobic discourse.[121] To put it simply, narrators' descriptions of the overweight as farm animals, or of black women with 'tetas opulentas',[122] are a far cry from what today is often termed the 'politically correct', and have rightly been called out by critics for their role in perpetuating what most now recognise as devastating stereotypes. However, if we delve beyond the surface of such language, and analyse the texts as a whole, it is evident that Azevedo in fact resisted naturalising representations of race, kinship, and even gender, despite his reproduction of them at times, proving remarkably deft at questioning these forms of relationality in society. Race and the patriarchal family in particular find no easy ideological home in his work, both presented in different ways as precarious, if powerful, social constructs, the former in *O mulato*, and the latter in *Casa de pensão*, where Nini stares in isolation at the hypocrisy and emptiness of 'family' values in a capitalist world, glimpsing a more visceral orientation of social relations. Curiously, then, an ostensibly white, male, normalising, 'scientific' perspective ultimately forges a critique of the intertwining pillars that ought to sustain its authority: racial supremacy, the hegemony of bourgeois, patriarchal codes, and of course the institutions of 'science' and literature, inasmuch as tragedy, allegory, folklore and superstition disrupt Zola's empirical experiment. Perhaps this disruption should come as little surprise: it was, after all, market capitalism, colonialism and the naturalisation of racial-national 'hierarchies' that, in the nineteenth century in particular, colluded to leave Brazil dependent on to the metropolitan centres whence these forces were unleashed.

There is one other way in which Azevedo's Naturalism carries the mark of its country, and here it seems pertinent to compare the structure of his Naturalist critique with that of Eça de Queirós. In many respects, there are striking similarities. Both expose a *parentesco postiço* that raises the possibility of a different way of forging societal bonds. So too do they evidently view Positivist thought, and by extension Naturalist writing, with a healthy pinch of scepticism. But in many respects their critiques operate in contrary motion. Eça, in *Os Maias* at least, takes on kinship at its ideological root, exploring the semantic excesses and shortcomings of its signifying system. Normative kinship is picked apart on its own terms to critique the problematic modes of relationality that it engenders. In *Casa de pensão*, however, the movement works in the opposite direction, with the critique of the contemporaneous socio-economic system — a hotchpotch of slavery, free markets and colonialism — reflected back allegorically in a 'deformed' family. As such, Azevedo relies on stereotypes, which doubtless relates to his differing canonical position to Eça. Interestingly, however, despite ample commentary on Azevedo's 'copies' of *O crime do Padre Amaro* and *L'Assommoir*, the possible influence of *O mulato* on the preeminent *Os Maias* has not been entertained, despite many striking similarities, which is probably symptomatic of the unidirectional manner in which transatlantic relations tend to be conceived, the reality proving somewhat more reciprocal. Indeed, there is one aspect in which *O mulato* and *Os Maias* converge remarkably in form and social critique: the motif of an Oedipal tragedy implicating a past of slavery and colonialism in the maladies of the present day. That both authors used (and adapted) Sophocles' tragedy as a tool with which to question a common set of historical processes testifies to the importance of understanding the movement as a phenomenon spanning both sides of the Atlantic, as well as to the continued close cultural contact between former coloniser and colonised in the decades following Brazilian independence, all too readily misinterpreted as plagiarism.

Aluísio Azevedo, therefore, the half-forgotten pioneer from Maranhão, ought surely to be remembered as a central figure in the Lusophone Naturalist movement, notable for his diverse and sometimes influential appropriation of alternative epistemologies to problematise the logic of desire, kinship and colonialism. In *O mulato* and *Casa de pensão*, the myths and allegories of the Romantics, as well as the looming and now-familiar influence of Sophocles, disrupt the narrative to renegotiate the nexus of (European) structures of power. Despite some slips into the language of prejudice, his work is much richer and more nuanced than a straightforward endorsement of *branqueamento* and the interests of the abolitionist bourgeoisie. Formally, too, Azevedo exhibits a willingness to borrow from a range of cultural traditions so that the ideas, to misquote Schwarz, are adapted to the time and place. Is this, perhaps, an early manifestation of the 'canibalização' [cannibalisation] in Brazilian culture that Oswald de Andrade identified and advocated aesthetically almost four decades later?[123] This is the question with which I would like to turn to the final text I will consider in this book, Adolfo Caminha's *Bom Crioulo*.

## Notes to Chapter 3

1. João de Cruz e Sousa, *Missal* (Rio de Janeiro: Magalhães & Cia Editores, 1893).
2. Adolfo Caminha, 'Norte e Sul', in *Cartas literárias*, ed. by Italo Gurgel (Fortaleza: UFC Edições, 1999), pp. 107–12.
3. Richard Burton, 'Terminal Essay', from *The Arabian Nights* (New York: Cosimo Classics, 2008), vol. x, pp. 63–260.
4. Thomas Skidmore, 'Racial Ideas and Social Policy in Brazil, 1870–1940', in *The Idea of Race in Latin America, 1870–1940*, ed. by Richard Graham (Austin: University of Texas Press, 1990), pp. 7–30 (pp. 11–12).
5. Caminha, p. 111.
6. Ibid., p. 11 (emphasis added).
7. Ibid., pp. 108–10.
8. Nelson Werneck Sodré, *O Naturalismo no Brasil* (Rio de Janeiro: Editôra Civilização Brasileira, 1965), p. 168.
9. See Marshall C. Eakin, 'Race and Identity: Sílvio Romero, Science, and Social Thought in Late 19th Century Brazil,' *Luso-Brazilian Review*, 22 (1985), 151–74 (pp. 164–65).
10. Ibid., p. 167.
11. Charles Darwin, *On the Origin of Species* (Oxford: Oxford World Classics, 1996).
12. Ibid., p. 153.
13. Josué Montello, 'A ficção naturalista', in *A literatura no Brasil*, ed. by Afrânio Coutinho (Rio de Janeiro: José Olympio, 1986), vol. IV, pp. 69–90 (p. 75).
14. Dorothy Loos, *The Naturalistic Novel of Brazil* (New York: Hispanic Institute in the United States, 1963), pp. 148–49.
15. See Lúcia Miguel Pereira, *Prosa de ficção (de 1870 a 1920)* (Rio de Janeiro: José Olympio, 1950), p. 126, and Flora Sussekind, *Tal Brasil, qual romance? Uma ideologia estética e sua história: Naturalismo* (Rio de Janeiro: Achiamé, 1984), p. 53.
16. David Brookshaw, *Race and Colour in Brazilian Literature* (London: The Scarecrow Press, 1986), pp. 41–49.
17. Murray Graeme MacNicoll, 'O Mulato and Maranhão: The Socio-Historical Context', *Luso-Brazilian Review*, 12.2 (Winter 1975), pp. 234–40 (p. 239).
18. Ibid., p. 238.
19. Published in 1891, this tale of a missionary's struggle against the unforgiving Amazon landscape, often cited as one of the first Brazilian Naturalist novels, is another obvious candidate for further study in my line of enquiry. See Inglês de Sousa, *O missionário* (Charleston, SC: Nabu Press, 2012). See also Sodré, p. 173.

20. See    <http://g1.globo.com/ma/maranhao/noticia/2014/03/interior-da-casa-onde-aluisio-azevedo-morou-em-sao-luis-esta-destruido.html> [accessed 29 September 2016].

21. Loos, p. 54.

22. See Antônio Cândido, 'De Cortiço a Cortiço', *Novos Estudos*, CEBRAP, 30 (July 1991), 111–29.

23. Cited by Sodré, p. 172.

24. See Maria Filomena Mónica, *Eça de Queirós* (Braga: Quetzal, 2001), p. 202.

25. Roberto Schwarz, 'As ideias fora do lugar', in *Ao vencedor as batatas* (São Paulo: Editora 34, 2000), pp. 11–31.

26. Roberto Schwarz, 'Nacional por subtração', in *Que horas são? Ensaios* (São Paulo: Companhia das Letras, 1987), pp. 29–48 (pp. 29–30).

27. Schwarz, 'As ideias...', p. 17.

28. Schwarz, 'Nacional...', p. 39.

29. Silviano Santiago, 'Eça, Autor de *Madame Bovary*', in *Uma literatura nos trópicos: ensaios sobre a dependência cultural* (Rio de Janeiro: Rocco, 2000), pp. 47–65 (p. 63).

30. Ibid., p. 53.

31. See Santiago, 'O entre-lugar do discurso americano', in *Uma literatura...*, pp. 9–26

32. See Nelson Vieira, *Portugal e o Brasil: a imagem recíproca (o mito e a realidade na expressão literária)* (Lisbon: Instituto de Cultura e Língua Portuguesa, 1991), p. 96.

33. Ibid., p. 96.

34. Adolfo Caminha, *A normalista* (Rio de Janeiro: Ática, 1998), p. 174.

35. Caminha, *A normalista*, pp. 32–33.

36. This is a reference to the passage in which Basílio sinks between Luísa's knees to teach her a new sensation. See Eça de Queirós, *O primo Basílio*, in *Obras completas de Eça de Queirós*, vol. 1, p. 223.

37. Regina Zilberman, 'Eça entre os brasileiros de ontem e hoje', in *Eças e outros: diálogos com a ficção de Eça de Queirós* (Porto Alegre: EDIPUCRS, 2002), pp. 7–21 (p. 19).

38. Carlos Eduardo Bezerra, *Adolfo Caminha: um polígrafo na literatura brasileira do século XIX (1885–1897)* (São Paulo: Editora UNESP, 2009), p. 362.

39. As Eça writes in a letter to Teófilo Braga, the novel was designed to 'destruir as falsas interpretações e falsas realizações' [destroy the false interpretations and false realisations] that supposedly rotted Portuguese society. See Eça de Queirós, *Correspondência* (Lisbon: Caminho, 2008), p. 135.

40. Eça himself addresses the criticism that *O crime* was a copy of Zola's *La Faute de l'Abbé Mouret* in the preface to the second edition.

41. Cited by Sylvio Lago in *Eça de Queirós: ensaios e estudos* (São Paulo: Biblioteca 24 horas, 2010), p. 89.

42. Josué Montello, *Aluísio Azevedo e a polêmica d''O Mulato'* (Rio de Janeiro: José Olympia, 1975), p. 3.

43. Loos, p. 42.

44. Cited by Loos, p. 43.

45. Loos, pp. 40–41. See also Coutinho, p. 76.

46. Cited by Luís Filipe Ribeiro, 'O Sexo e o Poder no Império: *Philomena Borges*', *Luso-Brazilian Review*, 30 (1993), 7–20 (p. 8).

47. Loos, p. 36.

48. Ibid., p. 31.

49. See Karl Marx and Friedrich Engels, *On Literature and Art* (New York: International General, 1974).

50. Berta Waldman identifies kinship as a central theme in *Casa de pensão*, relating it to the epistemological tensions in the narration. See introduction to *Casa de pensão*, 5th edn (São Paulo: Editora Ática, 1989), pp. 5–9 (p. 6). I will return to this insight in my subsequent analysis of the novel.

51. Cândido, p. 127.

52. For this argument, see, for example, Elizabeth A. Marchant, 'Naturalism Race, and Nationalism in Aluísio Azevedo's *O Mulato*', *Hispania*, 83 (2000), 445–53.

53. Daphne Patai and Murray MacNicoll mention that Azevedo 'limns the story of Oedipus', but

do not explore this facet in any depth. See Introduction to *Mulatto*, trans. by Murray Graeme MacNicoll, ed. by Daphne Patai (London: Associated University Press, 1990), p. 18.

54. See Valentim Magalhães, *Escritores e escritos* (Rio de Janeiro: Camiliano, 1889), p. 82.

55. Aluísio Azevedo, *O mulato* (São Paulo: Klick Editora, 1999), p. 3. All page references are to this edition.

56. MacNicoll, 'O *Mulato* and Maranhão', p. 239.

57. Loos, p. 44.

58. I thus disagree here with Josué Montello's book-length study of O *mulato*, which reads the novel almost exclusively through the lens of anticlericalism and what he claims is its 'concordância... perfeita' with O *crime do Padre Amaro*. See Montello, *Aluísio Azevedo...*, p. 3. As we shall see, Azevedo draws on a much wider range of influences in his structuring of O *mulato*, including local *maranhense* myths.

59. MacNicoll, p. 234.

60. As regards the novel's similarities with *Os Maias*, it is interesting to note that O *mulato* was published after Eça wrote *A tragédia da Rua das Flores* (1877–78) and before the publication of *Os Maias* chronologically, both novels that take incest as a central theme. In the lesser-known *A tragédia*, however, which was not published in Eça's lifetime, the incest occurs between mother and son, and in many ways *Os Maias*, with its banished mother and long-forgotten siblings, bears many more similarities to O *mulato*. Thus even if Eça did not take his cues from Azevedo in his concern with incest itself, the differences between *Os Maias* and *A tragédia* raise the possibility that Eça revised his approach after reading Azevedo's supposed 'copy' of O *crime*. See Eça de Queirós, *A tragédia da Rua das Flores* (Lisbon: Fernando Pereira, 1980).

61. Marchant, p. 450.

62. See Terence, *Andria*, with intro. by George Shipp (London: Bristol Classical Press, 2002).

63. Marchant, p. 448.

64. Sophocles, *Oedipus the King*, trans. by David Grene in *Sophocles I: Antigone, Oedipus the King and Oedipus at Colonus*, ed. by Mark Griffith and Glenn W. Most (London: Chicago University Press, 2013), pp. 71–143 (p. 92).

65. There is another kind of relationality, besides cousinship, that would allow for such a formulation, and that is if Raimundo were Ana Rosa's half-brother. This is the state of affairs in one of Azevedo's so-called 'pulp productions', O *homem*, in which Magdá gradually goes mad after her father forbids her from marrying her half-brother, Fernando. Again, in this novel, the consanguinity of the half-siblings is kept secret until they fall in love, and the incest taboo is called into question by Magdá's father himself, who asks, '[n]ão seria tudo aquilo um crime maior do que os seus passados amores com a mãe de Fernando?... Sim; estes ao menos não se baseavam em preconceitos e vaidades, baseavam-se nos instintos e na ternura' [would it all be a greater crime than his past love for Fernando's mother?... Indeed; these were at least not based on prejudice and vanity, but on instinct and tenderness]. The novel loses some, though not all, of its initial radical thrust as it follows Magdá's 'pathological' descent into madness, but it is nonetheless interesting as another instance in which Azevedo experiments with the greyer areas of the incest taboo. See Aluísio Azevedo, O *homem* (Rio de Janeiro: Livraria Garnier, 1923), p. 34.

66. I am here following the reading of Daphne Patai and Murray MacNicoll, who ask, '[m]ight not the function of the white-black character, suffering the stigma of race, be precisely to call into the question the entire system of coding [...] that sustains domination?' See introduction to *Mulatto*, p. 23.

67. Diogo, in fact, ever in defence of the status quo, is perhaps the only character who demonstrates understanding of race as a social construction, more so even than Raimundo. As he tries to convince Dias to shoot Raimundo at the end, he mentions Ana Rosa's developing baby, 'já se sabe, parecida com o pai...' [with its father's likeness, as we know] (p. 307), arguing that as long as Raimundo lives, the child will seek his true father — like Raimundo himself of course, as Azevedo hints at the possibility of tragic repetition through the generations. However, Diogo then implies that if Raimundo is killed, the true father of the child matters not the least, the pregnancy being, on the contrary, an advantage: 'vejamos agora o que sucederá se você seguir o

meu conselho: a rapariga chora por algum tempo, pouco, muito pouco, porque eu a consolarei com as minhas palavras; depois como precisa de um pai para o filho, casa-se com você, e aí está o meu amigo, de um dia para outro, feliz, rico, independente!' [let's see now what will happen if you follow my advice: the girl cries for a time, a little, only a little, because I will console her with my words; then, as she will need a father for the child, she marries you, and there we are my friend, from one day to the next, happy, rich, independent!] (p. 310). The child dies when Ana Rosa miscarries, and so this outcome is foreclosed, but it stands that Diogo realises that race is ultimately defined at the level of discourse, and not physiology.

68. See Peter Fryer, *Rhythms of Resistance: African Musical Heritage in Brazil* (London: Pluto Press, 2000), p. 74.

69. Inês Aguiar de Freitas and Paul Claval, 'Seasonality in Brazil', in *Seasonal Landscapes*, ed. by Hannes Palang et al. (Dordrecht: Springer, 2007), pp. 61–85 (p. 71).

70. See José Sousa dos Reis, *Bumba meu boi, o maior espectáculo do Maranhão* (Recife: Fundação Joaquim Nabuco, 1980), pp. 12–16.

71. Anonymous journalist, cited by Fryer, p. 75.

72. This version of story is taken from Fryer, p. 75.

73. This version is taken from <http://bumba-meu-boi.info/a-lenda.html> [accessed 17 November 2016].

74. See Eugene Genovese, '*Our Family, White and Black:* Family and Household in the Southern Slaveholders' World View', in *In Joy and in Sorrow: Women, Family, and Marriage in the Victorian South, 1830–1900*, ed. by Carol Bleser (New York: Oxford University Press, 1991), pp. 69–87.

75. Gilberto Freyre, *Casa-Grande e senzala: formação da família brasileira sob o regime da economia patriarcal* (Rio de Janeiro: Maia & Schmidt, 1933).

76. Mukuna, cited by Fryer, p. 74.

77. See, for example, Sílvio Romero's 1883 work, *Cantos populares do Brasil* (São Paulo: José Olympio, 1954), in which he brings together popular songs from his homeland.

78. <http://www.ornithos.com.br/escola/mitos-e-lendas/a-lenda-do-urutau-mae-da-lua/> [accessed 22 October 2016].

79. Eça de Queirós, *Correspondência*, p. 135.

80. Cândido, p. 115.

81. For the most prominent proponent of this reading, see Marchant, 'Naturalism, Race, and Nationalism...', in which she describes Raimundo as privileged uniquely with a 'positive portrayal', being an 'enlightened national type' (p. 448).

82. MacNicoll, p. 239.

83. Loos, p. 44.

84. I do not wish to claim, of course, that Azevedo's novel is in any way a defence of Maranhão's provincial ways; on the contrary, the criticism of its widespread racism, as a case in point, is particularly elaborate, and the author's derision for his compatriots is more than evident in his preface to the third edition (see *O mulato*, pp. 11–14). However, at the level of discourse and ideas, *O mulato* nonetheless appears to incorporate elements from both province and metropolis in its search for a Brazilian narrative voice.

85. One of most comic, and no less fine, examples of the problematic reception of science in *O mulato* is when Freitas mentions the *Cucurbitaceae* family of vegetables, to which the senile Dona Amância, 'a sentir o cheiro de uma intriga' [sniffing out a scandal], replies, 'Ah! são estrangeiros!... Já sei, já sei! é uma família de bifes, que está morando no Hotel da Boavista! É certo, agora lembro que ainda est'outr'dia uma sujeita ruiva... deve ser mulher ou filha do tal...' [Ah! Those foreigners!... I know who you mean! That British family staying at the Hotel da Boavista! Of course, now I remember; just the other day I saw a ginger woman... She must be the mother or daughter] (p. 160).

86. Patai and MacNicoll, for example, argue that *O mulato* 'portrays the continuing prominence of Portuguese immigrants in Maranhão'. See Introduction to *Mulatto*, p. 10.

87. Obesity is clearly used as an often-xenophobic trope of degeneracy in *O mulato*, typically used to mark exploitative capitalists. Already in the opening pages, '[v]iam-se deslizar pela praça os imponentes e monstruosos abdomens dos capitalistas' [the monstrous and imposing abdomens of the capitalists could be seen sliding across the square] (p. 19). The Portuguese in particular

are stereotyped as fat and interested only in capital. The enormous, floor-shuddering Lindoca, meanwhile, who balloons over the course of the novel, is described in the terms of a farm animal with 'banhas' [pork fat], her nose likened to a 'lombinho' [piece of loin] (pp. 79–80). Gradually confined to the household, she becomes an allegory for the immobility of *Maranhense* society.

88. Cândido identifies a similar current in *O cortiço* where, he argues, the narrator occupies the precarious position of the white Brazilian, quick to profess his racial superiority over the black protagonists, but hateful of the European, who works no harder than the Brazilian but who nevertheless 'acaba mais rico e mais importante' [ends up richer and more important]. See Cândido, p. 117.

89. The young, pale Portuguese boy, Gustavo de Vila Rica, is found altered at the end of the novel, losing his 'belas cores europeias' [handsome European complexion] and becoming pock-marked with venereal disease (p. 325).

90. Marchant, p. 448.

91. Freud, 'Further Recommendations in the Technique of Psycho-Analysis: Remembering, Repeating, and Working-Through', trans. from the German by Joan Riviere, in *The Standard Edition of the Complete Works of Sigmund Freud* (London: Hogarth Press, 1950), vol. XII, pp. 145–57 (p. 150). In the case of *O mulato*, it is not possible that Raimundo remembers the events of his father's escape from Grão-Pará, lived prior to his birth, although he nonetheless spends his infant years on the *fazenda*, witnessing both considerable wealth and the corresponding abuse of slaves, including his own mother. I thus deploy this Freudian insight here in a slightly augmented or societal sense, to stress the manner in which the traumas of the past return to disrupt the present when not sufficiently addressed or recognised.

92. ' — Não me toques! gritava o moço, com raiva, *levantando o chicote*' ['don't touch me!' shouted the young man angrily, *raising his whip*'] (p. 216, emphasis added).

93. See Robert Bernasconi and Anika Maaza Mann, 'The Contradictions of Racism: Locke, Slavery and the *Two Treatises*', in *Race and Racism in Modern Philosophy*, ed. by Andrew Valls (London: Cornell University Press), pp. 90–107 (p. 90).

94. Roberto Schwarz mentions this example in 'Misplaced Ideas...', including some highly charged barbs by nineteenth-century Brazilians on the matter. See Schwarz, p. 19. Modern-day parallels are all too compelling: the extraction and export of fossil fuels by countries who promote domestic use of renewable energy, for example, or the criticism of deforestation by those who continue to import and consume the resultant agricultural produce.

95. See Loos, pp. 40–41.

96. Here I am therefore developing the insights of Berta Waldman in her introduction to *Casa de pensão*, in which she argues that 'a casa de pensão guarda em si relações familiares, só que desencadeadas mediante pagamento' [the guesthouse does contain familial relations, but they are subject to payment], a dynamic that she relates to the tensions between Romanticism and Naturalism in the novel. See Waldman, pp. 6–7.

97. Lacan associates the Imaginary with the mother, and the Symbolic with the father. Malcolm Bowie discusses Lacan's abstraction of Freudian theory in this respect in *Lacan* (Cambridge, MA: Harvard University Press, 1991), pp. 57–58.

98. Angela Maria Rubel Fanini, 'Uma solução local para formas importadas em *Casa de pensão*', *Anuário de literatura: publicação do Curso de Pós-Graduação em Letras, Literatura Brasileira e Teoria Literária*, 8 (2000), 29–56.

99. Aluísio Azevedo, *Casa de pensão* (Rio de Janeiro: Ediouro, 1980). All page references are to this edition.

100. Capistrano was a student murdered by the brother of his former lover. The judicial case caused great sensation in Rio at the time. See Fanini, pp. 34–35. As with *O Barão de Lavos*, there is an engagement here with contemporary 'crimes of passion'.

101. Ibid., p. 48.

102. Ibid., p. 41.

103. Ibid., p. 46.

104. See, for example, Doris Summer, *Foundational Fictions: The National Romances of Latin America* (London: University of California Press, 1991), pp. 143–45.

105. Paul de Man, *Blindness and Insight: Essays in the Rhetoric of Contemporary Criticism* (Abingdon: Routledge, 1983), p. 208.

106. See <http://www.priberam.pt/dlpo/pensao> [accessed 4 November 2016].

107. Michel Foucault, *The History of Sexuality*, vol. I: *An Introduction*, trans. by Robert Hurley (New York: Vintage Books, 1978), pp. 27–28.

108. Émile Zola, *Au Bonheurs des Dames* (Paris: Fasquelle, 1962).

109. See Brookshaw, p. 49.

110. Maria Manuel Lisboa, 'A Mother is a Boy's Best Friend: Birth and Kinslaying in the Brazilian Foundation Novel', *Portuguese Studies*, 13 (1997), 95–107 (p. 98).

111. José de Alencar, *Iracema* (Rio de Janeiro: Ediçoes BestBolso, 2012).

112. Lisboa, p. 98.

113. See Vieira, p. 111.

114. Aluísio Azevedo, *O cortiço* (São Paulo, Editora Ática, 2005).

115. Madame Brizard's greatest pride is her 'rico pescoço' [rich neck], 'um grande pescoço pálido cheio de ondulações macias e fartas' [a large neck, pale and filled with soft, loose waves] (p. 80). The use of obesity here as a pejorative trope of greed and stagnation echoes that which we saw in relation to Lindoca and the Portuguese capitalists in *O mulato*.

116. Louis Philippe's ascension to the throne leads Monsieur Brizard and his wife to flee France for Brazil (p. 80).

117. Amélia's somewhat two-dimensional character is thus similar to that of Ana Rosa and perhaps the majority of high-society women in Azevedo's work. Marchant suggests on this basis that gender remains an 'unexplored realm', although two other novels, *Filomena Borges* and *O livro da sogra*, the latter a first-person narrative of an older lady sharing her thoughts on love and sex, are more complex in this respect. See, for example, Luís Filipe Ribeiro, 'O Sexo e o Poder no Império: *Philomena Borges*', *The Luso-Brazilian Review*, 30 (1993), 7–20.

118. Oscar Wilde, *The Picture of Dorian Gray* (London: Penguin Classics, 2003).

119. The perversion of the 'scientific' gaze in relation to the hysteric is arguably the central concern of the later *O homem*, which has as its protagonist the hysteric Magdá, tended to by a heartless and authoritarian doctor and her well-meaning but helpless father. There is very little written about the novel in recent times, and insufficient space to discuss it in any detail here, but it serves nevertheless as a more developed example of Azevedo's criticism of the potentially destructive application of 'science' and paternal authority even as he reproduces many of its tenets.

120. Cândido, p. 112.

121. MacNicoll, for example, arguably forecloses a discussion of racial politics in *O mulato* with his suggestion that such racialised discourse renders the novel unable to function as anything other than an 'exposé of provincial pettiness'. See MacNicoll, p. 239.

122. Azevedo, *O mulato*, p. 18.

123. Andrade characterised Brazilian culture as 'cannibalistic' in its unabashed digestion of imported models, a process he encapsulated with the famous lines, 'Tupi, or not tupi that is the question'. See Oswald de Andrade, 'Manifesto Antropófago', available at <http://www.ufrgs.br/cdrom/oandrade/oandrade.pdf> [accessed 21 March 2016].

# CHAPTER 4

# Adolfo Caminha

## Introduction

To consider, at the end of this book, Adolfo Caminha's *Bom Crioulo* [*The Good Creole*], with its similarities in plot to *O Barão de Lavos*, is not so much to return to where we began — the 'scientific' portrayal of deviance clustered around a same-sex relationship — as to observe how the model travels and changes with great innovation across the Atlantic. In the previous chapter, I argued that Azevedo, like his Portuguese counterparts, adapts the Naturalist model by introducing narrative currents that counter its fundamental principles, such as myth and allegory, and that these constitute an attempt to construct a Brazilian voice sensitive to the inadequacy of European thought in a supposedly independent Brazil. In Caminha's *Bom Crioulo*, as the title playfully suggests and as I shall argue, such adaptations become no less than the structuring principle of the work. As we have seen, the author of *A normalista* and 'Norte e Sul', which criticises the accompanying words to Cruz e Sousa's *Missal*, was deeply preoccupied with the reception and deployment of 'scientific' thought in Brazil, apparently mistrusting its enthusiastic replication in national discourse, even if he sometimes reproduced its logic in his own criticism. Like Azevedo, Caminha grew up in the 'underdeveloped' *Nordeste*, in neighbouring Ceará, and his admiration for the Positivist ideas of the *Escola do Recife*, of which he was an 'herdeiro intelectual' [intellectual heir],[1] was bound up nevertheless with an awareness of their potential complicity in naturalising the economic and cultural power of metropolitan centres, particularly with regards to climate, which was central to the racial-social theories of the time. However, Caminha is altogether a more enigmatic figure than Azevedo, having published a relatively small body of work and dying of tuberculosis at the age of just twenty-nine, a state of affairs compounded by the fact that *A normalista*, *Bom Crioulo*, his critical pieces, and his travel writings on the United States, *No país dos Yankees*, exhibit considerable differences in style.[2] Even so, the marginal, postcolonial condition of Brazil is at play in all of these works, and Caminha engages closely with the dilemma of misplaced ideas. Drawing considerably on Abel Botelho's *O Barão de Lavos*, then, and yet distorting the Naturalist narration such that the model is almost unrecognisable, *Bom Crioulo* serves, I hope, as an enlightening conclusion for my analysis of 'Naturalism against nature' and its tumultuous journey around the Lusophone world. As we shall see, the meaning of the novel is in fact constructed through the connections it fosters with other Portuguese and Brazilian texts, cementing its importance within a transatlantic movement whose contours it maps and negotiates.

By turning, moreover, to *Bom Crioulo* in light of the authors considered thus far, I hope to bring an intertextual perspective that sheds new light on what is perhaps one of the most puzzling works of Brazilian literature, having divided critics considerably to this day. Published amid great scandal in 1895, this 'audácia do século XIX' [audacity from the nineteenth century],[3] about the relationship between a runaway black slave and fifteen-year-old white deckhand, has been successively scorned, censored,[4] almost forgotten, 'rediscovered' in the closing years of the twentieth century, and today finally holds a place in the Brazilian literary canon, 'if not quite at its centre',[5] and is one of the most widely read novels from the Naturalist movement in Brazil. Surpassed perhaps only by *O cortiço* in this respect, it is now generally considered Caminha's finest novel, although critical consensus apparently extends little further. Soon after the novel's publication, Valentim Magalhães described it as a 'romance-pus, romance-poia, romance-vômito' [a pus novel, a rubbish novel, a vomit novel], only two days after Alves de Faria wrote in true *fin-de-siècle* spirit that 'apanha bem certas cenas e apesar [...] de descrever atos indecentes, reais, mas repulsivos, não desagrada ao leitor' [it captures certain scenes well and despite [...] describing indecent acts, real but repulsive, it doesn't displease the reader],[6] leaving readers wondering whether the book appealed to him despite, or because of, these 'indecent' scenes. After the great stir that the novel initially caused, however, *Bom Crioulo* 'lapsed into obscurity' in the twentieth century;[7] still in 1950, Lúcia Miguel Pereira wrote that novel contained 'certas cenas repulsivas' [certain repulsive scenes],[8] and the text's unusual explicitness appears to have left critics unwilling to engage with it seriously.

This reluctance changed markedly later in the century, when the American LGBT movement 'discovered' the novel and hailed it as 'a founding text of Brazilian gay literature',[9] sentiments typified in the 1980s English translation by Gay Sunshine Press with the altogether less subtle title of *The Black Man and the Cabin Boy*, which Cristiano Mazzei has since criticised for 'outing' the original text to attract a gay readership in the United States, softening the language of degeneration theory in relation to same-sex desire and reinforcing the element of the exotic.[10] There has since been a persistent tendency amongst critics to foreground 'homosexuality' in analysis and read the novel as an 'early apologia for gay rights'.[11] More recently, however, César Braga-Pinto has drawn attention to the importance of degeneration theory in *Bom Crioulo*, reading the novel against Cesare Lombroso's 'science' of criminal man and cautioning against analyses that overlook the pathological treatment of race, violence and homosexuality. It is curious indeed that a novel that describes the pleasures of the central relationship as 'contra a natureza' [against nature], reproducing all the 'stereotypes, prejudices and misinformation of the time',[12] has led to a number of readings that appear to celebrate its 'surprisingly modern approach towards issues of race, nationality, gender and sexuality'.[13] By bringing intertextuality into play, taking my cue from the novel's title and Elizabeth

Ginway's insight that *Bom Crioulo* is a 'cultural hybrid',[14] I hope to disentangle these contrasting readings and propose a different framework for understanding the text, whereby its principle concern is not 'homosexuality', still less gay rights, but lies rather in 'creolising' and renegotiating degeneration theory to imagine a 'viable' future for Brazil in an age of cultural and economic dependency.[15]

*Bom Crioulo* tells the story of Amaro, an escaped slave born in Brazil, who works as a sailor on an old merchant ship. In the years following his escape, he proves to be an exemplary worker, acquiring the nickname of 'Bom Crioulo' from his colleagues — who admire his figure of an 'homem robusto' [robust man] — and submitting himself, without complaint, 'à vontade superior' [to the will of his superiors] (pp. 26–27). The only sign of his propensity for destructive behaviour, which becomes increasingly clear over the course of the novel, is his tendency to 'de longe em longe [...] se chafurdar em bebedeiras que o obrigavam a toda sorte de loucuras' [degrade himself with bouts of drunkenness that drove him to all sorts of crazed acts] (p. 26). At the beginning of the story, however, he falls passionately in love with Aleixo, a young, blond teenager of pale skin and effeminate figure. Their budding relationship, which begins happily, leads them to rent an apartment in a garret on the Rua da Misercórdia, Rio de Janeiro, owned by a corpulent Portuguese lady named Carola Bunda, who, as we shall see, bears striking resemblances to the obese Madame Brizard of *Casa de pensão*. Carola is supposedly an old friend of Amaro, grateful towards him for having saved her life in the past. However, after a year of perfect love and 'gozo espiritual' [spiritual pleasure] (p. 69), Amaro is forced to work on a different ship, larger and more modern, which he is forbidden from leaving and where he is punished brutally for the slightest infraction of the rules. One day he flees the vessel, but drinks excessively in the city until landing himself in a fight with a Portuguese provocateur, after which he is arrested, returned to the ship and whipped mercilessly as punishment, requiring his convalescence in hospital. As such, Aleixo and Amaro spend months apart, leaving the latter increasingly jealous and imagining that Aleixo is with another man. Aleixo, however, is seduced by Carola Bunda herself, who thus betrays her old 'friend' without remorse, intercepting and destroying the desperate letter he writes to Aleixo in hospital. The intergenerational love triangle, portending imminent disaster, thus clearly echoes that of *O Barão de Lavos*, though with several important differences that I will return to later. Eventually, Amaro escapes from captivity in hospital and returns to the Rua da Misericórdia, where he learns definitively of his betrayal by his friend and lover from a local baker. Enraged, he murders Aleixo in broad daylight and the closing lines, in another nod to *Lavos*, depict him being carried away by policemen.

Despite what seems to be an invitation to identify with Amaro, surely the 'hero' of the story,[16] and with his plight, the language used in the novel reveals a more complex picture. As I have indicated, the narrator describes the sexual acts of the 'pederasta' — as Amaro is frequently described — as 'contra a natureza', reproducing theories of sexuality being developed at the time by figures such as Krafft-Ebing, and which aimed to establish 'homosexuality' (a term that, as we know, the movement itself invented) as a pathological abnormality.[17] Even if such language is less pointed and diffuse in *Bom Crioulo* than it is in *Lavos*, it arguably casts a wider pathological net with its close interaction with race, alcoholism and criminality, categories which, as we saw in the case of *Lavos*, readily overlap. Braga-Pinto's study is particularly adept at demonstrating how the protagonist presents a constellation of 'symptoms' that mark him as a 'pathological' being, going as far as to affirm that the novel is a 'case study' of degeneration theory and in particular of Lombroso's criminal anthropology.[18] It is in this spirit, certainly, that the narrator describes Amaro as a 'sistema de músculos' [system of muscles] and 'morbidez patológica' [pathological morbidity] (p. 21). It seems pertinent, too, to consider Robert Howes's claim that the central relationship, being necessarily non-generative, allows the author to avoid contemplating miscegenation as a form of integrating the freed slave into the new republic.[19] In this sense, the supposedly audacious homosexual relationship in fact serves to reinforce strict distinctions of race. Challenging the sexual orthodoxy for its own sake does not seem to have been Caminha's intention, and in the marginalising language deployed in relation to race and sexuality, we can hear the echo, even if dampened,[20] of *O Barão de Lavos*. Even though the recourse to Greek pederasty, and Platonic thought more generally, recalls other Lusophone novels from the period, Caminha, like Botelho, often re-inscribes the relationship in the terms of degeneration theory.

However, whilst the discourse of degeneration and criminality can explain much of the characterisation in *Bom Crioulo*, particularly with regards to Amaro, leaving a sizeable linguistic footprint, there are also clear signs that the author contemplates its tenets at a critical distance. Besides the twisting and intertwining of cultural loans in the novel's composition, which I will be exploring over the course of this chapter, I would like to mention two observations by critics that present a challenge to Braga-Pinto's claim that the novel is a 'case study' of degeneration theory. Firstly, Howes points astutely to the character of Herculano, an onanist with the unfortunate nickname of '*Pingas*' [Drip-Drop], scandalously caught in the act at the beginning of the novel, but who, at the end, appears:

> outro, admiravelmente outro, o Herculano — gordo, rosado, o olhar vivo e brilhante, sem melancolia, nem sombra alguma de tristeza. Perdera a antiga palidez que lhe dava um arzinho pulha de coisa à toa, falava desempenado, alto, e ria, como uma criança, por ninharias. (p. 136)

> [a new man, an admirably new man, Herculano — plump, rosy, with bright, lively eyes, free of melancholy, without a trace of sadness. He had lost his former pallidness that lent him a vacant air, and now spoke with confidence, loudly, and laughing like a child at trivialities.]

Instead of 'degenerating', as theories of sexuality would dictate, the onanist seems entirely rejuvenated. Howes interprets this detail as a rejection, on the part of the author, of some of the more extreme strands of degeneration theory.[21] However, the description of Herculano's health is particularly emphatic, the extensive list of attributes heightening the sense of admiration, involving words opposed in meaning to those typically associated with degeneration theory ('rosado', 'vivo', 'brilhante').

There is surely irony in Herculano's plump, ruddy appearance, the image of a healthy, well-fed man, when set against the dark prophesies of degeneration theory. Might this episode not also constitute a jibe on the part of the author at the theories that he nonetheless reproduces elsewhere which, to use Santiago's phrase, comes to surprise the original model?[22] Caminha appears to play with the imported theories, demonstrating, above all, a degree of critical distance that Braga-Pinto's reading, attentive to the similarities with the work of Lombroso, does not necessarily account for.

This independence of thought is alluded to in the analysis of another critic, this time by Celina Moreira de Mello, who uncovers 'uma discrepância entre o que autor pensa de seu romance e o romance que de fato ele escreveu' [a discrepancy between what the author thinks about his novel and the novel he actually wrote].[23] Although, in the article that he wrote in defence of *Bom Crioulo* after the torrent of criticism that followed its publication, Caminha describes his protagonist as 'um degenerado nato' [a born degenerate] with 'tendências *homossexuais*',[24] he does not make use of this term at any point in his novel. Mello perhaps exaggerates when she argues that this conspicuous lexical absence suggests the author believed 'que amar uma pessoa do mesmo sexo não era um crime, mas um destino' [loving someone of the same sex was not a crime, but a matter of destiny],[25] but it is nonetheless significant that Caminha seems not to have trusted this pseudoscientific term with which he was evidently familiar. Despite the word not being widely known or used at the time, the author still recognised it as one of the most authoritative and acceptable when the novel was criticised by prudish readers. Indeed, the criticism that surrounded the publication of *Bom Crioulo* warrants comment in itself, especially since it was marked by a series of speculations about the author's own sexuality.[26] Unfortunately, and still recently, some critics have continued the speculation, reproducing the Foucauldian notion of the 'will to know',[27] in which sexuality figures as a mysterious realm hiding inaccessible truths, identified by Anna Klobucka as a recurring theme within Lusophone studies.[28] In any case, it seems reasonable to suggest that such speculation would not have been welcome on the part of the author, and that he availed himself of 'scientific' language in an attempt to attenuate its influence. It is curious, in this context, that the word 'homossexual' does not appear in *Bom Crioulo*, implying a restriction of pseudoscientific thought in the narrative. Correspondingly, the scandal that the novel provoked, far greater than the relative feather-ruffling caused by the publication of Botelho's unapologetically 'pathological' work, *O Barão de Lavos*,[29] suggests that Caminha's narrative deeply offended bourgeois sensibilities in a way that Botelho's did not, and continued to do so well into the 1950s when Lúcia Miguel Pereira contemplated the novel. The scandal illustrates too the restrictions that contemporaneous discourses imposed on authors; several novels were censored or restricted at the time for lewd and homoerotic content,[30] and the space between the generally accepted 'pathological' genre, and writing that resulted in censorship, scandal and attacks on the author, appears to have been constrictively small. Nevertheless, one can deduce that Caminha pondered considerably over the theories that he read before reproducing them, and that he was quite willing to adapt and play with them, doubtless more than Botelho was, and despite considerable risk to his personal reputation.

## The Creolisation of Degenerescence

In light of this apparent critical distance on the part of the author in relation to degeneration theory, I now wish to explore the ways in which he distorts its principles. The imbrication and creolisation of other literary and philosophical influences that work against Positivist theories, which I claimed to be an important feature of Azevedo's work, is key to Caminha's reworking of European precedents. Several critics have commented upon the emergence of other literary styles in the novel, in particular the gothic; Leonardo Mendes identifies the role this latter plays in shrouding sexuality with an air of mystery, as reflected in the description of the old *corveta* [corvette] as 'um grande morcego apocalíptico de asas abertas sobre o mar' [a giant, apocalyptic bat, spreading its wings over the sea] (p. 15), or of the attic on the Rua da Misericórdia, in which the previous occupant dies of yellow fever, left abandoned during Amaro's absence to gather cobwebs and mildew. However, like Azevedo in *Casa de pensão*, Caminha also borrows from Romanticism, including an (anti-)foundational love triangle reminiscent of Alencar's *Iracema*, to which I will return later. Christian mythology also plays a significant role in this context. One night, when Amaro is unable to sleep on the ship's deck, he gazes at the stars, imagining them 'cantando o hino triunfal da ressurreição' [singing the triumphant hymn of the resurrection] (p. 34), suggesting a new beginning in his life. Later, when the *corveta* heads towards its destination in Rio, he wishes for the journey never to end in order to remain forever with Aleixo, in a wonderfully poetic sentence:

> desejaria que a viagem se prolongasse indefinidamente, que a corveta não chegasse nunca mais, que o mar se alargasse de repente submergindo ilhas e continentes numa cheia tremenda, e a velha nau, só ela, como uma coisa fantástica sobrevivesse ao cataclismo, ela somente, grandiosa e indestrutível ficasse flutuando, flutuando por toda a eternidade. (p. 41)

> [he wished for the journey to go on forever, for the corvette never to arrive, for the seas to rise up without warning and drown islands and continents in a tremendous flood, and for the old ship, alone in the world like something magical, to be the sole survivor of the cataclysm, majestic and unsinkable, floating, floating for all eternity.]

There are clearly utopian resonances in the eternal journey of the *corveta*,[31] audible in the calm repetition of the word 'flutuando', and in the appearance of the vessel, 'grandiosa e indestrutível', dreamed in the subjunctive. The metaphor of the flood also recalls the myth of Noah's Ark, in which the world undergoes a moral purge that ends, importantly, in another new beginning. Like the 'hino da ressurreição', this image harmonises with the foundational love triangle akin to those of Brazilian Romanticism, underscoring the novel's status as a text not just written at the beginning of a new era in the nation's history, but comprising a confluence of discourses participating actively in a renegotiation of national identity. Moreover, as with the forays into mystery and metaphysics in *O mulato*, such references to fantastical and oneiric visions constitute a strategic retreat from the tenets of 'scientific' writing which, as we shall see, again provides the key to the development of a 'viable' future for Brazil.

Having drawn attention to the plurality of styles that *Bom Crioulo* synthesises, which is in many respects anticipated by Azevedo's writing, I would now finally like to turn to the ways in which these function within the text. I shall begin with a literary model that has already been widely commented upon by critics, and one that echoes Eça's and Azevedo's use of tragedy (albeit Greek) in their novels, that of Shakespeare's *Othello*. As Daniel Rhinow demonstrates, *Othello* was a remarkably popular play in *fin-de-siècle* Brazil, fascinating authors[32] and audiences alike with what critics of the time, drawing links between race and violence, described as the 'paixões ocultas e selvagens' [hidden, wild passions] of the hero.[33] Braga-Pinto argues that the reference to Shakespeare, in this context, serves to reinforce the 'degeneracy' of the protagonist. Such a view, however, assumes that Caminha himself shared this popular take on the Moor of Venice. For this reader, and although parallels between the impassioned Othello and the *crioulo* assassin of Rio are easily drawn, there is a decisive difference between the play and the novel. In *Othello*, Iago exploits the protagonist's *hamartia*: his jealousy. There is no indication that Desdemona has been unfaithful, any insinuations of adultery being instead the result of a conspiracy plotted by Iago, including the fateful handkerchief planted in Cassio's quarters. In *Bom Crioulo*, however, as in *Lavos*, suspicions of treachery prove to be correct, implicating betrayal as a factor — alongside his heritage — leading to the murder at the end.

When Amaro escapes slavery and begins paid work for the first time, he believes in a future of freedom and contentment, 'sonhando histórias de viagem' [dreaming of tales of adventure] (p. 33), and even carving small wooden ships in his excitement prior to embarking on his maiden voyage, when he appears surrounded by well-wishers:

> Parecia-lhe ouvir ainda na proa do transporte, como as últimas reminiscências de um sonho, a voz dos companheiros abraçando-o:
> — Adeus, ó Bom Crioulo: sê feliz! (p. 34)

> [On the prow of the ship, the voices of his companions seemed to linger in the air, like a half-forgotten dream, embracing him:
> 'Farewell, Bom Crioulo: be happy!']

The voices of his companions, vague and perhaps dreamed, wish him a life of happiness, embracing him in a show of brotherhood reminiscent of Benedict Anderson's concept of 'horizontal camaraderie' and 'fraternity', with which the nation creates an imagined community to which each individual supposedly belongs,[34] a republican discourse we saw widely disrupted in the novels of Eça. In the same vein, Amaro is led to believe that Carola Bunda is a friend who does not judge by appearances:

> [Carola] não se importava de cor e tão-pouco se importava com a classe ou profissão do sujeito. Marinheiro, soldado, embarcadiço, caixeiro de venda, tudo

era a mesmíssima coisa: o tratamento que lhe fosse possível dar a um inquilino, dava-o do mesmo modo aos outros. (p. 64)

[[Carola] didn't care about skin colour and nor was she bothered about the class or profession of her guests. Sailors, soldiers, seafarers, salesmen, it was all very much the same to her: whatever she did for one guest, she did for all the others.]

The pretence to egalitarian treatment echoes the liberal constitution of Brazil that had just brought an end to slavery and the imperial regime. There is already a hint of irony here in the paradoxical use of the superlative in the word 'mesmíssima'. Amaro, as it transpires, is systematically betrayed by these supposedly liberal ideals. In the first instance, after being transferred to another vessel, he quickly learns that life on a ship which he is forbidden to leave differs little from his prior enslavement. 'Escravo na fazenda, escravo a bordo, escravo em toda parte... E chamava-se a isso servir a pátria!' [slave on the plantation, slave on board, slave the world over... And that's what they call serving the homeland!] (p. 60), he comments, in stark contrast to his optimistic departure at the beginning of the novel. Furthermore, the fact that Amaro is effectively enslaved on the second ship creates the conditions for the amorous betrayals of Aleixo and Carola, excluding the 'slave' from the love triangle that develops. Carola proves particularly cruel and calculating, seducing Aleixo in full knowledge of her friend's love for him, acting to prevent any communication between them, destroying Amaro's love letter, and dissuading Aleixo from visiting him in hospital. Despite her miniature liberal manifesto, she describes the impassioned letter as 'coisas de negro' [the stuff of negroes], remarking that 'negro é raça do diabo' [negroes are the Devil's race] and 'quem o conhecer que o compre' [if anyone finds him I hope they buy him] (pp. 128–31), openly advocating slavery. All the promises of community and happiness that once motivated Amaro's commitment to the national project reveal themselves, at this stage, to be false and deceitful. Ginway describes the love triangle as 'exactly the same' as that of *Othello*, with Amaro the Othello, Carola the Iago, and Aleixo the innocent Desdemona.[35] It is difficult, however, to claim that Aleixo is 'innocent' when he derides Amaro for his low social position, contemplating the possibility of finding a man of greater influence, and even imagining that he is 'sacrificando a saúde, o corpo, a mocidade... ora, não valia a pena!' [sacrificing his health, body, youth... it just wasn't worth it!] (p. 80). Indeed, in contrast to Desdemona, Aleixo turns out to confirm, rather than demystify, all of the hero's suspicions.

This 'betrayal' of Shakespeare by Caminha in his reproduction of *Othello* surely has the effect of encouraging sympathy for the protagonist; perhaps it is this that has led to readings that view the novel as 'an eloquent defence of Amaro',[36] or even of gay rights. It seems beyond doubt, at least, that the author invites the reader to look not just to the hereditary factors, but also to the circumstantial ones — a series of betrayals — implicated in the novel's violent conclusion. Indeed, only after his first punishment as a 'free' man does Amaro begin to change the good behaviour that earns him his nickname, treating his superiors 'com desdém' [with disdain] and 'maldizendo-os na ausência' [cursing them behind their backs] (p. 39). Rather than linking this apparent sympathy for Amaro to a defence of his sexual practices, however, I propose reading this adaptation of *Othello* as, above all, an attempt to emphasise the importance of the environment in governing the destiny of individual and nation.

In the previous chapter, I mentioned that theories of degeneracy typically hinged on questions of heredity and environment, with little overall consensus on which was most influential in the course of the individual's life. Those that drew on Darwin tended to stress the importance of heredity (since it was this that determined one's suitability for the environment),[37] whilst those that drew on Lamarck and Spencer, whose ideas remained popular in Brazil even after the landmark publication of *The Origin of Species*, argued that the environment had the potential to alter hereditary characteristics.[38] In Brazil, Sílvio Romero found himself at the confluence of these differing perspectives, at first seeking national 'salvation' in the *branqueamento* hypothesis (which sought to 'improve' the nation's 'stock') and gradually turning towards the Lamarckian view; Marshall Eakin identifies a definitive change in his thought after 1888,[39] when he emphasises the 'transformative power of social forces', and even before this, the education of the populace to achieve what he called '*a conquista da inteligência sobre o fatalismo da natureza*' [*the victory of intelligence over the fatalism of nature*].[40] Of course, such thinking is fraught with contradictions, but Romero's late interest in the power of environment meant that it was widely and seriously considered by Brazilian intellectuals of the time as a way out of disastrous predictions for the nation's future, these seemingly inevitable conclusions of European thought. We have seen already how Azevedo, for example, becomes ever more interested in the environment in his works, shifting the narrative focus from the mulatto to the *cortiço* over the course of his literary career and, already in *O mulato*, handing ultimate victory to Maranhão itself. In *Bom Crioulo*, the power of the environment is made explicit; it seems no coincidence, for example, that pederasty and masturbation are rife aboard a ship devoid of women. When it comes to the author's reworking of Shakespeare, then, and the reader is encouraged to look at the transformative impact of the protagonist's circumstances in his violent crime at the end, it seems that this latter is presented in the novel as the principle means of working — to quote from *Bom Crioulo* itself — '*contra a natureza*'.

With the relationships in *Bom Crioulo* essentially barren, as we have seen, Caminha circumvents the miscegenation hypothesis and presents the environment as the principle agent capable of fighting 'against nature'. Perhaps these two structuring forces, apparently opposed to each other, go some way to explaining the much-commented 'contradictions' in the narrative, which Mello describes as '*uma ambiguidade tão feroz que quase destrói o romance*' [an ambiguity so ferocious that it almost destroys the novel].[41] In this sense, although the protagonist is apparently presented as a 'born degenerate', we are also invited to contemplate, with the distorted reference to Shakespeare's *Othello*, whether or not the murder would have occurred, had the murderer not been betrayed so completely. Seen in this light, the possibility of identification with Amaro, which is also to share his suspicions of Desdemona's betrayal, becomes part of a process in which the supposed inevitabilities of heritage are covertly refuted.

I mentioned earlier that one of the effects of 'creolising' the Naturalist discourse, typified by the (ab)use of Shakespearean tragedy, consists of forging a way out of a wider, national 'degeneration'. The word 'crioulo' of the novel's title and eponymous protagonist refers, in the context of nineteenth-century Brazil, to a person of African descent born in Brazil and, in a more general sense in the colonial age, to a descendant of Europeans, born and brought up overseas.[42] Its meaning, therefore, traverses opposing notions of nature and environment including, importantly, education. To allow the environment to work 'against nature', as happens (or more precisely, does not happen) in *Bom Crioulo*, is also to allow something inherited to develop under the influence of the surrounding cultural environment. Caminha conceives this 'creolising' process at several levels of literary composition. The protagonist is compelled to attempt a reconciliation of his inherited characteristics with the environment in which he finds himself. On a more allegorical level, meanwhile, the new republic must contemplate and accommodate (if only minimally) the freed slave that it has inherited. Finally, the novel itself 'inherits' Naturalism and degeneration theory as a structuring discourse and appropriates it, creolising it, indeed, to account for a different socio-political context. In this space in between European Naturalism and Caminha's novel, the ground is cleared for a renegotiation of degeneration theory to imagine a 'viable' future nation.

### *Bom Crioulo* as (anti-)Foundational Novel

If, therefore, we can model the literary and even ideological structure of *Bom Crioulo* as a creolisation of discourses, one that seeks to adapt and adjust these to the socio-political context, I would now like to illustrate and strengthen this reading by considering the central love triangle as 'foundational' of the nation, and which can again be compared productively with that of *Iracema*, José de Alencar's 'fantasy of American-European miscegenation'[43] that I discussed in the previous chapter. Earlier I drew attention to *Bom Crioulo*'s foundational tactics with Caminha's use of Christian mythology, and the novel's love triangle bears clear similarities, if also interesting differences, to Alencar's foundational text. The markedly divergent figuration of the love triangle in *Bom Crioulo* when compared with *Iracema* is reminiscent of the sterile inversion encountered in *Casa de pensão*, so much so that this latter work ought to be considered as a significant literary influence, alongside *O Barão de Lavos*. Indeed, Madame Brizard is herself many years older than Coqueiro and 'educates' him in quasi-motherly fashion. Once more, the relations in the novel are best approached in relation to the dialogues they foster with other Lusophone authors, characterised by the degradation of the nineteenth-century love triangle and the weakening of patriarchal power.

In *Casa de pensão*, as I argued, Madame Brizard appears as an ideological inversion of Iracema: overweight, European, old and sterile. Carola differs little from Madame Brizard in character; she also runs a guesthouse, is Portuguese, overweight, middle-aged, seductive, calculating, selfish and childless. Caminha — characteristically perhaps — was evidently not concerned with disguising any debt to Azevedo, but Carola also warrants comparison with the bourgeois, if ultimately adulterous, Elvira in *O Barão de Lavos*, from whom she differs in important ways. Most notably, whilst Elvira is seduced by Eugénio in *Lavos*, Carola becomes a powerful temptress in *Bom Crioulo*, inviting Aleixo to take a bath with her, undressing him lasciviously, and thus reversing the dynamic of seduction. Treating Aleixo as 'filho' seven times in the novel, she is a Brizard-like anti-mother, incorporating Lusophobia, identified by Nelson Vieira as a growing sentiment in nineteenth-century Brazil,[44] into the contemporaneous, misogynistic representation of woman readily dichotomised into angel or whore. In this respect, her nickname 'Bunda' [Bottom] is every bit as intriguing as Amaro's: besides endowing her with a 'dangerous' sexual appetite, it is possible, in accordance with his use of the word 'crioulo', that Caminha was alluding to the word 'bundo', derived from 'kimbundu', popularly used to refer to any black African language and, by racist extension, 'linguagem incorreta'.[45] Thus whilst the *bom crioulo* — ostensibly the outsider — fights for a place in society, Carola Bunda, the exploitative *Portuguese* lady who ought to speak the language as a native, is subtly marked as the outsider herself, with wordplay that renegotiates notions of belonging in post–independence Brazil.

In addition to the Lusophobic inversion of the mother figure, a further discrepancy arises with *Iracema*, and also with *Casa de pensão* and *Lavos*: the incorporation of the 'freed' (or escaped) black slave into what Howes describes as 'one of the first [Brazilian novels] to have a pureblooded black as its hero'.[46] *Iracema*, by contrast, is a particularly conspicuous candidate for what Roberto Schwarz describes as 'as ideias fora do lugar' [misplaced ideas], and Schwarz himself devotes a whole essay to the 'contradictions' in the work of Alencar, although he is careful to describe these as illuminative strengths rather than literary weaknesses.[47] Thus in *Iracema*, the total absence of slaves is at odds with a nation sustained by a slave economy, and the European, in the form of Martim, is virtuous and generative despite the reality of continued exploitation; these contradictions illustrate the inescapably precarious position of Brazilian intellectuals of the time, who could neither abandon European ideas nor implement them convincingly in their country. In *Bom Crioulo*, however, Caminha launches a reactive attempt to reassemble the love triangle of *Iracema*, and indeed *Lavos* and *Casa de pensão*, with parts better representative of the new Brazilian nation: Aleixo, the working-class, white Brazilian, Carola, the Portuguese capitalist, and Amaro, the freed black slave. Here, the repeated exchange of ruinous, often pederastic, and always allegorical love triangles between the Lusophone Naturalists — that literary game of Chinese whispers — is made particularly visible.

It might seem that, even if *Bom Crioulo* strives for a more appropriate representation of society than its predecessors, the same deadlock is reached as in *Casa de pensão*, characterised by childlessness and an *apparent* refutation, on the allegorical plane, of a national future, this overshadowed by a monstrous European mother and the absolute exclusion of the slave. As Ginway suggests, *Bom Crioulo* depicts a 'cultural impasse' in nineteenth-century Brazil.[48] Indeed, the inherited demographics do not in themselves point to any possible route towards progress. However, one could argue that Caminha's dialogue with other novels is so extensive that, returning to the creolisation hypothesis, another kind of fecundity is subtly restored at the level of the text. Caminha appropriates the pederastic relationship of *Lavos*, the ageing temptress of *Casa de pensão*, and in an inverted sense, the foundational allegories of *Iracema* and the Brazilian Romantics, fusing them with the story of *Othello*. These models are then adapted to account for the exploits of slavery and colonialism in Brazil, both of which apparently foreclose any generative future. And by placing these issues centre stage, rather than behind the curtain, as in *Iracema*, the author draws readers' attention to the contemporaneous environment and its role in reinforcing the troubling cultural impasse, necessitating a novel, creolised discourse and a new basis for national belonging. Once more, it is through the environment, and not race and heredity, that a way forward is found, with ideas adapted to the place, and not the place to the ideas.[49] If *Iracema* depicts national generation, and *Casa de pensão* sterility, *Bom Crioulo* restores the former not by depicting it but by performing it in creole. The result is a shift in focus from the 'viability' of the inherited demographics to the viability of the very symbolic universe in which these are represented and understood. The novel might thus even be read as a meditation on the shifting location of meaning in postcolonial contexts, where all systems of knowledge seem but half-truths in perpetual need of renegotiation.

## The Dialogue with *O Barão de Lavos*

Caminha's interaction with other literary texts might therefore be read as an aesthetic and ideological position in itself, reminiscent of Oswald de Andrade's 'Manifesto Antropófago', in which Brazilian cultural production is characterised principally by its 'cannibalisation' of European trends, famously exemplified in the witty phrase, 'Tupi, or not tupi that is the question'.[50] *Bom Crioulo* performs a similar distortion and interweaving of European models — including, of course, Shakespeare — to that found in Andrade's own manifesto. Other critics have pointed to the influence of Camões's *Os Lusíadas* in the novel, and in particular of contemporaneous journalism such as that surrounding the naval revolt of 1893.[51] However, for the purposes of this study, I would now like to return to *O Barão de Lavos* as a key literary precedent for Caminha's 'creole' novel, continuing to explore the latter's construction of meaning through deferral to other authors and thinkers.

The correspondences between *Lavos* and *Bom Crioulo* are difficult to pass over: an intergenerational love triangle, a pederastic relationship enacted in a hideaway city apartment, the subsequent betrayal of the hero by the woman and his teenage lover, the demise of the hero, and his final handover to the police at the end. So too are the love triangles deployed to represent, allegorically speaking, differing elements of Portuguese and Brazilian society. If the economy of the Western world could be said, until the abolition of slavery in Brazil at least, to have consisted of four main classes — the aristocracy, the bourgeoisie, the proletariat, and slaves — *Lavos* deals primarily with the first three, and *Bom Crioulo* with the latter three. That only the capitalist classes and the proletariat are dealt with by both novels reflects the gradual erosion of the aristocracy and slavery over the course of the century, the former primarily in Europe, and the latter in the Americas, though this should of course be conceived as one process rather than two separate ones.[52] The different thematic focus of the novels can thus help us to organise them within the literary and socio-economic space of the Lusophone world and beyond.

My analysis of *Lavos* focused closely on its narrative structure whereby, I argued, the so-called 'pathological' approach leads to a representation that is both reductive and productive, surprisingly generative in its obsession with degeneracy. Central to this process is the irresolvable dialectical movement between the voice of the doctor-narrator and that of the Baron in free indirect discourse which, despite its remarkably transgressive perspective, becomes a justification, more often than not, for the doctor's diagnosis. I compared this state of affairs to Bakhtin's concept of the monological narrative, in which characters exist purely to confirm the views of the narrator,[53] if also to conclude that, at times, the narrative creates space for other subjectivities and epistemologies. There are evidently traces of this logic in *Bom Crioulo*; the thoughts of the characters are typically related in free indirect discourse and often work against the nature of the narration. For example, when Amaro contemplates relinquishing any hope of seeing Aleixo again, he says to himself, 'Abandoná-lo, porquê? Porque era negro, porque fora escravo? Tão bom era ele como o imperador!...' [Abandon him, why? Because he was black, because he'd been a slave? He was every bit as worthy as the Emperor!] (p. 135). His fervent conviction that his blood is no inferior to that of the emperor himself contrasts clearly with the words of the narrator, who describes Amaro as a 'morbidez patalógica'. Amaro's words are strikingly reminiscent of those of the Baron of Lavos when he learns that he is not the only pederast in Lisbon: 'E porque não?... Que fizera ele de condenável, no fim de contas?...' [And why not?... What crime was he guilty of, in the end?], a remark that the narrator dismisses immediately as a 'vibração da insânia' [wave of madness].[54] In *Bom Crioulo* and *Lavos*, then, if in different measure, free indirect discourse both challenges and confirms the views of the narrator over the course of his tale.

However, the narrator of *Bom Crioulo* is much less consistent in his descriptions of the protagonist. Although, in *Lavos*, the doctor-narrator insists upon characterising the Baron's relations with Eugénio as 'abonimações', 'andromania' and 'neuropatia', in *Bom Crioulo*, the narrator uses other words to describe love that echo those that the protagonist himself uses in free indirect discourse. Aleixo, for example, at the beginning of the relationship, is described as enjoying 'a perpétua alegria dos que não têm cuidados' [the perpetual happiness of the carefree] (p. 70), suggesting the blissfulness of first love.[55] In the paradise of their room on the top floor — hidden far away from the street, unlike the Baron of Lavos's cell — the pair is described as an ideal couple:

> Ficavam em ceroulas, ele e o negro, espojavam-se à vontade na velha cama de lona, muito fresca pelo calor, a garrafa de aguardente ali perto, sozinhos numa independência absoluta, rindo e conversando à larga sem que ninguém os fosse perturbar — volta na chave por via de dúvidas... (p. 71)

[In their underwear, he and the negro stretched out freely on the old canvas bed, cool and fresh in spite of the heat, with a bottle of rum at their side, alone in absolute independence, laughing and talking at length with no one there to disturb them — turning the key in the lock just in case...]

The details offered by the narrator, such as the old bed which, far from reflecting the 'degeneracies' of the couple, is found 'muito fresca pelo calor', create a utopian space safeguarded by the locked door, resisting, like the onanist Herculano, the discourse of pathology. The diminutive 'sozinhos', meanwhile, suggests affection on the part of the narrator, apparently absent in some of the more overtly Naturalist passages. In the same vein, in the honeymoon phase of their relationship, the narrator describes the three main characters as 'como uma pequena família, não tinham segredos entre si, estimavam-se mutuamente' [like a little family, there were no secrets between them, they held each other in equal regard] (p. 73), language manifestly at odds with the phrase 'contra a natureza', and indeed decidedly inclusive in its invocation of normative kinship to describe the queer family. Once again, the word 'pequena' connotes affection; there is even a childlike simplicity in the phrasing, with main clauses subordinated between commas, quite at odds with the precise, clinical style of a narrator-doctor. In *O Barão de Lavos*, by contrast, the narrator describes the love triangle of Sebastião as 'a desamparada ruína do seu nome' [the unhinged ruin of his name],[56] the undoing, rather than the tentative formation of a family. Here the shift in the representation of kinship when the story travels across the Atlantic is especially visible. Although the doctor of *Lavos*, outside free indirect discourse, is incapable of regarding Sebastião's pederastic relationship as anything other than a corruption of heterosexual love, Caminha, from time to time, allows antiscientific language to disperse through the narrator's discourse, weakening definitively the cordon sanitaire that separates the protagonist's 'pathologies' from the bourgeois reader. Like creole languages, the narration plays with the imported model to create a version in which old distinctions are lost and new connections are made. Indeed, whilst *Lavos* depicts the end of an old aristocratic family, excluded from society by the new science of the bourgeoisie and so comforting the bourgeois reader, Caminha makes space for the new citizen, the freed slave fighting for social recognition in the wake of abolition. It is by adapting the original model in this manner that the reader can hear that which Lopes-Júnior describes as 'uma subjectividade outra' [an other subjectivity].[57] What certain critics, therefore, have interpreted as contradictions in the novel that almost lead to its destruction[58] can, on the contrary, be read as a space of highly productive betrayals that seek a novel, generative discourse capable of incorporating new voices.

The dialogue with *O Barão de Lavos* concludes at the end of *Bom Crioulo* when, in another transparent reference to Botelho's text, police arrive at the scene of Aleixo's murder. The altered representation of the ending confirms Caminha's willingness to establish a plurality of voices articulated in terms beyond those of degeneration theory. In *Lavos*, I argued, the closing lines create a seamless transition between the perspective of the narrator and that of the policemen examining the Baron's body, in a resounding victory for the bourgeoisie and its 'sciences' of degeneracy. In *Bom Crioulo*, the narrative focuses instead on the process of examination itself:

Muitas vistas dirigiam-se para o sobradinho.

Aleixo passava nos braços de dois marinheiros, levado como um fardo, o corpo mole, a cabeça pendida para trás, roxo, os olhos imóveis, a boca entreaberta. O azul-escuro da camisa e a calça branca tinha grande chumaço de panos. Os braços caíam-lhe, sem vida, inertes, bambos, numa frouxidão de membros mutilados.

A rua enchia-se de gente pelas janelas, pelas portas, pelas calçadas. Era uma curiosidade tumultuosa e flagrante a saltar dos olhos, um desejo irresistível de ver, uma irresistível atração, uma ânsia!

Ninguém se importava com o outro, com o negro, que lá ia, rua abaixo, triste e desolado, entre as baionetas, à luz quente da manhã: todos, porém, queriam ver o cadáver, analisar o ferimento, meter o nariz na chaga...

Mas um carro rodou, todo lúgubre, todo fechado, e a onda dos curiosos foi se espalhando, se espalhando, até cair tudo na monotonia habitual, no eterno vaivém. (pp. 152–53)

[All eyes turned towards the house.

Aleixo was being carried away in the arms of two sailors, like a bundle of clothes, his body soft and his head hanging limp, purple, with motionless eyes and his mouth half open. His dark blue shirt and white trousers were wrapped in an enormous cloth bandage. His mutilated limbs fell at his side, loose and inert.

People flooded to their windows and doors, filling the street. Their eyes flamed with tumultuous curiosity. There was an insatiable desire to watch, an irresistible allure, a thirst!

No one paid any attention to the other man, the negro. Off he went, sad and desolate between bayonets in the hot morning sun: everyone, however, wanted to see the corpse, analyse the injury, stick their beak into the wound...

But a carriage rolled past mournfully with its windows shut, the wave of onlookers slowly dissipated, and everything returned to normal in the eternal ebb and flow.]

The pathological perspective is seen in the second paragraph, with words such as 'inertes' and 'membros mutilados' reducing Aleixo to a sum of physical parts. However, this perspective is not made consistent with that of the narrator, as in *Lavos*, but rather with the multitude that rushes to observe the blood and gore, with a perverse 'desejo irresistível de ver, uma irresistível atração, uma ânsia!'. This uncontrollable urge is thus articulated in the same — pathological? — terms as Amaro's own attraction to Aleixo, with remarkably similar syntax, his strength of will 'irresistivelmente dominada pelo desejo de unir-se ao marujo, como se ele fora de outro sexo, de possuí-lo, [...] de gozá-lo!...' [irresistibly will overwhelmed by the desire to unite with the deckhand, as though he were of the other sex, [...] to enjoy him!...] (p. 42). As in the case of Nini in *Casa de pensão*, or of Raimundo's mirror-gazing in *O mulato*, what ought to be the 'perverse' object of pathological study — the hysteric, the negro, the murder of Aleixo — in the end reveals, on the contrary, the perversion of the study itself. In a similar vein, whilst the policemen are the saviours of the bourgeoisie at the end of *Lavos*, here they are barely noticed as they lead Amaro away between bayonets: 'ninguém se importava com o outro'. His story of betrayal thus dissolves into the perverse observation of his crime and his return to captivity in the hands of a burgeoning criminal justice system. Only the narrator seems to grasp society's woeful indifference to '*o outro, o negro*' as the usual monotony returns, Amaro's plight lost in the 'eterno vaivém', in what can again be interpreted as a rejection of the Hegelian view of historical progress through ideological synthesis, sentiments reflected too in the novel's recourse to tragedy, with which the historic mistakes of colonialism again resurface to trouble the present. The clear distancing of the narrator's perspective from that of *Lavos* and degeneration theory at the end, tapering into the poetic language of 'a onda de curiosos [...] se espalhando, se espalhando', once again demonstrates Caminha's attempt to rework imported discourses in a way that gives voice to the forgotten and repressed.

To bring together the claims about *Bom Crioulo* that I have made in this chapter, I would like to discuss one particular passage from the novel that efficiently illustrates Caminha's creolisation of imported styles to represent a different social reality. These are the three paragraphs detailing the violent punishment that Amaro receives after his fight with the Portuguese provocateur:

> E, como da outra vez, Bom Crioulo emudeceu profundamente sob os golpes da chibata. Apanhou calado, retorcendo-se a cada golpe na dor imensa que o cortava d'alto a baixo, como se todo ele fosse uma grande chaga aberta, viva e cruenta..... Morria-lhe na garganta um grunhido estertoroso e imperceptível, cheio de angústia, comprimido e seco; dilatavam-se-lhe os músculos da face em contrações galvânicas; o sangue, convulsionado, rugia dentro, nas artérias, no coração, no íntimo da sua natureza física, palpitante, caudaloso, numa pletora descomunal!
>
> Ele sofria tudo com aquele orgulho selvagem de animal ferido, que se não pode vingar porque está preso, e que morre sem um gemido, com o olhar aceso em cólera impotente!
>
> Errava na luz intensa do meio-dia uma tristeza vaga e universal. Lá de fora, da barra, vinha, encrespando a água, um arzinho fresco impregnado de maresia. A cidade, em anfiteatro, cintilava entre montanhas na lânguida apatia daquela hora calmosa. O vulto do couraçado, largo e imóvel no meio da baía, com o seu enorme aríete, com a sua cobertura de lona, resplandecia destacado, longe dos outros navios, longe de terra, fantástico, arquitetural! (pp. 105–06)

> [And like the last time, Bom Crioulo fell silent under the lashings of the whip. He took them without making a sound, writhing with each strike in the immense pain that rocked him from head to toe, as though he were nothing more than an open wound, alive and raw... A faint, death-rattling groan died in his throat, full of anguish, dry and cut short; the muscles on his face dilated in electrical contractions; his convulsed blood roared inside him, in his arteries, in his heart, in his innermost physical nature, palpitating, torrential, in a terrific plethora!
>
> He bore the pain with the wild pride of a wounded animal, trapped and unable to take revenge, dying without a whimper, its eyes wide open in impotent rage!
>
> The fierce noon sun cast a vague, universal sadness. A gentle breeze blew from the faraway harbour, freshening the air with sea spray. The city shimmered in its amphitheatre of mountains, languishing in the sleepy heat of

> the day. The figure of the warship, vast and motionless in the middle of the
> bay, with its enormous ram at the prow, with its canvas roof, shone out from
> the other ships, far from land, fantastical, architectural!]

This passage is particularly noteworthy for its seamless fusion of literary influences. On the one hand, Amaro's convulsions, plethoras, choleras and 'contrações galvânicas' could be drawn from a contemporary medical textbook, establishing a pathological perspective. However, the style becomes increasingly poetic over the course of the episode, with 'scientific' phenomena giving way to more evocative images. The second paragraph metaphorises the punishment, comparing Amaro to an injured animal: still the language of Naturalism, perhaps, but losing its pathological edge. Finally, when the narration moves to a panoramic description in the last paragraph, the reader is presented with an image of modernity — the city and the enormous new battleship — but dressed with curiously Romantic language. The vessel sits motionless in the idyllic Guanabara bay, surrounded by 'um arzinho fresco'. Even the city, ever the fascination of the Naturalists, does not grow and rot as an organism but shimmers between the mountains (dramatically metaphorised as an amphitheatre) in the midday sun. Meanwhile, Caminha develops a peculiar sense of rhythm over the course of the passage. The short clauses describing his physical symptoms create a tension and shortness of breath reproduced in subsequent paragraphs, all of which end in exclamation marks. In the final sentence, too, the repetition of 'com' and 'longe' adds to the sense of rhythm. Indeed, the distinct rhythm of the passage, reaching its climatic moments in the repeated exclamation marks, evokes the atmosphere of a chant, a spell, or even an epic poem.[59] Why would Caminha juxtapose the language of pathology with the rhythm and style of an incantation? The two discourses stand clearly at other ends of the literary and ideological field. It is as though the searing pain of Amaro's punishment demands an urgency and intensity of expression that the detached Naturalist perspective cannot match. As in Azevedo's O mulato, the inclusion of narrative currents that restrict Naturalist principles gestures towards their inadequacies in representing the (post-) colonial world, and in this case, significantly, in relation to flagellation, one of the most enduring and traumatic images of slavery. Creolising the Naturalist discourse in this manner, Caminha forges an alternative system of representation for his country of study, one that differed markedly from those of Zola and Abel Botelho.

The word crioulo derives from Latin 'creare' (to create): surprisingly generative resonances, perhaps, for a novel described by critics as a 'case study' of degeneration theory and in which no one bears children. It is this generative potential of creolisation, however, that the author of Bom Crioulo exploits particularly astutely, blending the Naturalist discourse with other, apparently contradictory styles to accompany the process by which the freed slave, born in, brought to but never indigenous to Brazil, fights for a place in the new republic. By appropriating Naturalism and adjusting it to account for different social realities, Caminha both restricts and reworks degeneration theory, allowing environment to work against nature, and thus echoing the later work of Sílvio Romero by seeking to weaken the pessimistic implications of fin-de-siècle thought in Brazil. At the same time, recalling the other Lusophone Naturalists, he includes a pederastic relationship that has the effect of bypassing the other 'way out' of national degeneration, the miscegenation hypothesis. It is this relationship, perhaps, together with the sympathy we are invited to feel for the protagonist, that has led some to argue that the novel functions as an early defence of homosexuality. On the contrary, I would argue that Caminha is much more interested in salvaging the nation from the stigma of degeneration theory than he is in the homosexual. Similarly, I hope to have demonstrated how the supposed narrative inconsistencies in *Bom Crioulo* can be read not as signs of an author who hovered indecisively above a library of European texts, but rather as betrayals of imported models, productive, creative and adapting ideas to the place. Indeed, if we follow the creolisation hypothesis, it is possible to synthesise a range of critical observations that may seem contradictory at first sight.

Perhaps the true queer dimension of *Bom Crioulo*, therefore, is not the central pederastic relationship but the rejection of any faithful adhesion to the discourses of the age, which also suggests an author highly critical of what he read and equally conscious of the fate of Brazilian intellectuals left with inadequate representative models born of Europe. My decision to begin and end with *Lavos* and *Bom Crioulo* was of course strategic: viewed against each other, their formal differences become especially apparent. One could certainly argue that, in this particular journey across the Atlantic, degeneration theory is turned on its head such that the representation of 'deviance' in *Lavos* translates, in *Bom Crioulo*, to deviance in representation. As I mentioned earlier, the crisis moves from one of individual and imperial bloodline to the very symbolic order in which notions of bloodline, belonging, empire and relationality are articulated. In this sense, *Bom Crioulo* anticipates what Karl Posso finds in the novels of Silviano Santiago and Caio Fernando Abreu: an 'indecidabilidade' in the discourse as a strategy for challenging 'os termos relacionais pelos quais a sociedade ortodoxa, heterossexista, funciona' [the terms of relationality on which orthodox, heterosexual society operates],[60] disturbing the imposed linearity and binary conflicts of heteronormative society. In a similar vein, reading the queer in *Bom Crioulo* as, above all, a problematisation of representation itself, leads us to its most radical aspect, which is surely its willingness to challenge not so much sexual norms per se as the nexus of discourses that sustained the balance of power in Western world, looked upon from its cultural and economic periphery. The novel demonstrates too the transatlantic connections and dialogues that the Lusophone Naturalists cultivated; indeed, it might be argued that the novel can only be fully understood in relation to these. As such, it is unfortunate, for this reader, that *Bom Crioulo* has not received the same recognition in the Brazilian canon as *Iracema*. For however much the Brazilian Naturalists' sympathy for the slaves' cause can be explained by their supposed allegiances to liberal capitalism, it seems undeniable that Caminha transcended the dictates of his social class, troubling the language with which power was wrought in the nineteenth century, including, especially, that of Naturalism and degeneration theory, which were the choice aesthetic systems for the 'modernising' middle classes. In this respect, this enigmatic author from Ceará, who proved remarkably brave in his determination to write *contra a natureza*, was truly visionary.

## Notes to Chapter 4

1. Carlos Eduardo Bezerra, *Adolfo Caminha: um polígrafo na literatura brasileira do século XIX (1885–1897)* (São Paulo: Editora UNESP, 2009), p. 15.
2. Bezerra argues on these grounds that Caminha is a polygraph, at ease in a range of literary registers, including journalism.
3. Editor's note to Adolfo Caminha, *Bom Crioulo* (Lisbon: Sistema Solar, 2014). All page references are to this edition.
4. See Robert Howes, 'Race and Transgressive Sexuality in Adolfo Caminha's *Bom Crioulo*', *Luso-Brazilian Review*, 38 (2001), 41–62.
5. César Braga-Pinto, 'Othello's Pathologies: Reading Adolfo Caminha with Lombroso', *Comparative Literature*, 66 (2014), 149–71 (p. 151).
6. Cited by Howes, p. 43.
7. Ibid., p. 45.
8. Cited by Leonardo Mendes in *O retrato do Imperador: negociação, sexualidade e romance naturalista no Brasil* (Porto Alegre: EDIPUCRS, 2000), p. 28.
9. See David Foster, 'Adolfo Caminha's *Bom-Crioulo*: A Founding Text of Brazilian Gay Literature', in *Gay and Lesbian Themes in Latin American Writing* (Austin: University of Texas Press, 1991), pp. 14–20.
10. See Cristiano Mazzei, 'How Adolfo Caminha's *Bom-Crioulo* Was "Outed" through its Translated Paratext', in *A Companion to Translation Studies*, ed. by Sandra Bermann and Catherine Porter (Chichester: John Wiley and Sons, 2014), pp. 310–22.
11. Howes, p. 45.
12. David White, Review of the English translation of *Bom Crioulo* by Gay Sunshine Press, *Library Journal*, 107 (1982).
13. Howes, p. 41.
14. Elizabeth Ginway, 'Nation Building and Heroic Undoing: Myth and Ideology in *Bom-Crioulo*', *Modern Language Studies*, 28 (1998), 41–56 (p. 52).
15. A shorter version of this argument is laid out in David J. Bailey, 'As traições de Adolfo Caminha: *Bom Crioulo* e a "crioulização" do *naturalismo*', *Portuguese Literary and Cultural Studies*, 29 (2017), 119–42.
16. Howes, p. 41.
17. Michel Foucault, *The History of Sexuality*, trans. by Robert Hurley, 3 vols (London: Random House, 1979), I: *An Introduction*, p. 43.
18. Braga-Pinto, p. 151.
19. Howes, p. 56.
20. This is the conclusion of Howes, for example, who argues that *Lavos* is 'controlled by the tenets of degeneration theory' to a much greater degree than *Bom Crioulo*. See Howes, p. 52.
21. Howes, p. 52.
22. Silviano Santiago, 'Eça, Autor de *Madame Bovary*', in *Uma literatura nos trópicos: ensaios sobre a dependência cultural* (Rio de Janeiro: Rocco, 2000), pp. 47–65 (p. 53).
23. Celina Moreira de Mello, *Crítica e movimentos estéticos: configurações discursivas do campo literário* (Rio de Janeiro: Viveiros de Castro, 2006), p. 154
24. Cited by Mello, p. 154 (emphasis added).
25. Ibid., pp. 154–55.
26. Howes, p. 43.
27. See Foucault, *The History...*
28. Anna M. Klobucka, 'Was Camões Gay? Queering the Portuguese Literary Canon', conference paper delivered at the Annual Convention of the Modern Language Association, 28 December 2007, available at <https://www.academia.edu/5165187/Was_Cam%C3%B5es_Gay_Queering_the_Portuguese_Literary_Canon> [accessed 20 August 2019].
29. Robert Howes, 'Concerning the Eccentricities of the Marquis of Valada: Politics, Culture and Homosexuality in Fin-de-Siècle Portugal', *Sexualities*, 5 (2002), 25–48 (p. 33).
30. See Alessandra El Far, *Páginas de sensação* (São Paulo: Companhia das Letras, 2004).

31. See Foster, p. 15, for a discussion of *Bom Crioulo*'s utopian spaces.
32. Including, for example, Machado de Assis, in his famous tale of adultery (or of a husband's paranoia), *Dom Casmurro* (Lisbon: Guerra e Paz, 2016).
33. Rhinow, cited by Braga-Pinto, pp. 167–69, and Ginway, pp. 47–48.
34. See Benedict Anderson, *Imagined Communities* (London: Verso, 2006), p. 7.
35. Ginway, pp. 47–48.
36. Foster, p. 20.
37. See Charles Darwin, *On the Origin of Species* (Oxford: Oxford World Classics, 1996).
38. See, for example, Derek Freeman et. al., 'The Evolutionary Theories of Charles Darwin and Herbert Spencer', *Current Anthropology*, 15 (1974), 211–37 (pp. 214–15).
39. Marshall C. Eakin, 'Race and Identity: Sílvio Romero, Science, and Social Thought in Late 19th Century Brazil', *Luso-Brazilian Review*, 22 (1985), 151–74 (p. 167).
40. Romero, cited by Arthur Orlando, in *Ensaios de Crítica* (São Paulo: Editorial Grijablo, 1975), p. 86 (emphasis added).
41. Mello, p. 153.
42. See   <http://michaelis.uol.com.br/moderno/portugues/index.php?lingua=portugues-portugues&palavra=crioulo> [accessed 22 March 2016].
43. Maria Manuel Lisboa, 'A Mother is a Boy's Best Friend: Birth and Kinslaying in the Brazilian Foundational Novel,' *Portuguese Studies*, 13 (1997), 95–107 (p. 98).
44. Nelson H. Vieira, *Brasil e Portugal: a imagem recíproca (o mito e a realidade na expressão literária)* (Lisbon: Instituto de Cultura e Língua Portuguesa, 1991), p. 105.
45. See <http://www.priberam.pt/dlpo/bundo> [accessed 5 May 2016].
46. Howes, p. 42.
47. See Roberto Schwarz, 'A importação do romance e as suas contradições em Alencar', in *Ao Vencedor as Batatas* (São Paulo: Livraria Duas Cidades, 2000), pp. 33–82 (p. 72).
48. Ginway, p. 45.
49. Indeed, as I have indicated elsewhere, the 'whitening solution', refuted or at least circumvented in *Bom Crioulo*, is the example par excellence of the adaptation of the place to the ideas.
50. See Oswald de Andrade, 'Manifesto Antropófago', available at <http://www.ufrgs.br/cdrom/oandrade/oandrade.pdf> [accessed 21 March 2016].
51. Bezerra, in his study (p. 384) discusses the appearance of the ship *Luís de Camões* in the novel, which I will return to shortly, and more broadly discusses Caminha's interest in journalism. Howes mentions Caminha's protests at naval punishments as a young cadet as a possible influence (see Howes, p. 45), whilst Mendes (p. 216) points to the Naval Revolts of 1881–84 that saw the government bombarded by the navy for remaining in power unconstitutionally.
52. Thus the greatest supporters of abolition in Brazil were the middle classes, who endorsed liberal ideas largely as a means to diminish the influence of the slave-owning classes associated with the monarchy. To them, freed slaves presented a new potential workforce that could consolidate their growing power. See, for example, David Brookshaw, *Race and Colour in Brazilian Literature* (London: The Scarecrow Press, 1986), pp. 41–49.
53. See Margaret Payras Phyllis, 'Monologism', in *Encyclopedia of Contemporary Literary Theory: Approaches, Scholars, Terms*, ed. by Irena R. Makaryk (London: University of Toronto Press, 1993), p. 596.
54. Abel Botelho, *O Barão de Lavos* (Porto: Lello & Irmão, 1982), p. 380.
55. Aleixo, indeed, although attracted to the basic financial security that Amaro can offer him, shows far more enthusiasm in the relationship than Eugénio does in *Lavos*, whose interest in the Baron is purely financial. During Amaro's absence, for example, he is unable to forget him, thinking often of his 'musculatura rija' [solid muscles] and 'natureza extraordinária' [extraordinary nature] (p. 112). By raising the degree of reciprocity in this manner, Caminha renders their relationship subtly more legitimate, since it does not rest solely upon financial interest as in *Lavos*, or indeed the relations in *Casa de pensão*.
56. Botelho, p. 312.
57. Francisco Lopes-Júnior, 'Uma subjectividade outra', in *Toward Socio-Criticism: Selected Proceedings of the Conference 'Luso-Brazilian Literatures: A Socio-Critical Approach'*, ed. and with an intro. by

Roberto Reis (Tempe: Center for Latin American Studies, Arizona State University, 1991), pp. 67–75.

58. Mello, p. 153.

59. I alluded earlier to the influence of Camões, and this passage, with its brave hero and focus on naval life, perhaps carries echoes of *Os Lusíadas*. Elsewhere, the reference to Camões is more pointed, with the appearance of a boat named *Luís de Camões*, carrying on its prow 'uma figura de óleo, que tanto podia ser a do grande épico como a de qualquer outra pessoa barbada' [a figure painted in oil, who was no more similar to the great epic poet than any other bearded man] (p. 145). The fact that the left eye is missing, and not the right, a mistake that Amaro does not notice, serves as yet more evidence that Caminha had a nuanced understanding of 'misplaced ideas' in his country. See also Bezerra, p. 384.

60. Karl Posso, *Artimanhas de sedução: homossexualidade e exílio* (Belo Horizonte: UFMG Press, 2009), p. 234.

# CONCLUDING REMARKS

This study has involved a journey beginning with an obscure work of social pathology from fin-de-siècle Portugal, moving to the centre of the Portuguese canon to consider the novels of Eça de Queirós, and then over the Atlantic to Brazil, where the Naturalists never quite reached the same canonical status, even if their works did enjoy immense popularity and engaged extensively with the movement in Portugal and France. There is evidently a great diversity in the works considered; on the surface at least, the differences between, say, Botelho and Eça could hardly be starker. However, closer scrutiny in fact reveals a series of dialogues and treacherous interplays between the authors, these most lucid and apparent when representing the family, whose undoing always entails a 'queering' of science itself. Thus *Bom Crioulo*, as I have argued, retells *O Barão de Lavos* and other queer love stories in a concertedly different idiom, limiting considerably the presumed supremacy of 'science'. Our journey from *Lavos* to *Bom Crioulo* therefore returns us to the question I posed in the introduction: what if to be a Naturalist writer in Portuguese was, in practice, to write against Naturalism — to refashion it, corrupt it, and turn it on its head?

Certainly, Eça, Azevedo and Caminha dare to dwell upon the insufficiency of the discourses that they nevertheless deploy. Even Abel Botelho, who could be considered the most 'faithful' to the scientific turn, generates the same symbolic excess that he strives to isolate and remove, using allegory, for example, to develop a particularly Portuguese 'pathology'. Allegories of empire and nationhood, strikingly, are common to all of the texts, apparently at odds with the Realist-Naturalist 'reality effect' described by Roland Barthes. Criticism of Naturalism has often focused on its supposed failures on its own 'scientific' terms, stemming from the fundamental contradiction in its structuring principle which, in the introduction, I set in the context of mankind's troubled relationship with the 'natural' world, of which we are observers but never an integral part. Thus Naturalism tended to disguise the subjective aspect of narration and produce the supposedly 'natural' reality that it claimed only to describe and analyse. Meanwhile in Portugal and especially Brazil, with notable exceptions to which I have referred, the movement was judged further against Zola's own model, set up to 'fail' twice over. However, I hope to have shown how adjustments to Zola's model, in Lusophone Naturalism at least, often seek to deal with the very contradiction of his formula since, as countries on the economic and cultural periphery variously imagined as 'degenerate', sharing the same, now-fractured (post-)colonial space, Portugal and Brazil experienced the Positivists' attempted transformation of culture into nature particularly keenly.

Hence the rethinking, on both sides of the Atlantic, of the Portuguese imperial project as a historic mistake with ongoing repercussions: cultural *'decadência'* in fact leads to a series of meditations on the logic of colonialism and (re)production through which *decadência* itself is conceived. If Lusophone Naturalism is, in other words, a series of 'queer' reiterations, drawing on texts from within and beyond its own (post-)colonial space, it consistently challenges structures of power by reimagining relations of kinship. These claims are indeed interrelated, insofar as the exploration of race, gender, bloodline, sexual desire and the incest taboo, themselves so central to power relations in the Western world, necessarily pressures the language that naturalises their reality, consciously or otherwise.

To illustrate these assertions we can return to that passing remark by António Cândido which I have cited elsewhere in this book and would now like to address from a different perspective. Pointing to the widespread incidence of non-normative desire in Lusophone Naturalism, Cândido argues that its authors oversaw a 'degradação do enfoque naturalista' [degradation of the Naturalist focus], such that 'as coisas de sexo' [sexual matters] came to be seen in a scandalous, and therefore antinaturalist, manner. 'É como se nas sociedades mais atrasadas [...] o provincianismo tornasse difícil adotar o Naturalismo com naturalidade' [it is as though in backward societies [...] provincialism made it difficult to adopt Naturalism naturally].[1] Here, as António Carlos Santos has argued, Cândido produces the 'unnaturalness' that he sets out to identify, reading non-normative desire as a symptom of misplaced ideas rather than an integral part of their renegotiation.[2] It remains a useful claim, however, because it nevertheless points to an implicit link between discourse and kinship that I have been addressing throughout this study. Changing the logic slightly, we could argue instead that the difficulty in adopting Naturalism as 'natural' in these countries in turn spurred attempts to adapt it, leading to a renegotiation of the naturalising language in which kinship and relationality were articulated, ideas that Cândido himself unwittingly deploys, and that worked to construct the backward, 'degenerate' periphery of Naturalist discourse. Thus, for example, allegorically sterile anti-mothers, such as Carola and Madame Brizard, or the spectre of a 'queer' Dom Sebastião, disrupt the Naturalist model and the 'natural' family in the same move, sounding the death knell for centuries of desire and conquest that, in the end, did little to secure the long-term prosperity of Portugal, and still less for Brazil. The same could be said of Eça's exploration of the ambiguity in the terminology of kinship, or of Azevedo's use of the Oedipus myth, or of Caminha's creolisation of Naturalism to work against the influence of heritage and bloodline. To refashion the bonds of kinship is, in some sense, to write against naturalising, essentialist representations in general, since it gestures towards an alternative, imagined pattern of social organisation, or at least pressures the established one as 'natural'.

How this process of renegotiation plays out in each author's work tells us much about their respective countries and positioning within society and the literary canon. Thus Eça and Botelho both reimagine the family in their depictions of a country in economic decline in relation to its northern neighbours, an old imperial power engulfed by the new industrial, capitalist order dominated by

Britain and France. The disruption to the patriarchal family also testifies to social upheavals in class and gender dynamics and to an emerging concept of a deviant 'homosexuality' that had been showcased in various scandals in *fin-de-siècle* Portugal. Meanwhile, the allegorical appearance of Dom Sebastião, common to the work of both authors, demonstrates the extent to which this mysterious monarch continued to exert a pull on the Portuguese imaginary centuries after his disappearance, imputing transhistorical meaning into individual 'pathologies' to supplement what is otherwise presented as the study of 'reality' and the present day. References to Greek conceptions of desire and beauty, and to tragedy in the case of Eça, pose a similar challenge to the preeminence of Naturalist approaches to human experience, rewriting the strict rules of love, or at least drawing on an older book. But whereas in *Lavos*, non-normative kinship is principally a malady of the aristocracy, confirming (almost) the righteousness of an ascendent bourgeoisie, Eça associates normative kinship with a crisis of nation, empire, knowledge and representation, deconstructing its terms, and calling for a comprehensive reassessment of relationality. As such, his vision, the development of which entails a gradual shift towards dubious, first-person narration, was many times keener than that of Botelho, and his place in the canon is surely justified, even though the works of both authors reflect the same ideological context in compelling ways and constitute important moments in a diverse movement. Thus despite the myth of Sebastião being upheld in *Lavos*, decades after its reworking in *Basílio* to dispute grandiose narratives of Portuguese history, Botelho still implicates his country's imperial past — through allegory and the extraordinary appearance of a 'degenerate' black priest — in the perceived woes of the present.

Further differences emerge, however, when we compare these works to those from Brazil. Here, even in less canonical, popular works, there is a still greater willingness to alter the Naturalist model formally, introducing other epistemological currents that work against its influence, from Romanticism and the gothic to epic poetry and myth — not to mention tragedy, an innovation common to both sides of the Atlantic, developed apparently in tandem by Azevedo and Eça. Again, these adaptations lead us to the distinct national context, one in which the intellectual culture was imported and 'inauthentic', and which, prior to adaptation at least, was always out of place in a slave economy. Above all, however, the Brazilian texts are more concerned with imagining a 'viable' national future, which can be understood in the context a tenuous First Republic that was supposedly racially disadvantaged, deemed by some to be insurmountably so, and which was still yoked to European colonialism and the consequences of slavery. This participation in the building of a new nation, which stands in contrast to the Portuguese texts that dwell on a past of 'mistakes' and a future of death and oblivion — or at best eternal moonlight — is consistent with the general trend of literary production in nineteenth-century Latin America, which often sought a basis for national progress and belonging. And as misplaced ideas par excellence, Naturalism and degeneration theory required considerable adaptation if they could ever gesture towards a generative future for Brazil.

There are other important conclusions to be drawn from the interaction of the Portuguese and Brazilian texts that relate to the countries' close, if troubled, history before and after Brazilian independence, which saw the same royal family continue to govern on the pretext of maintaining close relations. One, which is hardly new, is the widespread presence of Lusophobia in *fin-de-siècle* Brazil, perhaps part of the same nationalist turn that characterises Latin American literature from the period, and reflective of the manner in which colonial practices continued to endure. Of particular interest here, however, is the way in which the Portuguese pretence to good kinship, as demonstrated in their desire to maintain the pan-continental monarchy, is reflected back in Brazilian Naturalism as its monstrous inversion, indeed the very inviability of kinship, in the form of a sterile mother. As Francisco de Magalhães asked of Luso-Brazilian relations in 1880, approaching the issue in identical terms, 'que diabo de trapalhada de parentesco é esta?' [what the devil is this bungled kinship?].[3] Thus as much as Portugal itself struggled to find a place in the new world order, the representation of the Portuguese in these works makes it clear that it continued to be perceived as an exploitative power and remained closer to centres of dominance than Brazil. This insight is consistent with Boaventura de Sousa Santos's claim that Portuguese identity in the nineteenth century was semi-peripheral, characterised by being *both* marginal to the Western world and centre of its own diminishing one.[4] In this context, Eça's stay-at-home Sebastianic figures, not to mention his critique of Portugal's ongoing complicity with plantation slave economies in *Os Maias*, seem all the more radical, joining the anti-colonial chorus of the Brazilian Naturalists seen in the equally childless mothers of *Casa de pensão* and *Bom Crioulo*. These common motifs and critiques also testify to the way in which Naturalism in Portuguese charts the social and political contours of the (post-)colonial Lusophone world, crossing borders (and returning home, in the case of Eça) in the search for national identity.

A somewhat less orthodox, but no less important, conclusion in this direction relates to the degree to which Brazilian and Portuguese Naturalists altered and refined each others' works to create a tentative transatlantic movement that wrote against Naturalism in mutually productive ways. On the one hand, the Brazilians drew heavily on Naturalist works from Portugal, often shifting their focus to explore social concerns peculiar to their country. Hence *A normalista* and *O mulato*, for example, retell *O crime do Padre Amaro* and *O primo Basílio* so as to draw attention to the culture of misplaced ideas and slavery. But on the other hand, as I have argued, these same authors exerted a degree of influence in Portugal. The most obvious example is Eça de Queirós, who seems to have refined his tale of incest in *Os Maias* after reading *O mulato*. Both works adjust the myth of Oedipus to explore the incest taboo and expose the hypocrisy of the replacement of slavery with liberal, free-market capitalism, though as with *Lavos* and *Bom Crioulo*, the former sees this replacement chiefly in relation to the demise of the Portuguese society and especially its aristocracy, and the latter in terms of the open wounds of slavery in Brazil. Other recurrent motifs, however, cannot be understood as 'originating' in Portugal, being passed playfully from author to the author. The characteristic nineteenth-century love triangle is perhaps the greatest victim of the Lusophone

Naturalists' literary mischief, seemingly discarded in favour of Platonic idealism in *O primo Basílio*, rendered sterile with age disparities in *Casa de pensão*, and then scandalously brought down by pederasty in *Lavos* and *Bom Crioulo*. In each case, the operation of homosocial desire is called into question, foreclosing a (re)productive future, albeit with varying degrees of critical sharpness and reliance on stereotypes. Another such motif, which relates to the former, is the vacuity and insufficiency of the terms of kinship, a central theme for Eça and Azevedo in particular, where brotherhood and paternity are rarely more than a façade, and never what they at first seem. In this respect, despite the differing positions of Portugal and Brazil in the Western world at the time, we can perhaps speak of 'Lusophone Naturalism' as, at its high points at least, a transatlantic circulation of ideas that sought to adapt and subversively reiterate 'scientific' representations of the human in countries that, in different measures, suffered the continuing (and increasing) conflicts and disappointments initiated by Portuguese colonialism. Again, the global perception of a backward and decadent Lusophone world may in fact have created the conditions for a radical, transnational questioning of the language in which such notions were articulated.

It is therefore little surprise that the writers in question often used similar techniques to rework Naturalism in their countries. Allegory is undoubtedly one of these, despite Cândido's assertion that it is not used by Eça.[5] After all, it is a particularly effective vehicle for moving from the representation of kinship and degeneracy to one of nationhood — and back again, often corruptively. Although it is doubtless not unique to Lusophone Naturalism, it is a defining characteristic. But perhaps the most intriguing formal adaptation to appear consistently in Caminha, Azevedo and Eça, again developing seemingly in tandem, is the recourse to the ancient tradition of tragedy. Whether *Othello* or *Oedipus Rex*, the existential threat to Naturalist principles is clear: how can humanity be understood in terms of logical, scientific laws if subject to the whims of the gods or, perhaps worse still, chaos and disorder? By the same token, in these works, the Hegelian notion of social progress is refuted by the suggestion that the traumas of the past — slavery, exploitation and above all colonialism — will always return to overshadow attempts to ignore and forget them.[6] Ironically, then, in Portugal as in Brazil, tragedy returns from the distant past to sabotage precisely what Zola's formula risks repressing: the unpredictability, ambiguity and especially, in these cases, plurality of human experience. In this sense, Eça and the *Geração de '70*, who bemoaned their failure to transform their country, were not the only *vencidos da vida*; the phrase could, with relative ease, be extended to characterise Azevedo and Caminha, tragedy being perhaps its most candid manifestation in their novels. But even if they acknowledged defeat, in writing against Naturalism, these writers displayed remarkable insight into how the representation of culture as nature — one side of a binary problem that troubles the world no less today than it did then — formed an integral part of perpetuating power structures in the Western world. The exchange and mutual deployment of motifs and techniques might even be read as itself a renegotiation of postcolonial relations both within and beyond the borders of the Lusosphere.

Naturalism was perhaps the last literary movement to draw so significantly on Positivist principles before Modernism shook the epistemological foundations of Western thought, and its critical regard has rarely reached the heights of that which it enjoyed in the *fin de siècle*. Eça de Queirós is a notable exception in this respect, and it is hoped this book has revealed yet more ways in which his work continues to surprise, fascinate and amuse. Few, if any, picked apart the ideology of the nineteenth-century world more thoroughly than he, and his aesthetic trajectory can be better understood in relation to the constraints on relationality that other Lusophone Naturalists, questioning the (il)logic of colonial history, also grappled with. As for the remainder of the movement in Portugal and Brazil, there are doubtless ways in which it, too, can be reconsidered. As Furst and Skrine suggest, 'Naturalism succeeded best where it appeared to fail'.[7] Indeed, perhaps the Lusophone Naturalists, in writing against nature, redeem the movement by supplementing Zola's model. One could even argue that, all the more for being Naturalists from the world's oldest and now-marginalised (post-)colonial space, they understood the inseparability of discourse and power; their movement established, to be sure, a highly critical and discursive idiom. These are questions still to be explored and developed; I have little doubt that the wealth of Naturalist literature in Portuguese, of which I have considered only a selection, will shed new light on them. As the tension between 'nature' and 'culture' seems far from resolved and new discourses emerge, in Brazil and elsewhere, to police race and sex, listening to the voices of those that have lived and challenged these conflicts remains a rewarding task.

## Notes to the Conclusion

1. António Cândido, 'De cortiço a cortiço', *Novos Estudos* (CEBRAP) 30 (July 1991), 111–29 (p. 127).
2. António Carlos Santos, 'O naturalismo sob o olhar modernista: Cândido e a crítica a Aluísio Azevedo', *Crítica Cultural*, 6 (2011), 557–63 (p. 561).
3. Cited by Nelson H. Vieira, *Brasil e Portugal: a imagem recíproca (o mito e a realidade na expressão literária)* (Lisbon: Instituto de Cultura e Língua Portuguesa, 1991), p. 78.
4. Boaventura de Sousa Santos, 'Entre Próspero e Caliban: colonialismo, pós-colonialismo e interidentidade', *Novos Estudos*, 66 (2003), 23–52.
5. Cândido, p. 114.
6. Here I am thus extending the conclusions of Maria Manuel Lisboa, who discusses the use of tragedy to disrupt Naturalist thought in Eça, to the movement as a whole. See Maria Manuel Lisboa, 'Uma caixa de charutos, uma caixa de fósforos ou como o mundo acaba', in *Teu amor fez de mim um lago triste: ensaios sobre 'Os Maias'* (Lisbon: Campo das Letras, 2000), pp. 333–93.
7. Lilian R. Furst and Peter N. Skrine, *Naturalism*, The Critical Idiom (London: Methuen, 1971), p. 71.

# BIBLIOGRAPHY

*Primary Texts*

AZEVEDO, ALUÍSIO, *Casa de pensão* (Rio de Janeiro: Ediouro, 1980)
——*O cortiço* (São Paulo: Editora Ática, 2005)
——*O homem* (Rio de Janeiro: Livraria Garnier, 1923)
——*O mulato* (São Paulo: Klick Editora, 1999)
BOTELHO, ABEL, *O Barão de Lavos* (Porto: Lello, 1982)
——*O livro de Alda* (Porto: Lello, 1984)
CAMINHA, ADOLFO, *Bom Crioulo* (Lisbon: Sistema Solar, 2014)
——*A normalista* (Rio de Janeiro: Ática, 1998)
——'Norte e Sul', in *Cartas literárias*, ed. by Italo Gurgel (Fortaleza: UFC Edições, 1999), pp. 107–12
QUEIRÓS, JOSÉ MARIA DE EÇA DE, 'O brasileiro', in *Obras de Eça de Queirós* (Porto: Lello e Irmão, 1948), vol. XXV, pp. 397–402
——'O Francesismo', in *Obras de Eça de Queirós* (Porto: Lello e Irmão, 1948), vol. II, pp. 813–27
——*Obras completas de Eça de Queirós* (Lisbon: Círculo de Leitores, 1980)
——*A tragédia da Rua das Flores* (Lisbon: Fernando Pereira, 1980)
——*Correspondência* (Lisbon: Caminho, 2008)

*Other fictional works*

ALENCAR, JOSÉ DE, *Iracema* (Rio de Janeiro: Edições BestBolso, 2012)
BRONTË, CHARLOTTE, *Jane Eyre* (London: Penguin, 2006)
CAMÕES, LUÍS DE, *Os Lusíadas* (Porto: Porto Editora, 2006)
CASTELO BRANCO, CAMILO, *A brasileira de Prazins* (Lisbon: Ulisseia, 1994)
CRUZ E SOUSA, JOÃO DE, *Missal* (Rio de Janeiro: Magalhães & Cia Editores, 1893)
DOSTOEVSKY, FYODOR, *Notes from Underground*, trans. by Richard Pevear and Larissa Volokhonsky (London: Vintage Classics, 1994)
FORSTER, E. M., *Maurice* (London: Penguin, 1972)
HUYSMANS, JORIS-KARL, *Against Nature*, with intro. by Nicholas White and trans. by Margaret Maulden (Oxford: Oxford University Press, 1998).
MACHADO DE ASSIS, JOAQUIM, *Dom Casmurro* (Lisbon: Guerra e Paz, 2016)
SOPHOCLES, *Oedipus the King*, trans. by David Grene in *Sophocles I: Antigone, Oedipus the King and Oedipus at Colonus*, ed. by Mark Griffith and Glenn W. Most (London: Chicago University Press, 2013), pp. 71–143
SOUSA, INGLÊS DE, *O missionário* (Charleston, SC: Nabu Press, 2012)
TERENCE, *Andria*, with intro. by George Shipp (London: Bristol Classical Press, 2002)
VICENTE, GIL, *Auto da Índia* (Porto: Porto Editora, 2018)
WILDE, OSCAR, *The Picture of Dorian Gray* (London: Penguin Classics, 2003)
ZOLA, ÉMILE, *Au Bonheurs des Dames* (Paris: Fasquelle, 1962)

——*Nana* (Paris: Ligaran, 2015)

——*Rome*, trans. by Ernest Alfred Vizetellt (London: Macmillan, 1901)

——, Preface to the first edition of *Thérèse Raquin*, trans. by Andrew Rothwell (Oxford: Oxford University Press, 1992)

### Critical works

ALSTON, ISABELLA, and KATHRYN DIXON, *Anatomical Anomalies* (Charlotte, NC: TAJ Books, 2014)

ANDERSON, BENEDICT, *Imagined Communities* (London: Verso, 2006)

ANDRADE, OSWALD DE, 'Manifesto Antropófago', available at <http://www.ufrgs.br/cdrom/oandrade/oandrade.pdf> [accessed 21 March 2016]

AYDEMIR, MURAT, *Indiscretions: At the Intersection of Queer and Postcolonial Theory* (Harleem: Colophon, 2011)

BAILEY, DAVID J., 'Com o odioso guarda-chuva entre os joelhos: Queer Male Desire, Weak Paternity, and Kinship Trouble in the Novels of Eça de Queirós', *The Modern Language Review*, 111 (2016), 413–33

——'As traições de Adolfo Caminha: *Bom Crioulo* e a "crioulização" do *naturalismo*', *Portuguese Literary and Cultural Studies*, 29 (2017), 119–42

BAKHTIN, MIKHAIL, *The Dialogic Imagination*, ed. by Michael Holquist and trans. by Caryl Emerson and Michael Holquist (London: University of Texas Press, 1982)

BALFOUR, ARTHUR, *Decadence* (Cambridge: Cambridge University Press, 1908)

BARCELLOS, JOSÉ CARLOS, *Literatura e homoerotismo em questão* (2006), available at <http://www.dialogarts.uerj.br/admin/arquivos_emquestao/%5B1%5Dlit_e_homo.pdf>

BARTHES, ROLAND, 'The Reality Effect', in *The Rustle of Language*, trans. by Richard Howard (Berkeley: University of California Press, 1989), pp. 141–48

BAUER, HEIKE, 'Measurements of Civilisation', *French Cultural Studies*, 17 (2008), 93–108

BERARDINELLI, CLEONICE, 'José Matias', in *Convergência Lusíada*, 13 (1996)

BERNASCONI, ROBERT, and ANIKA MAAZA MANN, 'The Contradictions of Racism: Locke, Slavery and the *Two Treatises*', in *Race and Racism in Modern Philosophy*, ed. by Andrew Valls (London: Cornell University Press), pp. 90–107

BERRINI, BEATRIZ, *Eça e Machado* (São Paulo: FAPESP, 2005)

——*Portugal de Eça de Queiroz* (Lisbon: Imprensa Nacional–Casa da Moeda, 1986)

BEZERRA, CARLOS EDUARDO, *Adolfo Caminha: um polígrafo na literatura brasileira do século XIX (1885–1897)* (São Paulo: Editora UNESP, 2009)

BLOOM, HAROLD BLOOM, *The Western Canon: The Books and School of the Ages* (London: Harcourt Brace, 1994)

——*The Anxiety of Influence* (Oxford: Oxford University Press, 1973)

BORDALO PINHEIRO, RAFAEL, *O funeral...*, in *A Paródia*, 1 (1900), pp. 292–93, Biblioteca Nacional de Portugal

BOSWELL, JOHN, 'Revolutions, Universals, and Sexual Categories', in *Hidden From History: Reclaiming the Gay and Lesbian Past*, ed. by Martin Duberman, Martha Vicinus and George Chauncy (London: Penguin, 1991), pp. 17–36

BOUISSAC, PAUL, *Semiotics at the Circus* (Berlin: Walter de Gruyter, 2010)

BOWIE, MALCOLM, *Lacan* (Cambridge, MA: Harvard University Press, 1991)

BRAGA, PEDRO, *O touro encantado da Ilha dos Lençóis: o sebastianismo no Maranhão* (Petrópolis: Editora Vozes, 2001)

BRAGA-PINTO, CÉSAR, 'Othello's Pathologies: Reading Adolfo Caminha with Lombroso', *Comparative Literature*, 66.2, Duke University Press (2014), 149–71

BROOKSHAW, DAVID, *Race and Colour in Brazilian Literature* (London: The Scarecrow Press, 1986)

BURTON, RICHARD, 'Terminal Essay', from *The Arabian Nights* (New York: Cosimo Classics, 2008), vol. x, pp. 63–260

BUTLER, JUDITH, *Antigone's Claim: Kinship Between Life and Death* (New York: Columbia University Press, 2000)

CAMPOS MATOS, ALFREDO, *Eça de Queirós: uma biografia* (Lisbon: Edições Afrontamento, 2009)

CÂNDIDO, ANTÔNIO, 'De Cortiço a Cortiço', *Novos Estudos*, CEBRAP, 30 (July 1991), 111–29

CAPUTO, JOHN D., *The Prayers and Tears of Jacques Derrida: Religion Without Religion* (Bloomington: Indiana University Press, 1997)

CARVALHO, MARIA DE, 'Eça de Queirós e a ópera no século XIX em Portugal', in *Revista Colóquio/Letras*, 91, May 1986, pp. 27–37

CARVER, T., and S. A. CHAMBERS, 'Kinship Trouble: Antigone's Claim and the Politics of Heteronormativity', in *Politics and Gender*, 4 (December 2007), 427–49

CASTIGLIA, CHRISTOPHER, 'Rebel Without a Closet' in *Engendering Men: The Question of Male Feminist Criticism*, ed. by Joseph A. Boone and Michael Cadden (London: Routledge, 1990)

CASTRO, EDUARDO VIVIEROS DE, 'The Gift and the Given: Three Nano-essays on Kinship and Magic', in *Kinship and Beyond: The Genealogical Model Reconsidered*, ed. by Sandra Bamford and James Leach (Oxford and New York: Berghahn Books, 2009), pp. 237–68

CATROGA, FERNANDO, 'Raça e História', in 'Historiografia de Oliveira Martins: entre a arte e as ciências sociais', *Revista da Universidade de Coimbra*, 38 (1999), 397–453

COLEMAN, ALEXANDER, *Eça de Queirós and European Realism* (New York: New York University Press, 1980)

COMTE, AUGUSTE, *A General View of Positivism*, trans. by J. H. Bridges (Cambridge: Cambridge University Press, 2009)

CRYLE, PETER, 'Foretelling Pathology: The Poetics of Prognosis', *French Cultural Studies*, 17 (2006), 107–22

CUROPOS, FERNANDO, *L'Émergence de l'homosexualité dans la littérature portugaise (1875–1915)* (Paris: L'Harmattan, 2016)

DARWIN, CHARLES, *On the Origin of Species* (Oxford: Oxford World Classics, 1996)

DE MAN, PAUL, *Blindness and Insight: Essays in the Rhetoric of Contemporary Criticism* (Abingdon: Routledge, 1983)

DERRIDA, JACQUES, 'From *Shibboleth*', in *Acts of Literature*, ed. by Derek Attridge (London: Routledge, 1992), pp. 370–413

—— 'Signature Event Context', in *Limited Inc* (Evanston, IL: Northwestern University Press, 1997), pp. 1–25

—— '...That Dangerous Supplement...' in *Of Grammatology*, trans. by Gayatri Spivak (Baltimore, MD: Johns Hopkins University Press, 1997), pp. 141–65

DINTER, ANNEGRETE, *Der Pygmalion-Stoff in der europäischen Literatur: Rezeptionsgeschichte einer Ovid-Fabel*, in *Studien zum Fortwirken der Antike*, vol. xi (Heidelberg: Carl Winter Universitätsverlag, 1979).

EAKIN, MARSHALL C., 'Race and Identity: Sílvio Romero, Science, and Social Thought in Late 19th Century Brazil,' *Luso-Brazilian Review*, 22 (1985), 151–74

EL FAHL, ALANDA, 'José Matias: um amor fora de lugar', in *Fólio — Revista de Letras*, vol. 6, n. 2, pp. 11–23

EL FAR, ALESSANDRA, *Páginas de sensação* (São Paulo: Companhia das Letras, 2004)

ELLMAN, RICHARD, *Oscar Wilde* (New York: Random House, 1988)

ENGELS, FRIEDRICH, *The Origin of the Family, Private Property and the State* (London: Penguin, 1986)

FANINI, ANGELA MARIA RUBEL, 'Uma solução local para formas importadas em *Casa de pensão*', *Anuário de literatura: publicação do Curso de Pós-Graduação em Letras, Literatura Brasileira e Teoria Literária*, 8 (2000), 29–56

FELDMAN, BURTON, *The Nobel Prize: A History of Genius, Controversy, and Prestige* (New York: Arcade Publishing, 2013)

FERREIRA, ANA PAULA, 'Amores vicários: "José Matias" e o pânico homo/heterossexual', in *Congresso de Estudos Queirosianos: IV Encontro Internacional de Queirosianos* (Coimbra: Livraria Almedina, 2000), vol. I, pp. 327–37

FLUDERNIK, MONIKA, *The Fictions of Language and the Languages of Fiction: The Linguistic Representation of Speech and Consciousness* (London: Routledge, 1993)

FOSTER, DAVID, 'Adolfo Caminha's *Bom-Crioulo*: A Founding Text of Brazilian Gay Literature' in *Gay and Lesbian Themes in Latin American Writing* (Austin: University of Texas Press, 1991), pp. 14–20

FOUCAULT, MICHEL, *The History of Sexuality*, Volume I: *An Introduction*, trans. by Robert Hurley (New York: Vintage Books, 1978)

—— *Madness and Civilization: A History of Insanity in the Age of Reason* (New York: Vintage, 1965)

—— 'The Means of Correct Training', in *Discipline and Punish: The Birth of the Prison*, trans. by Alan Sheridan (London: Penguin, 1991), pp. 170–94

—— 'A Preface to Transgression', in *Language, Counter-Memory, Practice*, ed. by Donald F. Bouchard, trans. by Donald F. Bouchard and Sherry Simon (New York: Cornell University Press, 1980), pp. 29–52

FREEMAN, DEREK ET AL., 'The Evolutionary Theories of Charles Darwin and Herbert Spencer', *Current Anthropology*, 15 (1974), 211–37

FREITAS, INÊS AGUIAR DE, and PAUL CLAVAL, 'Seasonality in Brazil', in *Seasonal Landscapes*, ed. by Hannes Palang et al. (Dordrecht: Springer, 2007), pp. 61–85

FREUD, SIGMUND, *Civilisation and its Discontents*, trans. by David McLintock (London: Penguin, 2002)

—— 'Fetishism,' in *The Standard Edition of the Complete Psychological Works of Sigmund Freud*, trans. by James Strachey in collaboration with Anna Freud (London: Hogarth Press, 1961), vol. XXI, pp. 152–59

—— 'Further Recommendations in the Technique of Psycho-Analysis: Remembering, Repeating, and Working-Through', trans. from the German by Joan Riviere, in *Standard Edition*, vol. XII, pp. 145–57

—— *The Interpretation of Dreams*, trans. by James Strachey (Harmondsworth: Penguin, 1976)

—— 'On Narcissism: an Introduction', in *Standard Edition*, vol. XIV, pp. 73–103

—— 'Three Essays on the Theory of Sexuality', in *Standard Edition*, vol. XVII, pp. 125–248

—— *Totem and Taboo*, trans. by Abraham A. Brill (New York: Cosimo Classics, 2009)

FREYRE, GILBERTO, *Casa-Grande e senzala: formação da família brasileira sob o regime da economia patriarcal* (Rio de Janeiro: Maia & Schmidt, 1933)

—— *Integração portuguesa nos trópicos* (Lisbon: Junta de Investigações do Ultramar, 1958)

FRIER, DAVID, 'Transcender o passado ou perder-se no passado? À procura de comunidades imaginadas n'*A ilustre casa de Ramires* e n'*A cidade e as serras*', *Queirosiana*, 21–22 (2010–11), pp. 57–73

FRYER, PETER, *Rhythms of Resistance: African Musical Heritage in Brazil* (London: Pluto Press, 2000)

FUKUYAMA, FRANCIS, 'The End of History?', *The National Interest* (Summer 1989), available at <http://www.wesjones.com/eoh.htm>

FURST, LILIAN R. and, PETER N. SKRINE, *Naturalism*, The Critical Idiom (London: Methuen, 1971)

GENOVESE, EUGENE, 'Our Family, White and Black: Family and Household in the Southern Slaveholders' World View', in In Joy and in Sorrow: Women, Family, and Marriage in the Victorian South, 1830–1900, ed. by Carol Bleser (New York: Oxford University Press, 1991), pp. 69–87

GINWAY, ELIZABETH, 'Nation Building and Heroic Undoing: Myth and Ideology in Bom-Crioulo', Modern Language Studies, 28 (1998), 41–56

GILBERT, SANDRA M., and SUSAN GUBAR, The Madwoman in the Attic: The Woman Writer and the Nineteenth-Century Literary Imagination (New Haven, CT: Yale University Press, 2000)

GLASSÉ, CYRIL, 'Cain and Abel' in The New Encyclopedia of Islam (New York: Rowman & Littlefield, 1989)

GREEN, JAMES N., Beyond Carnival: Male Homosexuality in Twentieth-Century Brazil (Chicago, IL: Chicago University Press, 1999)

GUERRA DA CAL, ERNESTO, A relíquia, romance picaresco e cervantesco (Lourenço Marques: Sociedade de Estudos de Moçambique, 1972)

HALPERIN, DAVID, 'Sex Before Sexuality: Pederasty, Politics, and Power in Classical Athens', in Hidden From History: Reclaiming the Gay and Lesbian Past, ed. by Martin Duberman, Martha Vicinus and George Chauncy (London: Penguin, 1991), pp. 37–53

HAMILTON, GEMENNE and BONNEUIL, The Anthropocene and the Global Environmental Crisis: Rethinking Modernity in a New Epoch (New York: Routledge, 2015), Google ebook

HIGGS, DAVID, ed., Queer Sites: Gay Urban Histories Since 1600 (London: Routledge, 2002)

HOWES, ROBERT, 'Concerning the Eccentricities of the Marquis of Valada: Politics, Culture and Homosexuality in Fin-de-Siècle Portugal', Sexualities, 5 (2002), 25–48

——'Race and Transgressive Sexuality in Adolfo Caminha's Bom Crioulo', Luso-Brazilian Review, 38 (2001), 41–46

——'Abel Botelho', in Who's Who in Gay and Lesbian History from Antiquity to World War II, ed. by Robert Aldrich and Garry Wotherspoon (London: Routledge, 2001), pp. 73–78

IRIGARAY, LUCE, This Sex Which is Not One, trans. by Catherine Porter and Catherine Burke (Ithaca, NY: Cornell University Press, 1985)

JOHNSON, HAROLD, 'A Pedophile in the Palace', 2004, available at <http://people.virginia. edu/~hbj8n/ pedophile.pdf> [accessed 28 April 2014]

JÚNIOR, ANTÓNIO SALGADO, História das Conferências do Casino (Lisbon: Cooperativa Militar, 1930)

KAPLAN, CORA, Sea Changes: Essays on Culture and Feminism (London: Verso, 1986)

KLOBUCKA, ANNA, 'Libaninho', in Reading Literature in Portuguese, ed. by Cláudia Pazos-Alonso and Stephen Parkinson (Oxford: Legenda, 2013)

——'Border Crossings: Transnationalism and Sexuality in Gombrowicz's Trans-Atlantyk and Eça de Queirós's A Cidade e as Serras' (paper presented at the conference Intra Muros, Ante Portas: Iberian and Slavonic Cultures in Contact and Comparison, Universidade de Lisboa, May 2008)

——'Was Camões Gay? Queering the Portuguese Literary Canon', conference paper delivered at the Annual Convention of the Modern Language Association, 28 December 2007

LACAN, JACQUES, 'Seminar on the Purloined Letter,' in Écrits, trans. by Bruce Frink (London: W. W. Norton and Co., 2007)

KRAFFT-EBING, RICHARD VON, Psychopathia Sexualis: The Classic Study of Deviant Sex, trans. by Franklin S. Klaf with an intro. by Joseph LoPicclo (New York: Arcade Publishing, 1965)

LAGO, SYLVIO, Eça de Queirós: Ensaios e Estudos (São Paulo: Biblioteca 24horas, 2010)

LEHAN, RICHARD, Realism and Naturalism: The Novel in an Age of Transition (Madison: The University of Wisconsin Press, 2005)

LEMOS, ANTERO VIEIRA DE, *Eça de Queiroz, o seu drama e a sua obra* (Porto: Edição do Autor, 1945)

LÉVI-STRAUSS, CLAUDE, *The Elementary Structures of Kinship*, trans. by James Harle Bell and John Richard von Sturmer (Boston, MA: Beacon Press, 1969)

LIMA, ISABEL PIRES DE, *As máscaras do desengano* (Lisbon: Editorial Caminho, 1987)

LIMÃO DE ANDRADE, MARIA RAQUEL, 'A homossexualidade no masculino e no feminino: para uma abordagem sociológica dos romances de Abel Botelho, *O Barão de Lavos* e *O Livro da Alda*' (unpublished master's thesis, Universidade Lusófona, 2003; copy held at Biblioteca Nacional de Portugal)

LISBOA, MARIA MANUEL, 'A Mother is a Boy's Best Friend: Birth and Kinslaying in the Brazilian Foundation Novel', *Portuguese Studies*, 13 (1997), 95–107

—— *Teu amor fez de mim um lago triste: ensaios sobre 'Os Maias'* (Porto: Campo das Letras, 2000)

—— *Uma mãe desconhecida: amor e perdição em Eça de Queirós* (Lisbon: Imprensa Nacional–Casa da Moeda, 2008)

LOMBROSO, CESARE, *Criminal Man* [1876], trans. and with intro. by Mary Gibson and Nicole Hahn Rafter (London: Duke University Press, 2006)

LOOS, DOROTHY, *The Naturalistic Novel of Brazil* (New York: Hispanic Institute in the United States, 1963)

LOPES-JÚNIOR, FRANCISCO, 'Uma subjetividade outra', in *Toward Socio-Criticism: Selected Proceedings of the Conference 'Luso-Brazilian Literatures: A Socio-Critical Approach'*, ed. and with intro. by Roberto Reis (Tempe: Center for Latin American Studies, Arizona State University, 1991), pp. 67–75

MACEDO, HÉLDER, introduction to *The Maias*, trans. by Patricia McGowan Pinheiro and Ann Stevens (London: Everyman, 1986)

MACHADO, ÁLVARO MANUEL, *A Geração de '70: uma revolução cultural e literária* (Lisbon: Instituto de Cultura e Língua Portuguesa, 1986)

MACNICOLL, MURRAY GRAEME, 'O Mulato and Maranhão: The Socio-Historical Context', *Luso-Brazilian Review*, 12.2 (1975), 234–40

MAGALHÃES, VALENTIM, *Escritores e escritos* (Rio de Janeiro: Camiliano, 1889)

MARCHANT, ELIZABETH A., 'Naturalism Race, and Nationalism in Aluísio Azevedo's *O Mulato*', *Hispania*, 83 (2000), 445–53

MARTINS, ANTÓNIO COIMBRA, *Ensaios queirosianos* (Lisbon: Publicações Europa-América, 1967)

MARTINS, OLIVEIRA, *Elementos de antropologia* (Lisbon: Guimarães Editora, 1954)

MARX, KARL, and FRIEDRICH ENGELS, *On Literature and Art* (New York: International General, 1974)

MAZZEI, CRISTIANO, 'How Adolfo Caminha's *Bom-Crioulo* Was 'Outed' through its Translated Paratext', in *A Companion to Translation Studies*, ed. by Sandra Bermann and Catherine Porter (Chichester: John Wiley and Sons, 2014), pp. 310–22

MELLO, CELINA MOREIRA DE, *Crítica e movimentos estéticos: configurações discursivas do campo literário* (Rio de Janeiro: Viveiros de Castro, 2006)

MENDES, LEONARDO, *O retrato do Imperador: negociação, sexualidade e romance naturalista no Brasil* (Porto Alegre: EDIPUCRS, 2000)

MERCHANT, CAROLYN, *Reinventing Eden: The Fate of Nature in Western Culture* (London: Routledge, 2003)

MEY, JACOB L., *When Voices Clash: A Study in Literary Pragmatics* (Berlin: Mouton de Gruyter, 1999)

MÓNICA, MARIA FILOMENA, *Eça de Queirós* (Braga: Quetzal, 2001)

MONIZ, EDMUNDO, *As mulheres proibidas: o incesto em Eça de Queirós* (São Paulo: J. Olympio Editora, 1993)

Montaigne, Michel, 'On Affectionate Relationships', in *The Complete Essays*, trans. by M. A. Screech (London: Penguin, 2004), pp. 205–19

Monteiro, Joaquim Gomes, *Vencidos da vida: relance literário e política da segunda metade do século XIX* (Lisbon: Edição Romano Tôrres, 1944)

Montello, Josué, *Aluísio Azevedo e a polêmica d''O Mulato'* (Rio de Janeiro: José Olympio, 1975)

——'A ficção naturalista', in *A Literatura no Brasil*, ed. by Afrânio Coutinho (Rio de Janeiro: José Olympio, 1986), vol. iv, pp. 69–90

Moog, Clodomir, *Eça de Queirós e o século XIX* (São Paulo: Delta, 1966)

Muñoz, José Esteban, *Cruising Utopia: The Then and There of Queer Futurity* (New York: New York University Press, 2009)

Nietzsche, Friedrich, *The Gay Science*, trans. by Josefine Nauckhoff (Cambridge: Cambridge University Press, 2001)

Orlando, Arthur, *Ensaios de Crítica* (São Paulo: Editorial Grijablo, 1975)

Owen, Hilary, *Mother Africa, Father Marx: Women's Writing of Mozambique, 1948–2002* (Lewisburg, PA: Bucknell University Press, 2007)

Patai, Daphne, and Murray MacNicoll, introduction to *Mulatto*, trans. by Murray Graeme MacNicoll, ed. by Daphne Patai (London: Associated University Press, 1990)

Pereira, Lúcia Miguel, *Prosa de Ficção (de 1870 a 1920)* (Rio de Janeiro: José Olympio, 1950)

Pereira, Miriam Halpern, 'Demografia e desenvolvimento em Portugal na segunda metade do século XIX', *Revista do Instituto de Ciências Sociais da Universidade de Lisboa*, 7 (1969), 85–117

Paryas, Phyllis Margaret, 'Monologism', in *Encyclopedia of Contemporary Literary Theory: Approaches, Scholars, Terms*, ed. by Irena R. Makaryk (London: University of Toronto Press, 1993), p. 596

Plato, *Symposium*, trans. by Benjamin Jowett (Rockville, MD: Serenity Publishers, 2009)

Ponte, Carmo Salazar, *Oliveira Martins: a história como tragédia* (Lisbon: Imprensa Nacional–Casa da Moeda, 1999)

Posso, Karl, *Artimanhas de sedução: homossexualidade e exílio* (Belo Horizonte: UFMG Press, 2009)

Quental, Antero de, 'Causas da decadência dos povos peninsulares nos últimos três séculos' (lecture delivered at the Casino de Lisboa, 22 March 1871, available at <http://www.arqnet.pt/portal/discursos/ maio01 html> [accessed 5 May 2017]

Reis, Carlos, *História da literatura portuguesa: o realismo e o naturalismo* (Lisbon: Publicações Alfa, 2001)

——*História crítica da literatura portuguesa* (Lisbon: Editorial Verbo, 1994)

——*Estatuto e perspectivas do narrador na ficção de Eça de Queirós* (Coimbra: Livraria Almedina, 1984)

Ribeiro, Luís Filipe, 'O sexo e o poder no Império: *Philomena Borges*', *Luso-Brazilian Review*, 30 (1993), 7–20

Romero, Sílvio, *Cantos populares do Brasil* (São Paulo: José Olympio, 1954)

Rothwell, Phillip, *A Canon of Empty Fathers* (Lewisburg, PA: Bucknell University Press, 2007)

Rubin, Gayle, 'The Traffic in Women: Notes on the Political Economy of Sex', in *Towards an Anthropology of Women*, ed. by Rayna Reiter (New York: Monthly Review Press, 1975), pp. 157–210

Said, Edward, *Orientalism: Western Conceptions of the Orient* (London: Vintage Books, 1979)

Sanches De Baena, Miguel, *Diário de D. Manuel: e estudo sobre o regicídio* (Lisbon: Publicações Alfa, 1990)

Santiago, Silviano, 'Eça, Autor de *Madame Bovary*', in *Uma literatura nos trópicos: ensaios sobre a dependência cultural* (Rio de Janeiro: Rocco, 2000), pp. 47–65

SANTOS, ANTÓNIO CARLOS, 'O naturalismo sob o olhar modernista: Cândido e a crítica a Aluísio Azevedo', *Crítica Cultural*, 6 (2011), 557–63

SARAIVA, ANTÓNIO JOSÉ, *As ideias de Eça de Queirós* (Lisbon: Gradiva, 2000)

SAUSSURE, FERDINAND DE, *Course in General Linguistics* [1916], trans. by Roy Harris (London: Bloomsbury, 2013)

SCHWARZ, ROBERTO, 'As ideias fora do lugar', in *Ao vencedor as batatas* (São Paulo: Editora 34, 2000), pp. 11–31

——'A importação do romance e as suas contradições em Alencar', in *Ao vencedor as batatas* (São Paulo: Editora 34, 2000), pp. 33–82

——'Nacional por subtração', in *Que horas são? Ensaios* (São Paulo: Companhia das Letras, 1987), pp. 29–48

SEDGWICK, EVE, *Between Men: English Literature and Male Homosocial Desire* (New York: Columbia University Press, 1985)

——*The Epistemology of the Closet* (London: Harvester Wheatsheaf, 1999)

SEITLER, DIANA, 'Queer Physiognomies; Or, How Many Ways Can We Do the History of Sexuality?' in *Criticism*, 46 (2004), 71–102

SERRÃO, JOAQUIM VERÍSSIMO, *História de Portugal* (Lisbon: Verbo, 1978)

SHOWALTER, ELAINE, *Sexual Anarchy* (London: Virago, 1992)

SILVEIRA, FABIANO, *Da criminalização do racismo: aspectos jurídicos e sociocriminológicos* (Belo Horizonte: Editora Del Rey, 2007)

SILVERMAN, KAJA, *Male Subjectivity at the Margins* (New York: Routledge, 1992)

SIMÕES, JOÃO GASPAR, *Vida e obra de Eça de Queirós* (Lisbon: Livraria Bertrand, 1973)

SKIDMORE, THOMAS, 'Racial Ideas and Social Policy in Brazil, 1870–1940', in *The Idea of Race in Latin America, 1870–1940*, ed. by Richard Graham (Austin: University of Texas Press, 1990), pp. 7–30

SODRÉ, NELSON WERNECK, *O Naturalismo no Brasil* (Rio de Janeiro: Editôra Civilização Brasileira, 1965)

SOMERVILLE, SIOBHAN, 'Scientific Racism and the Invention of the Homosexual Body,' *Journal of the History of Sexuality*, 5 (2016), 246–66

SONTAG, SUSAN, *Aids and its Metaphors* (New York: Farrar, Straus and Giroux, 1988)

SOUSA, FRANK DE, 'A Relíquia: do Realismo/Naturalismo a uma estética da imperfeição,' in Alfredo Campos Matos, *Suplemento ao Dicionário de Eça de Queirós* (Lisbon: Editorial Caminho, 2000)

SOUSA DOS REIS, JOSÉ, *Bumba meu boi, o maior espectáculo do Maranhão* (Recife: Fundação Joaquim Nabuco, 1980)

SOUSA SANTOS, BOAVENTURA DE, 'Entre Próspero e Caliban: colonialismo, pós-colonialismo e interidentidade', *Novos Estudos*, 66 (July 2003), 23–52

SPENCER, JANE, *Literary Relations: Kinship and the Canon, 1660–1830* (Oxford: Oxford University Press, 2005)

STEPHENS, ELIZABETH, 'Anatomies of Desire' in *Sexuality at the Fin de Siècle*, ed. by Peter Cryle and Christopher E. Forth (Cranbury, NJ: University of Delaware, 2008), pp. 25–38

SUMMER, DORIS, *Foundational Fictions: The National Romances of Latin America* (London: University of California Press, 1991)

SUSSEKIND, FLORA, *Tal Brasil, qual romance? Uma ideologia estética e sua história: Naturalismo* (Rio de Janeiro: Achiamé, 1984)

TARQUÍNIO DE SOUSA, OCTÁVIO DE, *A vida de D. Pedro I* (Rio de Janeiro: José Olympio, 1957)

VALÉRIO, ELISA, *Para uma leitura de 'Os Maias'* (Lisbon: Presença, 1997)

VIEIRA, NELSON, *Portugal e o Brasil: a imagem recíproca (o mito e a realidade na expressão literária)* (Lisbon: Instituto de Cultura e Língua Portuguesa, 1991)

WALDMAN, BERTA, Introduction to ALUÍSIO AZEVEDO, *Casa de pensão*, 5th edn (São Paulo: Editora Ática, 1989), pp. 5–9

WARNER, MICHAEL, 'Homo-Narcissism; or, Heterosexuality', in *Engendering Men: The Question of Male Feminist Criticism*, ed. by Joseph A. Boone and Michael Cadden (London: Routledge, 1990)

WELGE, JOBST, *Genealogical Fictions: Cultural Periphery and Historical Change in the Modern Novel* (Baltimore, MD: Johns Hopkins University Press, 2014)

WHITE, DAVID, Review of the English translation of *Bom Crioulo* by Gay Sunshine Press, in *Library Journal*, 107 (1 October 1982)

WILSON, MICHAEL L., 'The Despair of Unhappy Love: Pederasty and Popular Fiction in the Belle Époque, in *Sexuality at the Fin de Siècle*, ed. by Peter Cryle and Christopher E. Forth (Cranbury, NJ: University of Delaware, 2008), pp. 109–22

WYNN, MARTIN, *Planning and Urban Growth in Southern Europe* (London: Manswell, 1994)

ZILBERMAN, REGINA, 'Eça entre os brasileiros de ontem e hoje', in *Eças e outros: diálogos com a ficção de Eça de Queirós* (Porto Alegre: EDIPUCRS, 2002), pp. 7–21

ŽIŽEK, SLAVOJ, *Less Than Nothing: Hegel and the Shadow of Dialectical Materialism* (London: Verso, 2012)

## Archives and collections

*Diário de Notícias*, 6 September 1888, Biblioteca Nacional de Portugal.

*Diário do Governo*, no. 177 (Lisbon, 20 July 1912), pp. 2714–15, Biblioteca Nacional de Portugal

*Diário Popular*, 24 April 1886 — 5 August 1888, Biblioteca Nacional de Portugal.

## Internet sources

<http://bumba-meu-boi.info/a-lenda.html>
<https://en.oxforddictionaries.com>
<http://g1.globo.com/ma/maranhao/noticia/2014/03/interior-da-casa-onde-aluisio-azevedo-morou-em-sao-luis-esta-destruido.html>
<http://lisboaverde.cm-lisboa.pt>
<http://www.arqnet.pt>
<http://www.dicionarioweb.com.br>
<http://www.etymonline.com>
<http://www.ornithos.com.br>
<http://www.priberam.pt>

# INDEX

www.ingramcontent.com/pod-product-compliance
Lightning Source LLC
Chambersburg PA
CBHW080819250626
47159CB00011B/3444